Palgrave Studies in Classical Liberalism

This series offers a forum to writers concerned that the central presuppositions of the liberal tradition have been severely corroded, neglected, or misappropriated by overly rationalistic and constructivist approaches.

The hardest-won achievement of the liberal tradition has been the wrestling of epistemic independence from overwhelming concentrations of power, monopolies and capricious zealotries. The very precondition of knowledge is the exploitation of the epistemic virtues accorded by society's situated and distributed manifold of spontaneous orders, the DNA of the modern civil condition.

With the confluence of interest in situated and distributed liberalism emanating from the Scottish tradition, Austrian and behavioral economics, non-Cartesian philosophy and moral psychology, the editors are soliciting proposals that speak to this multidisciplinary constituency. Sole or joint authorship submissions are welcome as are edited collections, broadly theoretical or topical in nature.

Giandomenica Becchio

The Doctrine of the Separate Spheres in Political Economy and Economics

Gender Equality and Classical Liberalism

palgrave
macmillan

Giandomenica Becchio
University of Turin
Turin, Italy

ISSN 2662-6470 ISSN 2662-6489 (electronic)
Palgrave Studies in Classical Liberalism
ISBN 978-3-031-51261-2 ISBN 978-3-031-51262-9 (eBook)
https://doi.org/10.1007/978-3-031-51262-9

This Palgrave Macmillan imprint is published by the registered company Springer Nature Switzerland AG
The registered company address is: Gewerbestrasse 11, 6330 Cham, Switzerland

Paper in this product is recyclable.

This book is dedicated to my late mother
with infinite love and eternal gratitude

Contents

1 Introduction: The Doctrine of the Separate Spheres 1
- 1.1 Definition and Debate 4
- 1.2 Historical Timeline and Contents of This Book 10
- 1.3 A Note on Definitions 25
- References 26

Part I Escaping the Doctrine of the Separate Spheres (1700s–early 1900s): The Economists' Points of View

2 Educated Women as an Asset to Society: The Role of Classical Liberal Tradition in Modern Europe 33
- 2.1 Early Debates on the Doctrine of the Separate Spheres 36
- 2.2 Women's Access to Higher Education: Olympe de Gouges and Mary Wollstonecraft 45
- 2.3 Economic Ideas as Tools for Women's Emancipation: Sophie de Grouchy, Jane Marcet, and Harriet Martineau 56

2.4 Harriet Taylor Mill on Marriage and Divorce and Her Influence on John Stuart Mill 64
References 76

3 Women and the Job Market in Victorian England and Progressive America 83
3.1 Women at Work: The Economic Challenges of the Time 85
3.2 Debates Among Economists: Gender Discrimination in Employment and Pay 90
3.3 Women and the Economy: Crossing the Boundaries of the Private Sphere 104
3.4 Women and Immigration in the Progressive Era: Sex and Race Intersected 117
References 128

4 Women's New Path Toward the Public Sphere 135
4.1 The Economic Debate on Women's Suffrage 139
4.2 From 'True Womanhood' to the 'New Woman': The Evolution of the Marriage Debate 155
4.3 The Economic Debate on Prostitution 168
4.4 Women of Color Between Gender and Race Stereotypes 176
References 182

Part II The Doctrine of the Separate Spheres Between Rebirth and Rejection (1920s–early 2000s): Marriage Theory in Economics

5 Reviving the Doctrine of the Separate Spheres: The New Home Economics 191
5.1 The Cult of Domesticity Revised: Home Economics and Household Economics 194
5.2 Marriage Theory in Becker's New Home Economics: Combining Human Capital and Labor Economics 203

5.3 Becker's *Treatise on the Family*: The Doctrine of the Separate Spheres on Steroids 213
5.4 Beyond Becker: Standard Economics on Marriage Theory 218
References 227

6 Feminist Economics and the Doctrine of the Separate Spheres 235
6.1 Feminism, Gender Equality, Care, and the Doctrine of the Separate Spheres: Friends or Foes? 239
6.2 Challenging Becker's Economic Approach: Marriage Theory in Feminist Economics 246
6.3 Going Beyond the Doctrine of the Separate Spheres: Barbara Bergmann's Combination of Feminist Economics and Classical Liberalism Against Becker's Approach 258
6.4 Are the Separate Spheres Still Separate Today? 267
References 277

Index 287

1

Introduction: The Doctrine of the Separate Spheres

The history of women's emancipation is the history of how women gained access to public sphere, after traditionally being relegated to the domestic sphere by gender categories. Gender categories are a set of cultural roles that define appropriate behavior for the sexes. The history of trascending the separate spheres is encapsulated in the narrative of the 'quiet revolution', as described by Nobel laureate and Harvard economist Claudia Goldin. This revolution transformed the condition of women "from agents who work because they and their families 'need the money' to those who are employed, at least in part, because occupation and employment define one's fundamental identity and societal worth" (Goldin, 2006, 1).

This book is about the doctrine of the separate spheres within the history of economic ideas and theories. It sheds light on the origins of gender inequality within the two spheres, as seen and explained by economists who evaluated the doctrine of the separate spheres by measuring whether it was efficient or dysfunctional for overall social well-being. It shows how economists, implicitly and explicitly, adopted the doctrine of the separate spheres, either by reinforcing the gendered division of economic and social roles between men and women or by

G. Becchio, *The Doctrine of the Separate Spheres in Political Economy and Economics*, Palgrave Studies in Classical Liberalism,
https://doi.org/10.1007/978-3-031-51262-9_1

rejecting it and promoting gender equality. The doctrine of the separate spheres was used by major economists of the time to assess or evaluate important economic arguments. They mainly proceeded by examining two specific phenomena. First, the role of women within the domestic sphere led economists to analyze the condition of women within marriage, the economy of the family, and the division of labor within the household (Akerlof & Kranton, 2010; Baker & Jacobsen, 2007; Barker, 1995; Davis, 2011; Fitzpatrick, 1990). Second, the entry of women into the paid labor force, affecting their position in the public sphere, led economists to investigate the nature of job discrimination and gender-based segregation as well as other forms of gender inequality, such as the gender labor gap and gender pay gap (Averett et al., 2018; Berik & Kongar, 2021; Goldin, 1990, 2021).

Economists were especially interested in combining these two dimensions by considering the effects of married women entering the job market on the performance and well-being of society as a whole. Differently from Goldin's timeline which covers three phases of evolutionary changes (late nineteenth century to the 1920s; 1930s–1950; 1950s–1970s) and one revolutionary phase (late 1970s to the present), this book dates back the beginning of women's quiet revolution against the doctrine of the separate spheres to early modern time.[1]

An investigation into the narrative of the doctrine of the separate spheres implies a broader perspective than that of economists. In fact, the doctrine of the separate spheres has been adopted by philosophers and

[1] Goldin summarized her argument as follows. During Phase I, female workers in the labor market, as opposed to those working in the household or family business, were generally young, unmarried, and unskilled. Only a minority were professional workers, such as teachers and clerical employees. This group expanded massively in the 1910s. They usually exit the labor force once they got married. During Phase II, the labor force participation rate for married women increased mainly because of the enormous growth in high school enrollment and graduation that occurred between 1910 and 1930. During Phase III, married women's labor force participation continued to expand, female labor supply became more elastic and responsive to changes in wages, although married women remained the secondary earners in their households. Phase IV is the revolutionary one: women started to close the educational gap and have careers rather than jobs; they established themselves as professionals by asserting that their identity is shaped by their work rather than their role within a family: "women had longer horizons than did previous generations and an altered identity that placed career ahead, or on equal footing, with marriage. Wives were less often secondary workers, the flotsam and jetsam of the labor market" (Goldin, 2006, 19).

social scientists since antiquity, either to justify or reject the subjection of women. However, in this book, the economists' perspective is privileged, as are the specific contributions of British and American economists and social reformers from the examined time period. The emphasis on the Anglo-American tradition remains central, mainly because the notion of the separate spheres became a metaphor used to idealize women's place in that cultural context.

The emphasis on the doctrine of the separate spheres took place with the simultaneous emergence of two idealizations: the Victorian model of the family, based on men as breadwinners and women as angels of the house (Cott, 1977); and Tocqueville's representation of American women as moral guardians of the family and religion against democratic despotism (Cogan, 1989; Kerber, 1988; Lerner, 1986; Ross, 2006; Smith-Rosenberg, 1985).[2] The idealized image of women remained constant until the second half of the twentieth century. As Betty Friedan wrote:

> The suburban housewife – she was the dream image of the young American women and the envy, it was said, of women all over the world. The American housewife (…) was healthy, beautiful, educated, concerned only about her husband, he children, her home. She had found true feminine fulfillment. As a housewife and a mother, as was respected as a full and equal partner to men in his world (…). In the fifteen years after World War II, this mystique of feminine became the cherished and self-perpetuating core of contemporary American culture (Friedan, 1963, 18).

What Friedan described was the role of women as depicted within the doctrine of the separate spheres. The history of economic ideas and theories helps us understand a part of this process.

This book combines the traditional narrative adopted by historians of economic thought, which presents the point of view of professional economists of the time, including academic female economists, and the

[2] Influenced by Rousseau, Tocqueville emphasized the traditional division of labor between the genders despite the restriction on women's freedom. Nevertheless, there is also feminist literature that praises him (Locke & Hunt Botting, 2009).

more recent *herstory* approach, which offers a platform for the voices of women economic writers whose works, though well-known in their time, has been neglected, forgotten and omitted from the history of economic ideas (Kuiper, 2022). The economic point of view, expressed either by professional academic economists or by scholars and social reformers of the time who employed economic arguments, was hosted in the academic press as well as in the popular press. It helps to understand the complexity of women's paths toward the public sphere. The battle for gender equality in education, labor market, political realms as well as within the households was multifaceted. It implied the evolution of a society capable of transcending the dichotomy of the separate spheres and enabling the empowerment of women, guided by the principle of individual freedom, regardless of gender, ethnicity, and class.

1.1 Definition and Debate

The doctrine of the separate spheres is an example of the *social construction of gender*. It is rooted in the idea that public and private life are strictly separate: the doctrine asserts that certain areas of life, belonging to the public sphere, such as the economy and the political arena, are best suited for men, while certain areas of life, within the private sphere, such as the domestic dimension, are considered best suited for women. Indeed, according to the doctrine, if society is to be at its most functional and prosperous, men and women should adhere to the roles that align with their respective genders: men are required to perform their skills in the public sphere, while women are required to achieve their abilities in the private sphere (Cohen, 1989; Katz, 1992, 2000).

Matrimony (or marriage) and patrimony are two words that effectively represent the underlying principles behind the doctrine of the separate spheres. Rooted in the Latin words mater and pater, meaning mother and father, respectively, they reveal the distinct societal roles expected of women and men. Patrimony is masculine and encompasses a broad spectrum of material wealth; matrimony is feminine and specifically refers to marriage and family.

This distinction between the two spheres and their gender connotations was introduced in the Greek classical philosophy through the opposition between *oikos*, the domestic sphere of production and reproduction reserved for women and slaves, and *polis*, the public sphere of political discussions, deliberation, and collective decision-making exclusively reserved for free men. It was based on the idea that public and private realms are driven by different virtues: the public sphere was supposed to be ruled by masculine virtues, such as strength, courage, and competition, while feminine virtues, such as love, compassion, and cooperation, governed the private sphere. In Aristotle's *Ethics* and *Politics*, women were considered naturally inferior to men, and the argumentation for the separate spheres was a direct consequence of the inherent difference between men and women.[3]

As a matter of fact, this dichotomy established distinct social roles for men and women: the public sphere was seen as the domain of men, where virtuous men were strong, brave, and competitive, while the private sphere was considered the domain of women, where virtuous women were lovely, compassionate, and cooperative. This way of perceiving men and women as different moral and rational agents was rooted in the belief in substantial differences between men's and women's minds and decision-making capacity. Their different abilities were regarded as a direct consequence of their biological and sexual distinctions.

As the public sphere was the domain of power, men traditionally assumed the roles of leaders and patrons over women, whose subjection was the *natural* effect of their placement in the private sphere and the separation of the two spheres. Indeed, this dichotomy greatly affected the lives of both men and women. Gender stereotypes emerged and were constantly reinforced by a patriarchal system that insisted on the idea that

---

[3] Xenophon's *Oeconomicus* presented a picture of the exemplary wife of a landowner: uneducated, exclusively devoted to the household, and treated as a minor. In Plato's *Republic* the separate spheres were not applied as women may be guardians, and no property and family existed. However, in the *Laws*, family and property are back in the picture as well as the natural argument for the division of sexes/roles based on the *natural* differences between men and women. In Aristotle's *Ethics* and *Politics*, women were regarded as naturally inferior to men and the argument for separate spheres was a direct consequence of the different nature of men and women.

women, naturally inclined (so the argument went) toward love and care, must fulfill their purpose in a domestic sphere by becoming good wives and mothers; while men, naturally inclined toward bravery and force, were expected to pursue their ambitions in the public sphere, performing their *natural* role of breadwinners as well as good citizens involved in the army, the economy, and politics (Apple, 2006; Eibach & Lanzinger, 2020).

Any commitment of women in the public sphere was traditionally viewed as an exception, usually ostracized, seldom and barely tolerated, and most of the time neglected. Likewise, any involvement of men in the responsibilities within the domestic sphere was forged around the notion of the powerful figure of the *pater familias* and reduced to a matter of dominion over the members of his household, including their spouse, children, servants, and animals. The dynamics of the sexual dimension mirrored this patriarchal system: men played the role of masters of reproduction, entitled to pleasure, while women remained objectified, either sanctified into the role of motherhood or positioned as providers of pleasure for men in the role of concubines, prostitutes, and sex slaves.

Various attempts have been made to analyze the doctrine of the separate spheres (Amstrong & Squires, 2002; Helly & Reverby, 1997). Some scholars viewed women's confinement to the private sphere as the source of their oppression and encouraged women's participation in the public sphere, without specifically advocating for increased men's participation in the private (Friedan, 1963; Pateman, 1988). Other scholars revised the concept of the two spheres, by de-gendering them and depicting the private sphere as the realm of intimate human relations protected from the influence of the public sphere (Moller Okin, 1979; Young, 1990). Others redefined the concept of the public sphere as the realm of rational communication and the institutionalization of the ideal of equality (Habermas, 1989), by ignoring and neglecting the marginalization of women from the public sphere (Fraser, 1990).

Historians agree in considering the use of the metaphor of separate spheres as an ideology imposed on women and as a set of boundaries expected to be adhered by women. The doctrine played a central role especially within feminist theories, serving as an explanation of sexual inequality and as a normative framework for advancing feminist political goals.

However, although the doctrine of the separate spheres is a simplification in itself, the adoption of this label was quite complex, and reality has always been more multifaceted. Furthermore, the doctrine of the separate spheres avoided addressing the categories of race and class, as all discussions of the subject were centered around the experience of white middle-class women (Kerber, 1988). In fact, it wasn't until the 1980s that intersectionality was introduced in the study of the separate spheres (Fox-Genovese, 1988; Gray White, 1985; Jones, 1985).

Prior to the widespread of the Second Industrial Revolution, the domestic sphere included manifold aspects that were under the double umbrella of 'household' and 'family'. The concept of a household implied several dimensions, including economic production, consumption, and material culture, in addition to family ties. The concept of the family was equally complex, evolving over the centuries: from a large set of people involved, including relatives, friends, and servants, to a narrower definition that excluded individuals not connected through specific contracts (such as marriage) or blood ties.[4] Shared spaces denoting the domestic sphere also underwent historical changes: the boundaries of privacy progressively contracted as the number of household members decreased. Furthermore, until the early twentieth century, the home served as a location for the education of both girls and boys as well as a place of work for both women and men.

As Rotman (2006) pointed out, an absolute separation of spheres never truly existed. The lives of both women and men were more dynamic than what this rigid dichotomy implies.[5] Yet, starting from the nineteenth century, gender roles began to shape the narrative of the two separate spheres. Husbands were often portrayed as breadwinners and producers, while wives were depicted as homemakers, consumers, and caregivers. The notion of family as a primary social unit became widely

[4] Some empirical studies reveal that the term 'family' took a considerable amount of time to become widely accepted in everyday language (Spolsky, 2012).

[5] As Yentsch (1991) noted, public space was not entirely public, but it contained private components and private space also included elements of the public.

accepted by social scientists, while the concept of individuality lost its appeal (De Grazia & Furlough, 1996; De Vries, 2008).

Another important element to consider when introducing the doctrine of the separate spheres is the different roles of rules, legislation, and institutions, such as marriage. These were entitled to determine tasks and responsibilities and to prevent conflicts within the domestic sphere, affecting the position of both partners and measuring the inequality of status between genders (Moring, 2010).[6] Other forms of contract shaped various hierarchies, such as the master-servant relationship, which was supposed to be grounded on the figure of a benevolent *pater familias*, although the benevolence, which was often pretentious, revealed the inherent inconsistency of the patriarchal system (Sarti, 2020).

The feminization of the domestic sphere transformed the household into a place of unpaid work provided by women while the public sphere became the natural environment for men to perform their paid jobs.[7] There are several interpretations of this phenomenon which are basically affected by ideological stances. Detractors of capitalism used to align with Alice Clark's view (1919), which suggested that the Industrial Revolution broke the harmony of the household by confining women to domestic roles, whereas prior to the eighteenth century, both men and women shared the responsibility for production, which was entirely domestic. Conversely, supporters of capitalism maintain that the subjection of women was a phenomenon present in various historical epochs and not solely a result of the transition from a domestic economy to an industrial one. Instead, they contend that the capitalist system and free market opportunities allowed women to escape the private sphere, promoting their independence and involvement in the public arena.

The cultural notion of domesticity in relation to the role of women and their identity as social agents has been interpreted in different ways by feminist scholars (Kerber 1988).

[6] During the nineteenth century, the legal recognition of women's property rights was introduced, leading to significant changes in the dynamics of decision-making within households (Moses, 2008).

[7] The notion of unpaid work was introduced to describe the activities performed by women, such as housekeeping and caregiving, within the household for the family's well-being, and exploited by the head of the family, usually a male figure (Addabbo et al., 2010; Delphy & Leonard, 1992).

Some feminist historians regarded women as victims of the ideology of domesticity and tended to consider the emancipation of women as a reaction against women's subjection within the private sphere.

Others observed that the ideology of domesticity was often linked with the idea of women's moral superiority and attributed the emergence and development of nineteenth-century feminism directly *to* the cult of domesticity. As Lerner noted (1986), nineteenth-century feminists, both in America and in England, redefined the doctrine of the separate spheres by portraying women as more altruistic than men due to their maternal instincts. They believed that women's traditional role as nurturers could help rescue society from the destructiveness, competition, and violence created by men.

Finally, other feminist scholars regarded women's role within the private sphere as the foundation for a female subculture that led women to explore their uniqueness and embrace the notion of sisterhood.

Feminist scholars have especially scrutinized the institution of marriage as the primary source of women's subjection. Many have rejected the idea that the private sphere of marriage is a zone exempt from state interference, suggesting that it should be subject to norms of justice. They have also emphasized that abuse within marriage and inequality upon the dissolution of marriages are significant problems for women, who often find themselves in a weaker position.

Feminist thinkers also emphasize the clear disadvantages women face within marriage. Married women who work full-time usually face a 'second shift' by performing more housework than their husbands. This additional workload impacts their competitiveness in the labor market (Maushart, 2001). The gendered division of labor, economic dependence on marriage, and the primary responsibility for childcare make married women vulnerable, make exiting from marriage challenging, and may facilitate intra-house abuse (Brake, 2016; Card, 1996; Ferguson, 2016; Moller Okin, 1979). Hence, while many feminists have proposed reforms to improve the institution of marriage, others have argued for its abolition in order to reshape social expectations (Chambers, 2017). Inspired by Simone de Beauvoir's critique of marriage (1949) as the traditional fate imposed on women, they identify marriage as the primary tool that limits women's ambitions in the public sphere.

Despite these varying interpretations, feminist scholars and historians generally concur that when the feminization of the domestic sphere took hold, women's work became invisible. Furthermore, they agree that the differential education of boys and girls represents one of the most detrimental consequences of the doctrine of the separate spheres. The gender-stereotyped education enforced by this doctrine perpetuated the division of spheres and its impact on the lives of men and women: while boys were educated to be competitive in the job market and to acquire either technical or scientific knowledge; girls were trained for marriage market with their personal aspirations often discouraged if they didn't align with the expectations of becoming good wives. This was a primary factor contributing the denial of access to higher education for girls, a phenomenon that persisted either legally or in practice until the early twentieth century.[8]

1.2 Historical Timeline and Contents of This Book

This book is divided into two parts.

The first part of the book covers a period from the eighteenth century to the early twentieth century. It deals with the lengthy process of women's attempts to break free from the doctrine of the separate spheres, which had traditionally confined them to the domestic sphere. However, this process was not straightforward. Movements aimed at emancipating women from their marginalization within the domestic sphere often intersected with counter-movements that glorified women's roles within the private sphere, emphasizing their position as mothers who were

[8] In earlier times, only the most fortunate wealthy girls and women in some urban contexts would open their homes to host scholars and artists of various kind. The phenomenon of *salonnièrs* intensively grew during the nineteenth century in European and American cities, creating a network of cultural exchange that allowed for the cultural interaction between both genders, which had previously been denied. Salons served as a means to extend the influence of women into traditionally male-dominated realms of culture, politics, and the economy (Baird, 2014; Brown & Dow, 2011).

rhetorically depicted as guardians of the nation's prosperity and protectors of societal harmony as a whole. Nonetheless, it is crystal clear that early feminists and social reformers of the time began their struggle against the traditional subjection of women by criticizing the relegation of women to the private sphere and by encouraging women to become active participants in public sphere.

During the Middle Age and up until the seventeenth century, the doctrine of the separate spheres was never questioned, and it was mainly strengthened by religious authorities who upheld the belief that the differences between men's and women's minds, which implies a strict separation of natural and social roles, were in accordance with God's will. Hence, any form of equality between men and women was viewed as dysfunctional and against the natural order (*contra natura*). Against this vision, opponents of the doctrine of the separate spheres, such as John Locke, argued that the relegation of women to the domestic sphere was not justified by nature; rather it was an artificial and social construct that empowered men and perpetually reinforced the traditional subjection of women.

As mentioned earlier, a movement aimed at liberating human society from the doctrine of the separate spheres and promoting gender equality began during the modern age and became central within the classical liberal tradition, which is based on the idea of equality among all human beings, regardless of their gender. Most women scholars of the time, such as Olympe de Gouges and Mary Wollstonecraft, specifically fought against the doctrine of the separate spheres, viewing it as the origin of the subjection of women. Inspired by John Locke's idea that human beings entered the world as *tabula rasa*, with their personalities shaped by environment and education, they emphasized the crucial role of education and socialization in shaping female character and behavior. Between the seventeenth and late eighteenth centuries, three fundamental aspects of the doctrine of separate spheres were questioned: women's education, women's economic independence, and women's role within the institution of marriage (Akkerman & Stuurman, 1998; Botting, 2006).

Scholars of the time, especially women, insisted on the importance of liberating girls from an education aimed at preparing them exclusively for roles as wives and mothers. Instead, they encouraged women to study especially economic matters in order to get more acquainted with the possibilities of taking an active role in the economy. The popularization of political economy, largely attributed to scholars like Sophie De Grouchy, Harriet Martineau, and Jane Marcet, occurred in the early nineteenth century. This development played a pivotal role in spreading economic knowledge among women and encouraged them to advocate for economic independence, which would, in turn, enable them to participate more actively in the public sphere.

While the doctrine of separate spheres was never completely rejected, it was adapted and used to bolster the call for women's emancipation. By combining the notions of individual natural rights, the notion of women being as virtuous as men, and the notion of women's empowerment, many scholars of the time framed women's emancipation as a matter of public utility. They argued that providing women with a better education and economic independence would make them better suited to fulfill their essential roles as wives for the sake of the society as a whole.

More critical was the treatment of the institution of marriage, as it was conceived by early feminists of the time. Marriage was often depicted as a constraint for women, a form of slavery or legal prostitution that hindered women from flourishing as individuals. The most well-known formulation of marriage as a contract between equals and of divorce as the termination of such a contract, which should involve a reduction of any possible transaction costs was due to Harriet Taylor. Her husband, John Stuart Mill, later applied the principle of 'perfect equality' to men and women, advocating for a system that allowed neither power nor privilege for one gender, nor subjection and disability for the other (Mill, 1869).

The role of economists of the time in questioning the doctrine of the separate sphere became central when middle and upper-class women entered the workforce. This phenomenon was primarily the result of the struggle of the women's movement for higher education and had the immediate effect of altering the labor supply curve. Nonetheless, women often remained segregated into some specific sectors, which required low-profile workers, or faced a significant pay gap. This pay gap was implemented as a means to advance men's careers and deter women from pursuing their ambitions.

On one side, many economists, such as Marshall, Jevons, Edgeworth, and Webb in the United Kingdom, and Ely, Carver, and Taussig in the United States, regardless of their political visions, accepted the doctrine of the separate spheres and tried to explain the rationale behind it from an economic point of view. They argued that preserving the separate spheres was the most rational and morally sound way to organize society. They put forth a paternalistic argument, contending that married female workers would be diverted from their primary role as care-providers for their families. Furthermore, they asserted that women did not need any form of independence because they were already protected by their male counterparts, either fathers or husbands. To reinforce this vision based on the doctrine of the separate spheres, economists introduced the concept of subsistence wage for women and family wage for men in order to justify and rationalize the gender pay gap. Finally, they also debated about the opportunity of introducing protective legislation for women workers. The aim of such legislation was to decrease women's competitiveness in the labor market and prevent potential social problems that could arise from women's absence from their households. The moralistic argument in favor of the traditional gendered dichotomy between the public and private spheres affected female social reformers too. Some of them started to exalt a maternalistic approach, emphasizing the superiority of motherhood. This stance reinforced the segregation of women within the domestic sphere, by offering a rationale for their subjection.

On the other side, many British economists of the time as well as American economists and social reformers from the Progressive Era, mostly women, such as Fawcett, Collet, Kelley, and Breckinridge, considered the doctrine of the separate spheres inefficient from an economic perspective because the subjection of one part of society decreased the overall well-being of society. They rejected the notion of the family wage and factory legislation as reflections of the traditional subjection of women to men.

Phenomena such as urbanization, immigration, and the emancipation of people of color pushed women toward the public sphere, thereby redefining the boundaries of the separate spheres for both white American women of Anglo-Saxon origin (referred to as 'native') and other women from different backgrounds, including lower-income immigrants. Many middle-class native women assumed public roles as charity workers or social reformers, initiating fundraising activities aimed at providing education and professional training to female immigrants. In turn, these immigrant women started to become integrated into the process of Americanization by contributing to the flourishing of American society through upward mobility that spanned over generations (Abramitzky & Boustan, 2022; Anderson & Zinsser, 2000).

These macro phenomena, which dramatically affected the lives of women during the Progressive Era, were scrutinized by economists and social reformers of the time who often reinforced the doctrine of the separate spheres by incorporating elements of eugenics (Leonard, 2016). Even the critics of the doctrine of the separate spheres were not entirely free from the influence of eugenics, as in the case of Charlotte Perkins Gilman. She played a crucial role in proposing the image of a 'new woman' intended as a well-educated and compassionate social agent, unburdened by confinement within the private sphere. Perkins Gilman's new woman was envisioned as breaking free from the prevailing androcentric culture that had relegated women to servitude to men, which might become detrimental to the Anglo-Saxon race.

The path of women toward the public sphere was ostracized by the cult of domesticity, a counter-movement, that spread in America during the nineteenth century, aimed at reinforcing the doctrine of the separate spheres. It became a companion ideology of gendered spheres by advocating the strict separation between public and private life in middle-class families in the name of the notion of 'true womanhood'. It was based on the idea that women were expected to fulfill their natural roles of perfect and obedient wives as well as nurturing mothers who could instill traditional family values in their children, who were seen as the future of society.

The tension between the notions of 'true womanhood' and 'new woman' was tangible in the debate on marriage and the family which occurred among economists of the time. On one side, there were those who advocated for the preservation of the traditional institution of marriage in line with the separate spheres: they embraced arguments such as the family wage, the notion of true womanhood, and the idea of social harmony based on the traditional division of roles between men and women in the two spheres. On the other side, there were detractors of the doctrine of separate spheres who promoted gender equality within marriage and in the marketplace. They did so either by embracing moral principles of individual freedom and equality or by making economic arguments based on the principle of opportunity cost applied to the trade-off between women's time at work and their engagement at home.

The debate encompassed economists and social reformers with a range of ideological perspectives, including classical liberals, Marxists, and socialists, and, especially in the United States, libertarian thinkers.

Classical liberals could be found among both the supporters and critics of the doctrine of separate spheres.

Marxists, influenced by Engels' book on the origin of the family (1884), depicted capitalism and patriarchy as intertwined. In the Marxist view, the man/husband represented the bourgeoisie, while the wife, or the prostitute, symbolized the proletariat. This perspective held that when capitalist production and property relations were abolished, gender inequality and the commodification of women would automatically disappear. Among non-Marxist socialists, it was Charles Fourier who first used the status of women as the fundamental measure for evaluating social progress. Non-Marxist socialists rejected the idealization of the family based on natural ties and bonds. Instead, they emphasized the role of culture in shaping the family, which they saw as a place where men held dominion over women and children, considering them as their property (Moller Okin, 1979).

American libertarians, who were also detractors of the doctrine of separate spheres, promoted free love, rejected monogamy, and proposed the abolition of marriage, differently from classical liberals, who typically did not reject existing institutions (McElroy, 1992, 2022).[9] Libertarians adopted an argument similar to that used by Marxists, albeit from the opposite side of the political spectrum: they believed that the subjection

[9] As McElroy pointed out (1992, 2022), while classical liberals focused on restrictive social and cultural norms, libertarians focused on legal restrictions. American libertarians of the Progressive Era, including figures such as Voltairine de Cleyre, Lucy Stone, Lillian Harman, Angela Heywood, and many more, argued that achieving equality and dignity for both sexes was a path to anarchism. They regarded sexual liberation as a manifestation of social freedom.

of women would cease once the State was abolished. Instead of blaming capitalism and the economic structure of the society, as Marxists did, libertarians pointed their finger at the State and the political nature of the society. Both groups viewed patriarchy as an effect of something major, without delving into the nature of patriarchy *per se* and its effects that harm women's lives in non-capitalistic societies as well as in other forms of political structures, such as communities.

Besides the analysis of marriage and family, economists of the time scrutinized other topics related to the challenge against the doctrine of the separate. These included women's suffrage, prostitution, and, only partially, the intersection of gender and ethnicity which affected Black American women, whose condition of being women and persons of color made the path toward the public sphere more challenging for them.

By analyzing the opportunity cost of granting the vote to women: economists who supported female suffrage tried to explain that the benefits of women's enfranchisement would outweigh the costs; detractors of female suffrage argued that the costs would outweigh the benefits by diverting women's energy and time from their primary task of care-providers, thus reinforcing the doctrine of the separate spheres.

The economic debate on prostitution was also contingent on the acceptance or rejection of the doctrine of the separate spheres: some perceived prostitution as an economic and voluntary transaction between men and women that reproduced the dynamics of the 'natural' subjection of women to men; others considered prostitution as an effect of the economic imbalance between men and women in the labor market that disproportionately affected the lower-class population, especially women, who occupied the most disadvantaged position when it came to income levels across all classes.

Economists of the time did not deal specifically with the condition of women of color. Influenced by their adherence to eugenics, some perpetuated the notion that the quality of work performed by people of color was inferior. Combining this idea with the general belief that women were naturally low-skilled workers, it is evident that they could be seen, explicitly or implicitly, as racist and chauvinist.

However, the battle against both gender and race discrimination was central in many activists of the time who adopted moral as well as economic arguments. For instance, Sarah Grimké drew parallels between the conditions of women and the conditions of slaves. Yet, women of color tended to be more conservative than white female activists of the time: during the nineteenth century, they mainly adhered to the doctrine of the separate sphere by embracing the cult of true womanhood. Later, during the Progressive Era, they moved beyond the doctrine of separate spheres by embracing the ideal of the 'new woman'.

Between the 1920s and 1970s, significant strides were made toward achieving gender equality in Western society. It was a gradual process that took place at different times and in different countries. Key developments included changes in marriage legislation to curb women's subjugation to their husbands, women gaining full access to higher education and political rights, and the removal of legal barriers against women in the workforce. The sexual and cultural revolution, which occurred in the late 1960s in concomitance with the uprising of the second wave of feminism, transformed women's private life with legislative changes related to contraception, divorce, and abortion. These changes, at least in formal terms, allowed women to become the masters of their destiny and embark on the quiet revolution, as labeled by Goldin (1990, 2006, 2021). The doctrine of the separate spheres seemed to have been finally defeated, albeit tacit rules, social pressure, and enduring gender stereotypes have persisted.

Yet, the doctrine of the separate sphere resurged within economics. This resurgence, which occurred in standard economics, along with the reaction against it, which led to the rise of feminist economics, is the focus of the second part of this book covering the period between the mid-1900 and early 2000s. This section primarily explores the realm where the doctrine of separate spheres reemerged within economics, specifically, on the treatment of marriage theory (encompassing mate search and divorce) and the economics of the family (involving the division of labor within the household and decisions regarding childrearing), keeping in mind that while marriage and divorce are legally acknowledged institutions, the gendered division of labor among spouses is more intertwined with cultural norms and established conventions.

During the first half of the twentieth century, the doctrine of the separate spheres received a boost with the rise of home economics in the

United States. Home economics was intended as the scientific management of the household aimed at shaping families into ideal and efficient consumers. Women were seen as instrumental in efficiently directing and organizing household consumption. This way of considering the role of women in society was strictly tied to the cult of domesticity. Home economics courses introduced girls to manuals and educational materials that aimed to prepare them for their role as homemakers, wives, mothers, and care-providers (Agarwal, 1997; Elias, 2008; Nickols & Kay, 2015; Stage & Vincenti, 1997).

During the interwar period, household economics emerged as an enlargement of home economics. It was developed by Chicago economists, Marion Talbot, Hazel Kyrk, Margaret Reid, and Elizabeth Hoyt. They intended households as productive sectors modeled as a series of industries. Within these households, members produce goods and services for their own consumption, by using their own capital and their own unpaid labor. Although some differences in their stances on the cult of domesticity, household economists of the time did not completely deviate from accepting the traditional role played by women within the domestic sphere (Ironmonger, 2001; Walker, 2003).

Both home economics and household economics rejecting the exclusive focus on households as centers of nurturing, endearment, and affection, and instead analyzing the economic decisions made by families, they still tended to consider women in the traditional role of full-time homemakers and consumers, and "rationalized the belief that unpaid household labor was women's work and that women's work was not work at all" (Barker & Feiner, 2004, 24).

The analytical framework of household economics, combined with labor economics and human capital theory, paved the way for the emergence of what is commonly referred to as the new home economics. The combination of labor economics and human capital was initially introduced by economists Gary Becker and Jacob Mincer during the 1960s while they were at Columbia University. A decade later, Gary Becker further developed the field of new home economics during his time at the University of Chicago. Becker's new home economics was standard economics applied to the economics of the family.

Other economists of the time, such as Theodore Schultz, Milton Friedman, and many of their students, also made significant contributions to and enriched the field of new home economics over the course of two decades or more.[10] The culmination of the new home economics occurred with the publication of Becker's book, *Treatise on the Family* (1981 [1991]). Furthermore, the new home economics gained widespread recognition and momentum when Gary Becker was awarded the Nobel Prize in 1992. Currently, the application of standard economics to gender-related issues is typically referred to as the 'economics of gender'.[11]

As defined in Chapter IV, Becker's economic approach to gender issues can be thought as the doctrine of the separate spheres on steroids. It was based on a strict division of labor within marriages, with men assuming the role of breadwinners and women taking on the responsibilities of homemaking and caregiving. Becker considered the traditional division of labor between husbands and wives as an application of the theory of comparative advantages within married couples. According to him, an efficient household would allocate women's time mainly to the household sector and men's time mainly to the market sector. This division of labor maximizes market and household production. As he wrote: "analytically, these differences can be distinguished by the assumption that an hour of household or market time of women is not a perfect substitute for an hour of the time of men when they make the same investments in human capital" (Becker 1991, 38).

Hence, married couples benefit from economies of scale. In fact, with men having acquired a higher level of human capital than women, their role in the public sphere (as breadwinners) is considered efficient, as is

---

[10] As illustrated by Grossbard et al. (2023), Becker founded two workshops: the Labor Workshop at Columbia University in 1958 and the Applications of Economics Workshop at the University of Chicago in 1970. Jacob Mincer co-directed the Columbia workshop. Both workshops played a pivotal role in advancing research in household economics, labor economics, and the economics of human capital. They also significantly contributed to the development of the research agenda on marriage and fertility. The proportion of women participating in both workshops was relatively high and many of them followed Becker's approach.

[11] In Becchio's work (2020), the term 'gender economics' was used to denote standard economics applied to gender isssues.

the role of women in the private sphere, which is justified by their lower level of human capital.

According to Becker and other new home economists, the disparities between women and men are due to biological intrinsic differences between men and women that are reinforced by cultural factors: the combination of biological and cultural differences allows us to understand labor segregation of women in lower-skilled occupations as well as the gender pay gap.

Becker's patriarchal attitude was reinforced by two more elements. First, he considered a job market-oriented education for boys and a home-oriented education for girls as an efficient human capital investment strategy, thereby ignoring the circularity of his way of reasoning that resembled the discrimination of women. Second, he represented household preferences by adopting a single utility function that corresponded to the utility function of the male breadwinner. This male figure, in Becker's view, was not only the more rational economic agent within the family but also a fair agent, eventually able to correct any possible deviance in other members' behavior: this benevolent male figure corresponded to the traditional figure of *pater familias*, which had justified men's power over women and children for centuries.

Further developments in new home economics partially modified Becker's adoption of the doctrine of the separate spheres, albeit they never completely eliminated it:

> Economists were, nevertheless, sometimes too ready to apply the implications of long-run competitive equilibrium to the status of women and the current state of gender inequities, concluding that the current state – whatever it was – was natural, inevitable, economically efficient, and therefore not usefully subject to change or policy intervention (…) Becker' model of taste-based discrimination famously concluded that gender pay differences unwarranted by productivity differences would disappear in appropriately competitive markets and thus focused much subsequent empirical research away from richer models of discrimination that might have fit gender issues more comfortably and toward finding productivity-based explanations of the gender pay gap. He also constructed models that rationalized an extreme gender-based division of

labor in households and occupational segregation (Averett et al., 2018, 4).

Moreover, new home economists ignored the fundamental role played by social pressure, tacit rules, self-constraints, gender stereotypes, and obsolete family policies in the division of labor between men and women. For instance, in the career-family dynamics, they reduced women's decision to sacrifice their professional careers, choosing part-time jobs or avoiding extra hours, as well as business trips, in order to devote more time to unpaid work within the household as a matter of personal preference. They did not explore the historical and cultural origins of gender inequality which can lead to inefficiency and break down Pareto optimality in marriage (Lundberg & Pollak, 2003). They often described social norms as the effect of consensus rather than of struggles and tended to ignore that the labor market and marriage market are social institutions shaped by norms and rules rather than by inter-personal agreements based on individual preferences.

As Folbre (2021) pointed out, new home economists did not properly scrutinize the broad category of 'care' as a central feature within political economy. Care, which includes unpaid work, is intended as the production, development and maintenance of human capabilities. Traditionally performed by women, care work had contributed on one side to provide public goods, which benefitted the well-being of the society as a whole, and on the other side, it had increased women's economic vulnerability.[12] New home economists reduced the analysis of care, which is crucial within marriage theory and the economics of the family, to the analysis of cooperative bargaining models and the phenomenon of free-riding. For instance, they presented a model of childbearing as driven exclusively by its cost and preferences (Folbre, 2008). They paid no attention to the ethic of care, which, as summarized by Hawk (2011), assumes the primacy of relationship rather than autonomy and applies the principle

[12] As Moos wrote: "Domestic and care work – both paid and unpaid – have been a central issue for feminist economics. In contrast to mainstream economics formulations that have justified the gender division of labor in the household and the allocation of unpaid labor to women in the name of efficiency and harmony, feminist economists have viewed this gender division of work as the lynchpin of gender inequality" (Moos, 2021, 90).

of responsibility against a vision that depends upon individual utility, as in the standard economics' instrumental rationality.

A sharp critique of new home economics, which often implied a rejection of the methodological assumptions and the theoretical results of standard economics as a whole, occurred between the 1970s and 1980s, when feminist economists emerged (Becchio, 2020). Feminist economics considered standard new home economics, not just mainstream but *malestream*, meaning grounded on methodological assumptions heavily biased by gender stereotypes that have favored men. Furthermore, masculinity and male values have been considered universal standards to assess paradigms upon which standard economic theory had been shaped, reinforcing the traditional subjection of women in the economy (Nelson, 1993, 1996).

Feminist economics aimed to develop an alternative model to standard economics applied to gender issues. As Jacobsen (2018) summarizes, feminist economics faced six specific challenges: the development of models able to explain endogenous preferences; the rejection of rational choice theory; the emphasis on the role of gender stereotypes that favor men and determine the traditional division on labor; the analysis of the origins of institutions that privilege men and disadvantage women; the development of a more comprehensive economic model of caregiving.

Feminist economists began to explore alternative ways to explain the economics of the family that would align with the concerns and values of the feminist movement of the time, which encompassed a range of cultural perspectives from conservatism to radicalism. Feminist economists of the time specifically pointed out the inequality and unfairness in new home economics intra-house allocation, bargaining, and relationships that perpetuate the subordination of women. They rejected Becker's arguments, which justified men's dominance in in the public spheres as well as women's subordination in the private sphere of family and failed to consider that gender roles in both public and private spheres had reinforced patriarchy and discrimination against women. They provided a model of marriage that included unpaid work and care as well as power and obligation embedded in cultural and social norms, which were wrongly explained or simply ignored by marriage theory *à la* Becker, which was detrimental to a correct view of the economics of the family and ignored that traditionally men had neglected housework and child care (Barker & Feiner, 2004; Bergmann, 1986, 1995; Paterson & Lewis, 1999).

Feminist economists, like feminist scholars, did not converge into a unique model in terms of theory and policy. However, they did converge in rejecting the doctrine of the separate spheres and in considering it unfair and inefficient, being it grounded on a general cultural devaluation of women and social roles associated with women that led to gender discrimination in the public sphere as well as in the private one, regardless of the rhetoric narrative of the cult of domesticity and true womanhood. Nonetheless, some feminists and feminist economists who advocate for a radical transformation of society have suggested transitioning from the traditionally male-dominated world into a more emotionally and less competitive female-centric world. While aiming for equality, this cultural, political, and social shift in the balance of power from the male to the female side can inadvertently reinforce the doctrine of separate spheres, justified by the natural propensity of women to be more compassionate and cooperative. By following this path, the doctrine of the separate spheres may appear for some feminists more a friend than a foe.

Eliminating the doctrine of separate spheres does not necessitate shifting the balance of power from the male dimension to the female one. Rather, it implies adopting a realistic perspective that combines a long-run educational project to promote equal job opportunities for women as well as an equal share of responsibilities between partners when it comes to housework. These measures and commitments would effectively render the doctrine of the separate spheres obsolete.

Feminist economist Barbara Bergmann used to present the effects of the doctrine of the separate spheres as a 'sex-role caste system', based on traditional stereotypes that disadvantaged women and, consequently, had detrimental effects on society as a whole. As a matter of fact, she proposed a transition toward gender equality to be achieved when women would participate in the male sphere, and men would engage in the female sphere. This transition was based on classical liberal principles that advocate equal freedom and dignity for all individuals, regardless of gender, class, race, sexual orientation, and religious beliefs (Bergmann, 1998).

Going beyond the doctrine of the separate spheres allows our global society to reach gender inequality in both spheres. This process implies a double movement: women need to have a more significant presence in the public sphere, and men need to equally share responsibilities in the private sphere.

However, data reveal that we are still a long way from accomplishing these goals: *de facto* women continue to bear the double burden of paid work in the marketplace, where significant gender gaps persist, and unpaid care work at home, while men still hold more power in the public spheres and rarely share responsibilities in the private sphere.

This book aims to offer a historical perspective on the journey toward gender equality, as viewed through the lens of the doctrine of the separate spheres by male and female economists and scholars who adopted economics whether in support of or in opposition to the doctrine. Creating a comprehensive global history of the separate spheres would necessitate a substantial cultural effort and a vast amount of expertise beyond the scope of this author's capabilities. The book traces this history from the rise of classical liberalism in the eighteenth century to the split between standard economists and feminist economists in the 1990s. This investigation primarily encompassed Western society, where the doctrine of separate spheres was well-defined. The initial chapters concentrated solely on the Anglo-American society, with exclusive attention on the American experience in the subsequent sections, particularly as the doctrine gained prominence and experienced a resurgence there starting in the 1950s–1960s.

As mentioned earlier, the path toward gender equality remains long and challenging, yet numerous individuals are committed to persist in fighting the right fight.

1.3 A Note on Definitions

In this book, various labels are employed, and it is important to clarify their distinctions, starting with the title that distinguishes between 'political economy' and 'economics'. As this historical exploration begins with the contributions of early modern scholars who dealt with the multifaceted aspect of the doctrine of the separate spheres by adopting economic argument, the label 'political economy' is more appropriate. The second part, which illustrates more recent contribution from economists, either standard or feminist, required the adoption of the label 'economics'. This label denotes the technical aspect of the discipline that, at least in the intentions of mainstream economists, has separated itself from the political dimension.

The labels 'mainstream', 'neoclassical', and 'standard' are synonymous and they refer to the dominant paradigm within the economic theory that emerged in the second half of the twentieth century. As mentioned earlier, standard economics applied to gender issues, such as marriage theory and the economics of household and the family, was termed 'new home economics' in the 1970s, primarily based on the work of Gary Becker. Lately, as mentioned earlier, the official label used is 'economics of gender'.

Opposite to standard economics, there are heterodox economic approaches that criticize and reject the mainstream. Feminist economics emerged and is still considered a heterodox approach. Lately, the gap between the two approaches has been narrowing. New generations of scholars from both sides are converging toward more moderate positions and, as matter of fact, the academic job market suggests the opportunity to avoid radical perspectives.

The label 'feminist', which is historically correct when applied to 'feminist economics' and its history, may be problematic today, considering that it is less inclusive than the label 'gender', which encompasses a non-binary vision and includes other gender identities. Nonetheless, the majority of research on the economic condition of other gender identities as well as on same-sex partnership is still predominantly found in feminist economics rather than in the economics of the gender.

Finally, some labels, which are no longer commonly adopted in public debates and academic publications, have been used for the sake of coherence with the historical reconstruction presented in this book. As mentioned above, a binary language, based on men and women, has been employed; the label 'people/women of color' has been preferred, although it is sometimes used interchangeably with the label 'Black Americans'; the label 'prostitution' and 'prostitutes' have been used as well, as the label 'sex-workers' is out of context in the late nineteenth century.

References

Abramitzky, R., & Boustan, L. (2022). *Streets of Gold: America's Untold Story of Immigrant Success*. Hachette Book Group.

Addabbo, T. Arrizabalaga, M., & Owens, A. (2010). *Gender Inequalities, Households and the Production of Well-Being in Modern Europe*. Ashgate.

Agarwal, B. (1997). Bargaining and Gender Relations: Within and Beyond the Household. *Feminist Economics, 3*(1), 1–51.

Akerlof, G., & Kranton, R. (2010). *Identity Economics: How Our Identities Shape Our Work, Wages, and Well-Being*. Princeton University Press.

Akkerman, T. & Stuurman, S. (Eds.), (1998). *Perspectives on Feminist Political Thought in European History: From the Middle age to The Present*. Routledge.

Amstron, C., & Squires, J. (2002). Beyond the Public/Private Dichotomy: Relational Space and Sexual Inequalities. *Contemporary Political Theory 1*, 261–283.

Anderson, B., & Zinsser, J. (2000). *A History of Their Own*. Oxford University Press.

Apple, R. (2006). *Perfect Motherhood: Science and Childrearing in America*. Rutgers University Press.

Averett, S., Argys, L., & Hoffman, S. (Eds.). (2018). *The Oxford Handbook of Women and the Economy*. Oxford University Press.

Baird, I. (Ed.). (2014). *Social Networks in the Long Eighteenth Century: Clubs, Literary Salons, Textual Coteries*. Cambridge Scholars Publishing.

Barker, D. (1995). Economists, Social Reformers, and Prophets: A Feminist Critique of Economic Efficiency. *Feminist Economics, 1*(3), 26–39.

Baker, M., & Jacobsen, J. (2007). Marriage, Specialization and the Gender Division of Labor. *Journal of Labor Economics, 108*(4), 663–679.

Barker, D., & Feiner, S. (2004). *Liberating Economics: Feminist Perspectives on Families, Work and Globalization.* The University of Michigan Press.
Beauvoir (de), S. (1949). *Le Deuxième Sexe.* Gallimard.
Becchio, G. (2020). *A History of Feminist and Gender Economics.* Routledge.
Becker, G. (1981 [1991]). *A Treatise on the Family.* Harvard University Press.
Bergmann, B. (1986). *The Economic Emergence of Women.* Basic Books.
Bergmann, B. (1995). Becker's Theory of the Family: Preposterous Conclusions. *Feminist Economics, 1*(1), 141–150.
Bergmann, B. (1998, Spring). The Only Ticket to Equality: Total Androgyny, Male Style. *Journal of Contemporary Legal Issues, 9*, 75–86.
Berik, G., & Kongar, E. (Eds.). (2021). *The Routledge Handbook of Feminist Economics.* Routledge.
Botting, E. (2006). *Family Feuds: Wollstonecraft, Burke, and Rousseau on the Transformation of the Family.* State University of New York Press.
Brake, E. (2016). Equality and Non-Hierarchy in Marriage: What Do Feminists Really Want?. In E. Brake (Ed.), *After Marriage: Rethinking Marital Relationships* (pp. 100–124). Oxford University Press.
Brown, H., & Dow, G. (Eds.). (2011). *Readers, Writers, and Salonnières: Female Networks in Europe, 1700–1900.* Peter Lang.
Card, C. (1996). *Against Marriage and Motherhood. Hypatia, 11*(3), 1–23.
Chambers, C. (2017). *Against Marriage: An Egalitarian Defence of the Marriage-Free State.* Oxford University Press.
Clark, A. (1919). *Working Life of Women in the Seventeenth Century.* Routledge.
Cogan, F. (1989). *The All-American Girl: The Ideal of Real Womanhood.* University of Georgia Press.
Cohen, D. (1989). Seclusion, Separation, and the Status of Women in Classical Athens. *Greece and Rome, 36*(1), 3–15.
Cott, N. (1977). *The Bonds of Womanhood: "Women's Sphere" in New England, 1780–1835.* Yale University Press.
Davis, J. (2011). *Individuals and Identity in Economics.* Cambridge University Press.
De Grazia, V., & Furlough, E. (Eds.). (1996). *The Sex of Things: Gender and Consumption in Historical Perspective.* University of California Press.
Delphy, C., & Leonard, D. (1992). *Familiar Exploitation: A New Analysis of Marriage in Contemporary Western Societies.* Polity Press.
De Vries, J. (2008). *The Industrious Revolution. Consumer Behavior and the Household Economy, 1650 to the Present.* Cambridge University Press.
Eibach, J., & Lanzinger, M. (Eds.). (2020). *The Routledge History of the Domestic Sphere in Europe.* Routledge.

Elias, M. (2008). *Stir It Up: Home Economics in American Culture*. University of Pennsylvania Press.

Engels, F. (1884 [1972]). *The Origin of the Family, Private Property, and the State*. Pathfinder Press.

Ferguson, M. (2016). Vulnerability by Marriage: Okin's Radical Feminist Critique of Structural Gender Inequality. *Hypatia, 31*(3), 687–703.

Fitzpatrick, E. (1990). *Endless Crusade: Women Social Scientists and Progressive Reform*. Oxford University Press

Folbre, N. (2008). *Valuing Children: Rethinking the Economics of the Family*. Harvard University Press.

Folbre, N. (2021). *The Rise and Decline of Patriarchal Systems*. Verso.

Fox-Genovese, E. (1988). *Within the Plantation Household: Black and White Women of the Old South*. University of North Carolina Press.

Fraser, N. (1990). Rethinking the Public Sphere: A Contribution to the Critique of Actually Existing Democracy. *Social Text, 25*(26), 56–80.

Friedan, B. (1963). *The Feminine Mistique*. Norton and Company.

Goldin, C. (1990). *Understanding the Gender Gap: An Economic History of American Women*. Oxford University Press.

Goldin, C. (2006). The Quiet Revolution That Transformed Women's Employment, Education, and Family. *American Economic Review, 96*(2), 1–21.

Goldin, C. (2021). *Career and Family: Women's Century-Long Journey Toward Equity*. Princeton University Press.

Gray White, D. (1985). *Arn't I a Woman? Female Slaves in the Plantation South*. Norton and Company.

Grossbard, S. Beller, A., & Idmansour, I. (2023, forthcoming). Women and Economics Workshops Run by Gary Becker and Jacob Mincer at Columbia University and the University of Chicago. *Journal of Family and Economic Issues*. Available at https://humcap.uchicago.edu/RePEc/hka/wpaper/Beller_Grossbard_Fava_etal_2021_women-economics-workshops-becker-mincer.pdf

Habermas, J. (1989). *The Structural Transformation of the Public Sphere*. MIT Press.

Hawk, T. F. (2011). An Ethic of Care: A Relational Ethic for the Relational Characteristics of Organizations. In M. Hamington & M. Sander-Staudt (Eds.), *Applying Care Ethics to Business* (pp. 3–34). Springer.

Helly, D., & Reverby, S. (Eds.). (1997). *Gendered Domains: Rethinking Public and Private in Women's History*. Cornell University Press.

Ironmonger, D. (2001). Household Production. In N. Smelser & B. Baltes (Eds.), *International Encyclopedia of the Social & Behavioral Sciences* (pp. 6934–6939). Elsevier.

Jacobsen, J. (2018). Women and the Labor Market: A Feminist Perspective. In S. L. Averett, L. M. Argys, & S. D. Hoffman (Eds.), *The Oxford Handbook of Women and the Economy* (pp. 623–641). Oxford University Press.

Jones, J. (1985). *Labor of Love, Labor of Sorrow: Black Women, Work, and the Family from Slavery to the Present*. Basic Books.

Katz, M. (1992). Ideology and 'The Status of Women' in Ancient Greece. *History and Theory, 31*(4), 70–97.

Katz, M. (2000). Sappho and Her Sisters: Women in Ancient Greece. *Signs, 25*(2), 505–531.

Kerber, L. (1988). Separate Spheres, Female Worlds, Woman's Place: The Rhetoric of Women's History. *The Journal of American History, 75*(1), 9–39.

Kuiper, E. (2022). *A Herstory of Economics*. Polity Press.

Leonard, T. (2016). *Illiberal Reformers: Race, Eugenics and American Economics in the Progressive Era*. Princeton University Press.

Lerner, G. (1986). *The Creation of Patriarchy*. Oxford University Press.

Locke, J., & Hunt Booting, E. (Eds.). (2009). *Feminist Interpretations of Alexis de Tocqueville*. Pennsylvania State University Press.

Lundberg, S., & Pollak, R. (2003). Efficiency in Marriage. *Review of Economics of the Household, 1*(3), 153–167.

Maushart, S. (2001). *Wifework: What Marriage Really Means for Women*. Bloomsbury Publishing.

McElroy, W. (1992). *Freedom, Feminism, and the State*. Homes and Meier.

McElroy, W. (2022). *Liberty for Women. Freedom and Feminism in the Twenty-First Century*. Library of Congress.

Mill, J. S. (1869). *The Subjection of Women*. Longmans, Green, Reader, and Dyer.

Moller Okin, S. (1979). *Women in the Western Political Thought*. Princeton University Press.

Moring, B. (Ed.). (2010). *Female Economic Strategies in the Modern World*. Pickering & Chatto.

Moos, K. (2021). Care work. In G. BErik & E. Kongar (Eds.), *The Routledge Handbook of Feminist Economics* (pp. 90–98). Routledge.

Moses, J. (Ed.). (2008). *Marriage, Law and Modernity: Global Histories*. Bloomsbury Publishing.

Nelson, J. (1993). Gender and Economic Ideologies. *Review of Social Economy, 51*(3), 287–301.

Nelson, J. (1996). *Feminism, Objectivity and Economics*. Routledge.
Nickols, S., & Kay, G. (Eds.). (2015). *Remaking Home Economics: Resourcefulness and Innovation in Changing Times*. The University of Georgia Press.
Paterson, J., & Lewis, M. (Eds.). (1999). *The Elgar Companion to Feminist Economics*. Edward Elgar.
Pateman, C. (1988). *The Sexual Contract*. Polity Press.
Ross, C. (2006). Separate Spheres or Shared Dominions? *Transformation, 23*(4), 228–235.
Rotman, D. (2006). Separate Spheres? Beyond the Dichotomies of Domesticity. *Current Anthropology, 47*(4), 666–674.
Sarti, R. (2020). Constructing and Challenging Dependence. In J. Eibach and M. Lanzinger (Eds.), *The Routledge History of the Domestic Sphere in Europe 16th to 19th Century*, (pp. 79–98). Routledge.
Smith-Rosenberg, C. (1985). *Disorderly Conduct: Visions of Gender in Victorian America*. Oxford University Press.
Spolsky, B. (2012). *The Cambridge Handbook of Language Policy*. Cambridge University Press.
Stage, S., & Vincenti, V. (Eds.). (1997). *Rethinking Home Economics*. Cornell University Press.
Walker, S. (2003). Professionalization or Incarceration? Household Engineering, Accounting and the Domestic Ideal. *Accounting, Organizations and Society, 28*(7–8), 743–772.
Yentsch, A. (1991). The Symbolic Divisions of Pottery: Sex-Related Attributes of English and Anglo-American Household Pots. In R. McGuire & R. Paynter (Eds.), *The Archeology of Inequality* (pp. 192–230). Basil Blackwell.
Young, I. (1990). *Justice and the Politics of Difference*. Princeton University Press.

Part I

Escaping the Doctrine of the Separate Spheres (1700s–early 1900s): The Economists' Points of View

2

Educated Women as an Asset to Society: The Role of Classical Liberal Tradition in Modern Europe

This chapter addresses the interconnection among three fundamental aspects of the doctrine of separate spheres which were questioned between the seventeenth and late eighteenth centuries: women's education, women's economic independence, and women's role within the institution of marriage.[1] As Lerner wrote, the effects of the doctrine of the separate spheres on women in Western society is culturally rooted in the history of Mesopotamia, where:

[1] Marriage is a very ancient institution which might be dated back before 2350 B.C., when the evidence of a marriage ceremony between a couple in Mesopotamia was recorded. In ancient time, its primary purpose was to bind women to men, who became their owners. Men were often surrounded by concubines and polygamy was normally customary, because women were considered men's property regardless of their own status. Divorce and repudiation were commonly accepted especially in case of childless unions. Religion and love entered much later into the picture, roughly in the Middle Ages, when the power of the Church arose and forbad polygamy and divorce by setting up marriage as a sacrament upon which the Church was the sole institution able to rule it (Yalom, 2001). The concept of romantic love emerged especially in the literature, albeit the legal and practical subjection of women continued (Coontz, 2006).

G. Becchio, *The Doctrine of the Separate Spheres in Political Economy and Economics*, Palgrave Studies in Classical Liberalism,
https://doi.org/10.1007/978-3-031-51262-9_2

> female subordination within the family, becomes institutionalized and codified in law; prostitution becomes established and regulated; with increasing specialization of work, women were gradually excluded from certain occupations and professions. After the invention of writing and the establishment of formal learning, women are excluded from equal access to such education. The cosmogonies, which provide the religious underpinning for the archaic state, subordinate female deities to chief male gods, and feature myths of origin which legitimate male ascendancy. (Lerner, 1986, 54)

The doctrine of the separate spheres applied to marriage was formalized by the institution known as 'coverture'—from the French for "covering"—which persisted until early feminism emerged in the nineteenth century. It implied that married women gave up their maiden name in order to surrender their identity in favor of their husbands who became representatives of two people and, eventually, of their children by forming a family around a household that has been regarded as the fundamental unity of a society. If households flourish, societies follow along: households could flourish only if a strict division of labor between spouses was achieved. Regardless of their natural inclination, men were breadwinners while women must take care of everything related to the sphere of domesticity, including child raising (Barclay et al., 2020).

According to the doctrine of the separate spheres, married women were supposed to be economically dependent on their husbands. Their primary duties revolved around household management and caring for the family. The concept of the cult of domesticity, which defined their social role, could vary depending on their social status. Lower-class women often worked alongside their husbands, especially on farms, while middle and upper-class women were primarily confined to their roles as housewives and mothers.

Given this perspective, women's education was predominantly geared toward preparing them for roles associated with the cult of domesticity and motherhood. Women typically received only basic education or, in many cases, no education at all. In several countries, girls were restricted from attending primary schools and were entirely excluded from secondary education, not to mention higher education. This division of gender roles was widely accepted and remained unquestioned until a debate emerged between the end of the eighteenth century and the beginning of the nineteenth century.

The critique of the doctrine of the separate spheres emerged within the tradition of classical liberalism and the rising of the capitalist system. The influence of capitalism led to a division between the market and the household, resulting in shifts in the relationships between husbands and wives, as well as in the social roles of men and women. This transformation occurred during a period when individualism was gaining prominence, rendering patriarchy ideologically unsuitable for a maturing liberal market society, as argued by Locke.

The initial arguments against the doctrine of the separate spheres were grounded in the notion of natural rights (life, liberty, and private property), asserting that all individuals are inherently equal by nature and, therefore, equal before the law, regardless of their gender, ethnicity, personal income, and so forth.[2]

A following argument against the doctrine of the separate spheres focused on the notion of virtue: it argued that both sexes are equally virtuous or vicious and there are no neurological differences between them. The uniqueness of certain values traditionally associated with femininity, rooted in the emotional sphere, was considered complementary, rather than inferior, to masculine values based on rationality. The opposite roles and attitudes of women and men in the private and public spheres were seen as the result of traditional education that has differentiated their roles in the two different spheres.[3]

[2] The concept of natural rights served philosophers of the time to explained the emergence of the State as a result of a contract among peers aimed to build up a social system able of guaranteeing peace and prosperity by either alienating or delegating their power to a third part (the State).

[3] Among the scholars who were involved in this debate were Mary de Gournay (1622 [2002]), who was deeply influenced by Michel de Montaigne, and the (male) French philosopher Poullain de la Barre (1673). They both insisted on the fact that there were no neurological differences between men and women that could determine any different behavior between the sexes. Hence, any differentiation between the sexes was grounded in an unfair subjection of women.

A further argument against the doctrine of the separate spheres focused on the notion of power and played a central role in John Locke's support for the equality of the sexes before the law.

This debate centered around the opportunity for women to pursue higher education in order to improve their condition and enhance overall social well-being. Supporters of the doctrine of the separate spheres argued against allowing women to earn university degrees, claiming that educated women wasted their time studying when they should instead focus on taking care of the family, seen as the primary unit of a wealthy and healthy society. On the opposite side, those who rejected the doctrine of the separate spheres promoted women's education as a pivotal instrument to enrich overall well-being.

2.1 Early Debates on the Doctrine of the Separate Spheres

Christine de Pizan (1365–1430) was a forerunner among the critics of the doctrine of the separate spheres. Her attitude as well as her publications were inspired by her own personal experience: she earned her living from writing books and pamphlets of various genres. Her utopian novel, *Livre de la Cité des Dames* (1405 [1999]), was a celebration of the lives of famous women and it was a reaction to *Liber lamentationum Matheoluli* (*The Lamentations of Matheolus*) (ca. 1295) by Mathieu of Boulogne, or Matheolus, who accused women of making men's lives miserable and suggested not getting married, but having a mistress instead. He wrote:

> It's true that women are lazy, but they are always ready to do harm. An evil woman just gets worse, becoming even more evil and wicked. It would take far too long for me to tell you everything about them, so for brevity's sake I shan't. Woman is not wise in this respect, for in her eagerness to do harm she only brings about her own ruin. According to the law, as I understand it, woman is not rational, nor does her love reside deep in her heart, but is there on her gaze for everyone to see. She entrusts her honour openly to her eyes, yet they can't help but fail to protect it, since folly animates her gaze. With all her words, her chatter, and her talk, she

> could break a heart of glass; all her actions are stupid and foolish. Woman can do no good, indeed, goodness is destroyed and obliterated by her.[4]

The plot of De Pizan's books revolved around her dream of three virtues: Reason, Rectitude, and Justice, which led her to discover a visionary fortified city inhabited only by women divided into social groups: queens, warriors, poetesses, fortune tellers, scientists, martyrs, and saints. Some prominent figures prevailed in the city, including Roman Carmenta, who invented the alphabet; Minerva and Aracne, who elevated weaving to an art; and the great queens, Dido, Medea, Semiramis, and Penthesilea, who proudly challenged centuries-old misogynistic traditions.

Although De Pizan never questioned the doctrine of the separate spheres, she urged women to take control of their private lives and showcased the strength and bravery of many historical female figures to promote the recognition of women among the virtuous. This countered the medieval tradition of anti-feminism rooted in two different sources: Judeo-Christian theology (based on Eve's guilt, believed to have caused humankind's fall into eternal sin), and the medical science of classical antiquity (grounded in the idea that women were unable to regulate their toxic humor, as revealed by menstruation). Both of these aspects, moral fault and organic defect, contributed to the belief that women were destined to be dominated by men.

The French writer Marie de Gournay (1565–1645) shared De Pizan's perspective. In her works *The Equality of Men and Women* (1622) and *The Ladies' Grievance* (1626), she advocated for women's education. She argued that both sexes possessed the same virtues, and therefore, education should be aimed at enhancing moral values to create good citizens regardless of gender. According to her, the difference in cultural achievements between men and women was solely due to the unequal educational opportunities provided to boys and girls.

---

[4] As retrieved on August 11, 2023, at: http://www.theabsolute.net/misogyny/matheol.html.

She wrote:

> Blessed are you, Reader, if you are not of the sex to which one forbids all goods, depriving it of freedom. One denies this sex just about everything: all the virtues and all the public offices, titles, and responsibilities. In short, this sex has its own power taken away; with this freedom gone, the possibility of developing virtues through the use of freedom disappears. This sex is left with the sovereign and unique virtues of ignorance, servitude, and the capacity to play the fool, if this game pleases it. (1626)[5]

In England, a long tradition of authors, from John Knox to Robert Filmer, insisted on the notion of power in order to justify the division of roles between the sexes. They claimed that the public sphere was reserved for men only, in accordance with God's will. Knox argued that women were incapable of ruling a kingdom. Thomas Hobbes, while maintaining that the social contract was gender-neutral, claimed, without providing an explanation, that the state of nature was shaped by families within a patriarchal system. In this system, a family consisted of a man with his wife, his children, and servants treating his wife as either a child or a servant. Marriage, a product of civil law, followed the general principle of the social contract: women traded liberty and security by alienating their natural rights to their husbands (Hirschman, 2007). In his work *Patriarcha, or the Natural Power of Kings* (1680 [1969]), Filmer argued that men were the perpetual symbols of Adam, to whom God gave the power to rule on earth. Consequently, husbands were seen as the only legitimate heads of the family, just as kings were the only legitimate heads of a state, relegating women to the private sphere.

John Locke (1693) harshly criticized supporters of the doctrine of separate spheres by blending ethical and political arguments. He wrote that the ability to rule, whether a family or a country, depended exclusively on virtues such as intelligence, bravery, and temperance, which were shared by both men and women, who only differed physically (Nyland, 1993). Locke explicitly introduced the idea that the traditional division of roles between the sexes was a product of a patriarchal system

---

[5] As retrieved on August 13, 2023, at: https://www.degruyter.com/document/doi/10.7208/9780226305264-005/html.

that constantly reinforced the subjection of women by denying them proper education and, consequently, the possibility of active participation in the public sphere.

However, there was some ambiguity in Locke's position. On one side, he advocated sexual equality in terms of reason, education, property, marriage, divorce, and inheritance (Butler 1978). On the other side, he never denied the subordination of women to men (Moller Okin, 1979). He refuted the position expressed by Filmer's *Patriarcha* but granted men ultimate authority. He never supported suffrage for women, and he never questioned or explicitly criticized the institution of marriage. Quite the opposite, he considered marriage as the entry to full membership in society for women. Nonetheless, he recognized the importance of reforming the marriage contract in 1690, suggesting that the parties involved should negotiate it on equal terms and promoted equal parenting in terms of responsibilities and authority (Hirschman & McClure, 2007).

In France, François Poullain de la Barre (1648–1723) pointed out that the superiority of intellect was equally shared by all human beings regardless of gender. He rejected the traditional division between mind and body based on the Cartesian dichotomy of the mind as masculine and the body as feminine (Poullain de la Barre, 1673, 1674, 1675). According to him, women internalized this prejudice, making it natural for them to accept their subjection to men. The only way to overcome this situation and attain their own liberty was through education:

> if [women] were educated according to traditional methods, is to doubt if they were taught well and to wish to discover the truth themselves. As they make progress in this search for truth, they cannot avoid noticing that we are full of prejudices, and that it is necessary to get rid of them completely in order to acquire clear and distinct knowledge. (Poullain de la Barre, 1673, 119)

As Reuter (2019) pointed out, Poullain de la Barre referred to a normative concept of natural equality, and he developed a normative demand for equal opportunity, which was expected to be achieved mainly in the private sphere, i.e. within marriage.

Since the old times, Western societies often arranged marriages, with or without mutual consent. Marriages were primarily focused on property rearrangement. Criticism of arranged marriages increased in the early modern era when harmony in the domestic sphere, based on individuals' choices, assumed a more central role than in previous historical periods. However, the redistribution of resources between the involved families still played a fundamental role in marriage, especially in the upper classes, where arranged marriages remained common, and women had limited agency outside the domestic sphere (Hopkins & Norries, 2019).[6] Children were often betrothed at a very early age and married in their teens. Lord Halifax, in his *Advice to a Daughter* published in 1688, explained that one of the disadvantages of being a woman is that women were seldom permitted to make their own choice, especially when they got married.

The British philosopher Mary Astell (1666–1731) questioned: "if marriage is such a blessed state, how is it that there are so few happy marriages?". In 1712, Lady Mary Pierrepont Montagu, betrothed by her father to an Irish aristocrat she had never met, described her wedding arrangements as "daily preparations for my journey to Hell" (Moore, 2009).[7] Astell authored *A Serious Proposal to the Ladies, Parts I and II. Wherein a Method is offer'd for the Improvement of their Minds* (1694, 1697)[8] and *Some Reflections upon Marriage, Occasion'd by the Duke and Duchess of Mazarine's Case; which is also considered* (1700), both devoted to promoting women's self-improvement. The *Proposal* was an invitation to women to be "as perfect and happy as it's possible to be in this imperfect state," despite all the opportunities for improvement that were denied in the name of a supposed inferiority of women. In fact, women suffered from ignorance due to a limited education imposed by customs that were intentional outcomes of men's power over women:

---

[6] The Protestant Reformation redefined marriage by viewing secular love as a gift from God. Although the father figure lost his despotic power over household's members, he still retained full responsibility for their well-being.

[7] She escaped and married her lover, Edward Wortley Montagu, just days before the planned wedding.

[8] As retrieved on August 16, 2023, at: https://www.gutenberg.org/files/54984/54984-h/54984-h.htm.

> When a poor Young Lady is taught to value herself on nothing but her cloths, and to think she's very fine when well accoutered; when she hears say, that'tis Wisdom enough for her to know how to dress herself, that she may become amiable in his eyes, to whom it appertains to be knowing and learned; who can blame her if she lay out her Industry and Money on such Accomplishments, and sometimes extends it farther than her misinformed desires she should?[9]

Astell's solution, in her *Proposal,* was to establish a retreat from the world in order to make it possible for women to devote themselves to education and virtue without being tempted by vanity and frivolities, as they were accustomed to being and taught to do.

She wrote:

> For since GOD has given Women as well as Men Intelligent Souls, why should they be forbidden to improve them? Since he has not denied us the faculty of Thinking, why shou'd we not (at least in gratitude to him) employ our Thoughts on himself their noblest Object, and not unworthily bestow them on Trifles and Gaities and secular Affairs?

In this all-female community, women were expected to cultivate philosophy and meditation to improve their virtues. In Astell's *Reflections upon Marriage*, she highlighted the subjection of women once they got married. She encouraged women to focus on education as a means to become more virtuous rather than making every possible effort to find a husband who would likely become "a monarch for life". Happiness should not depend on other people's will, especially in the case of men who, once married, often turned into domestic tyrants. According to Astell, marriages based on 'Money, Wit, or Beauty' would soon collapse and make both spouses unhappy. The only path to happiness was through virtue, and the only means to achieve it was proper education that was still denied to women.

---

[9] As retrieved on August 16, 2023, at: http://digital.library.upenn.edu/women/astell/marriage/marriage.html.

Astell's purely philosophical argument, which did not advocate for women's access to equal rights but rather insisted on women's education as a tool to better fulfill the traditional role of being a good wife, led some critics to exclude her from the ranks of proto-feminist writers who challenged the doctrine of the separate spheres (Frye, 1997). Others considered Astell's emphasis on women's education, as well as her stance on gender equality, to be a fundamental contribution to the critique of the doctrine of the separate spheres (Broad, 2015; Webb, 2020).

Meanwhile, Daniel Defoe's *Roxana* (1724) and Samuel Richardson's *Pamela* (1740) were blamed for undermining the concept of arranged marriages and fueling expectations of romantic love. Their books were banned as dangerous readings for young women by François Fénelon, Archbishop of Chambray, in his *Instructions for the Education of a Daughter* (1687 [1713]). The prominent role of virtue as a tool for human and social improvement extended to the education of girls was the central argument in Fénelon's book. According to him, it was essential to provide women with a proper education as they were a fundamental element of the family, and families were the main constituents of civil society. He wrote:

"Virtue is as necessary for men as for women; and without entering upon the comparative good or ill which society experiences from the latter sex, it must be remembered that they are *one half of the human race*". Nonetheless, the education of girls was promoted by Fénelon in order to avoid their curiosity towards the public sphere. He wrote: "In such a state of lassitude, a young woman abandons herself to pure idleness; and idleness, which may be termed a languor of the soul, is an inexhaustible source of weariness and discontent. (…) This weariness and idleness, united with ignorance, beget a pernicious eagerness for public diversions; hence arises a spirit of curiosity, as indiscreet as it is insatiable".[10]

Hence, Fénelon had in mind a kind of education for women that reinforced the doctrine of the separate spheres rather than allowing them to make their own choices. Education for women was only aimed

[10] As retrieved on August 16, 2023, at: https://www.gutenberg.org/files/47621/47621-h/47621-h.htm.

at improving their performance within the household. Nevertheless, Fénelon included economics among the subjects to be taught to women, which they apparently disliked, as well as elements of jurisprudence to make them capable of properly managing the household.

More than Fénelon, it was Jean-Jacques Rousseau (1712–1778) who was the most influential philosopher of the time to believe in and reinforce the doctrine of the separate spheres. Firmly convinced that the differences between men and women were inherently natural and involved physical traits, characters, and minds, he argued that men and women must perform different roles within civil society. Men were meant for the public sphere (business, army, politics), while women were suited for the private domain (households and the family). Therefore, he believed that their education should be tailored to their respective roles.

In his work *Julie, or the New Heloise* (1761), Rousseau depicted the ideal 'private sphere,' where the main character serves as a virtuous model of a wife and mother. In his *Émile or Treatise on Education* (1762a), Rousseau argued for the importance of different educations for boys and girls to reinforce their distinct cultural roles and duties in society. According to him, men should be trained to govern and self-govern, while women should be educated to be obedient.

As pointed out by Hirschman (2007), Rousseau's sexism was political rather than theoretical. He was disgusted by his contemporaries who praised the major effects of civilization through the development of the arts and sciences and regarded the status of women as an indicator of the level of civilization. Rousseau believed that the modern world was morally corrupted by greed, egoism, and competition. According to him, women were functionally determined by their reproductive role. Therefore, contrary to those scholars who promoted education for girls to teach them moral values, Rousseau considered chastity as the most important virtue for women and their subordination as necessary for maintaining a natural patriarchal order.

In his work *The Social Contract* (1762b), patriarchy is seen as the golden age of isolated families. Women have innate qualities, such as shame and modesty, which make them unable to do anything outside the domestic sphere. Rousseau gave three reasons for the legitimacy of patriarchy: the family needs a final authority; the leardership must be in charge of men, who are the stronger of the two partners; children must be subjected to their fathers in order to learn and respect the fundamental role of authority, subjected to any affection: as fathers are never certain, children must be guided by respect rather than love (Moller Okin, 1979).

Like Edward Burke, Rousseau feared the transformation of the family into egalitarian terms and the subsequent loss of the patriarchal family based on the doctrine of separate spheres. Burke feared the destruction of patriarchy as a way to destroy morality and manners. He coined the term 'little platoon' to describe small communities like the family and claimed that without affection for kin and family, there is no affection for fellow citizens and the nation. Burke's argument anticipated Marxist feminists' and postfeminists' idea that the modern family emerged as a result of private property.

Rousseau admired and embraced the patriarchal rural family based on a moral code that allows the establishment of an authentic republic in popular sovereignty. He praised Aristotle's organicism, which was based on the idea that the State originates in the family. For Rousseau, society should maintain separate spheres between men and women because humans are solitary and peaceful beings, not social animals as in Locke's state of nature. Moreover, Rousseau considered procreation as a random act between strangers, and childbearing as an act of responsibility rather than an emotional bond between mothers and children.

He recognized that his vision contradicted the Enlightenment ideas of his time. In his analysis of the family and its transformation, Rousseau praised rural families (as opposed to bourgeois and aristocratic families) as instruments of republicanism, defending strict patriarchy which served as a tool to combat sexual corruption. Nonetheless, Rousseau rejected Filmer's correspondence between the patriarchal family and the patriarchal state.

While Mme. De Stael claimed Rousseau as a hero because he praised women as moral and civic educators, celebrating them as 'empresses' of the domestic sphere, Burke criticized Rousseau's educational system, based on creativity and contact with nature as presented in *Julie*, as an expression of the moral degeneration of French society (Botting, 2006). Rousseau's endorment of the separate spheres had a significant influence on Tocqueville, who emphasized the traditional division of labor between the sexes despite the restrictions on women's freedom. However, there is some feminist literature that praises Tocqueville. For instance, American educator Catharine Beecher (1800–1878) used Tocqueville as a resource to develop theories of self-governance for women, both as individuals and in groups (Locke & Botting, 2009).

2.2 Women's Access to Higher Education: Olympe de Gouges and Mary Wollstonecraft

The debate surrounding the doctrine of the separate spheres became central during the Enlightenment. In addition to the three arguments mentioned earlier—the notion of individual natural rights, the notion of virtue, and the notion of power—a socio-political argument emerged based on the recognition of the role of women as mothers and wives, seen as a matter of public utility.

In the sixth volume of the *Encyclopédie*, the subjection of women was depicted as a constructed result of patriarchy. Women's disadvantages within families and society were publicly recognized, especially within the legal framework and the economic realm, due to the denied access to education for women.[11]

One year before the beginning of the French Revolution, Olympe de Gouges (1748–1793) wrote the *Portrait of Women* (1788). In her pamphlet, de Gouges attacked the system by pointing out its patriarchal framework that "only allows us the right to please". She emphasized the lack of education for girls and the subjection of women to the private sphere: "We are fit only to manage a household. Women who are perceptive and aspire to take up literature are beings that society cannot tolerate; having no function within it, they inspire only tedium".

[11] During the French Revolution, several associations, such as the *Société fraternelle de l'un et l'autre sexe* and the *Société des républicaines révolutionnaires*, were founded and counted on more than two hundred members, exclusively women.

She suggested women be more confident in combining private duties and public commitment:

> I accept there is some basis for these differing principles but my belief is that women can unite the benefit of wit with household duties, even with the virtues of soulfulness, and the qualities of love: join to these beauties and a sweet nature and there, I accept, you would have a rare example. But who can aspire to perfection? We have no Pygmalion, unlike the Greeks, so therefore no Galatea either. In consequence, my dearest Sisters, we must be more indulgent amongst ourselves regarding our failings, hide them mutually and aim to become more favourable towards our sex.

De Gouges insisted on the idea that the subjection of women was often reinforced by a self-constrain attitude, which was mainly an effect of traditional chivalry education:

> Few women think like men, but there are a some; sadly, the greater number pitilessly join with the strongest party, without perceiving that they are themselves destroying the charms of their rule. How much we should regret the passing of that ancient Chivalry which our superficial men deem fantastical for it made women, at one and the same time, respectable and interesting! What pleasure delicate women must derive from the belief in the existence of this noble Chivalry, whilst now they are forced to blush at being born in a century when men seem to enjoy displaying towards women the opposite of these sentiments, so refined and respectful, that ennobled those happy days. Alas! who should one accuse: is it not always our imprudence, and indiscretions, my dearest Sisters?

Traditional education, according to de Gouges, had protected men from vanity: they compete for power and money, not for good-looking:

> If I imitate you, on this occasion, by revealing our faults, it is only to try and correct them. We all have them, our vagaries and our qualities. Men are organised in more or less the same way but they are more reasoned: they do not share in this rivalry of looks, wit, character, deportment, dress, that divides us and provides their amusement, their education, concerning us.

De Gouges also emphasized the notion of sisterhood, which was still lacking among women of the time:

> Ah! my Sisters, my dearest Sisters, is this what we reciprocally owe to ourselves. Men certainly tarnish each other a little, but not nearly as much as we do, and that is what (...) Fanaticism renders womankind even more inhumane. Oh Women, Women, whatever type, state or rank you belong to, become simpler, more modest, and more generous one to the other.

The pamphlet ends with an autobiographical note and an invitation to women to change their attitude and believe in themselves as the only way to overcome their subjection:

> I have often been reproached for not knowing how to compose myself in society; that the impulsiveness of my character shows me at a disadvantage; that otherwise I could be one of those adorable women, if I did not abandon myself so. I have often replied to this verbiage that I abandon myself no more than I compose myself; that I only know one kind of constraint, the weaknesses of Nature that humanity can only overcome through effort: and she who tames passion through self-esteem can justifiably call herself, the Forceful Woman.[12]

In 1790, de Gouges wrote a comedy in three acts, which was never staged, titled *The Necessity of Divorce*, in response to a National Assembly debate held on August 5, 1790, regarding divorce.[13] In her piece, she re-emphasized the importance of sisterhood: two cheated women resolved their despicable situation by being sensible and showing mutual respect and reciprocal trust. Against the stereotypes of either a heartbroken woman who cannot handle this kind of situation or a silly and superficial coquette who cannot care more about sharing a lover with others, the two protagonists were never depicted as victims, despite their sorrow

[12] As retrieved on August 20, 2023, at: https://www.olympedegouges.eu/docs/ba.Preface-pour-les-dames.pdf.

[13] A secular law in favor of divorce was finally decreed on September 20, 1792, by the National Assembly and modified in 1793 and 1794. From January 1, 1793, to June 17, 1795, nearly 6000 divorces were pronounced, 71% initiated by women. The law on divorce was revoked in 1816 during the Restoration and was not reinstated until 1844. Divorce by mutual consent was not fully re-established in France until 1975 (Godineau, 2004).

for having been betrayed. Moreover, De Gouges places the male cheater in a closet during the women's conversation to indicate that women can be rational and are entitled to show men how to properly behave and resolve any inconvenient situation. Nonetheless, the argument in favor of divorce is presented by a male character, Rosambert, who explains the advantages of divorce as such:

> "Through divorce, Father, you would place an innumerable mass of bachelors in the position of taking up marriage. They are reticent merely because they fear the eternity of marriage. More marriages would make it harder for libertines to illicitly search out girls, their numbers having decreased. Divorce gives you the means to propagate marriage by increasing its spread, by reducing the number of troublesome bachelors and, because the status of married individuals will depend on their behaviour, they will perforce become more circumspect. Finally, through the exercise of divorce, you gain the upper hand over vice and you avenge an oppressed virtue without using violent means. Couples who are at present living as though they were actually divorced are forced into sterility; when their position is altered by the changes that will take place they will become fecund again. You return a man to a wife who is made for him and a woman to a husband she finds suitable". And he went on: "with divorce there would be fewer unhappy households and fewer separations than might be envisaged since, the first, albeit false, tidings of this law made a deep enough impression on you for you to forget your failings and reunite more tenderly than ever".[14]

De Gouges' argument in favor of divorce was based on the fact that marriage left women in a powerless state, subjected to their husbands' will. Her views on marriage and divorce were articulated in her *Declaration of the Rights of Woman and the Female Citizen* (1791), a pamphlet that went beyond the question of divorce. It was one of the first publications openly directed against the doctrine of the separate spheres, where the author adopted a classical liberal argumentation.

The first article was about women being born free and remaining equal to men in rights, with social distinctions based only on common utility.

[14] As retrieved on August 11, 2023, at: https://olympedegouges.eu/docs/La-Necessite-du-divorce.pdf.

The second article claimed that the purpose of any political association is the preservation of the natural and imprescriptible rights of women and men. These rights include liberty, property, security, and, above all, resistance to oppression. This was an implicit reference to the oppression faced by women, who were relegated to the private sphere. The third article was about the principle of all sovereignty lying essentially in the Nation, which is the union of Woman and Man. The fourth article focused on the notion of liberty and justice, stating that it consists of "restoring to others all that belongs to them; hence the only limit to the exercise of the natural rights of women is the perpetual tyranny that man opposes to it and that these limits must be reformed by the laws of nature and reason". The fifth article was about the laws of nature and reason prohibiting all acts injurious to society. Again, this is an implicit accusation against constraints on women. The sixth and seventh articles were respectively an explicit request for women's suffrage and gender equality in the public sphere, as well as gender equality before the law and in courts. The seventeenth article was particularly important for the history of the doctrine of the separate spheres and its critique: it was about property that "belongs to both sexes, whether united or separated (upon divorce, property is split evenly between the involved parties, and property cannot be seized from women without reason)."

Influenced by the Enlightenment and the French Revolution, the British writer Mary Wollstonecraft (1757–1797) published *Thoughts on the Education of Daughters* (1787)[15] and *A Vindication of the Rights of Woman* (1792).[16]

The first book was inspired by Locke's *Some Thoughts Concerning Education* (1693). Wollstonecraft insisted on the importance of reading as the most rational pursuit for the minds of both women and men as well as the importance for women to earn and manage their own money.

Although the book was primarily focused on the institution of marriage, which Wollstonecraft saw "often [as] a state of discord", she emphasized that usually husbands have the power to harm their wives.

---

[15] As retrieved on August 15, 2023, at: https://www.gutenberg.org/cache/epub/67466/pg67466-images.html.

[16] As retrieved on August 15, 2023, at: https://www.gutenberg.org/cache/epub/3420/pg3420.html.

This, in turn, became a problem for children who usually depend on their mothers. According to the author, the common practice of early marriages was intended to perpetuate the subjection of women.

She wrote:

> In youth a woman endeavours to please the other sex, in order, generally speaking, to get married, and this endeavour calls forth all her powers. If she has had a tolerable education, the foundation only is laid, for the mind does not soon arrive at maturity, and should not be engrossed by domestic cares before any habits are fixed.

Furthermore, she pointed out that love grounded in romantic attraction, as described in novels, may destroy the peace of mind: "The passions also have too much influence over the judgment to direct [women] in this most important affair; and many women, I am persuaded, marry a man before they are twenty, whom they would have rejected some years after".

The only possible solution to avoid unhappy marriages is to provide education to girls before they get married. She continued: "When a woman's mind has gained some strength, she will in all probability pay more attention to her actions than a girl can be expected to do. And if she thinks seriously, she will choose for a companion a man of principle, and this perhaps young people do not sufficiently attend to, or see the necessity of doing". And insisted: "intellectual improvement, when our comfort here, and happiness hereafter, depends upon [education]". Young men, too, were used to getting married just upon returning the boarding school "when they are scarcely out of the state of childhood themselves".

Wollstonecraft concluded by considering that placing women in public spaces will improve the general well-being of society.

Her following book, *A Vindication of the Rights of Women*, was a plea to Talleyrand to grant equality of opportunity to women. This appeal went beyond merely extending the education given to upper-class boys to women. Instead it called for a development of a new curriculum for both sexes, mixing rational and emotional skills (Todd, 2002). The book was also a critique of Burke's *Reflections on the Revolution in France* (1790), asserting that Burke was defending his privileges against the new order that was emerging in France (Tomaselli, 2021).

Wollstonecraft's book is mainly directly against Rousseau's view on women and their education, as the following long quotation shows:

> "I firmly believe, that all the writers who have written on the subject of female education and manners from Rousseau to Dr. Gregory, have contributed to render women more artificial, weak characters, than they would otherwise have been". And she continued: "I now principally allude to Rousseau, for his character of Sophia is, undoubtedly, a captivating one, though it appears to me grossly unnatural; however, it is not the superstructure, but the foundation of her character, the principles on which her education was built, that I mean to attack (...) Rousseau declares that a woman should never, for a moment, feel herself independent, that she should be governed by fear to exercise her natural cunning, and made a coquetish slave in order to render her a more alluring object of desire, a sweeter companion to man, whenever he chooses to relax himself. He carries the arguments, which he pretends to draw from the indications of nature, still further, and insinuates that truth and fortitude, the corner stones of all human virtue, should be cultivated with certain restrictions, because, with respect to the female character, obedience is the grand lesson which ought to be impressed with unrelenting rigour. What nonsense! (...) Rousseau, and most of the male writers who have followed his steps, have warmly inculcated that the whole tendency of female education ought to be directed to one point: - to render them pleasing. 'Educate women like men,' says Rousseau, 'and the more they resemble our sex the less power will they have over us.' This is the very point I aim at. I do not wish them to have power over men; but over themselves. (...) I plead for my sex-- not for myself. Independence I have long considered as the grand blessing of life, the basis of every virtue-- and independence I will ever secure by contracting my wants, though I were to live on a barren heath. It is then an affection for the whole human race that makes my pen dart rapidly along to support what I believe to be the cause of virtue: and the same motive leads me earnestly to wish to see woman placed in a station in which she would advance, instead of

retarding, the progress of those glorious principles that give a substance to morality".[17]

Wollstonecraft's pamphlet was a masterpiece of classical liberal feminism. Rooted in the Enlightenment principle of the Reason's ability to govern passions and emotions, serving as a tool to build a civil society where individual freedom prevails over privileges of any sort, Wollstonecraft pointed out that half humanity was subjected to the other half without any reasonable justification and against the principle of Reason:

> "women are excluded, without having a voice, from a participation of the natural rights of mankind (…) Contending for the rights of woman, my main argument is built on this simple principle, that if she be not prepared by education to become the companion of man, she will stop the progress of knowledge and virtue; for truth must be common to all, or it will be inefficacious with respect to its influence on general practice (…) the prevailing notion respecting a sexual character was subversive of morality".

The division of roles between men, aimed at performing in the public sphere, and women, aimed at being devoted to the private sphere, was the result of gender stereotypes stemming from different education for girls and boys. This kind of education was intended to reinforce the role of the female figure as a wife and mother subjected to fathers, husbands, and eventually grown-up sons, as well as to strengthen the male figure as a leader not only in the public domain but also in the private one.

Wollstonecraft's plea continued by introducing a political argument against this strict division of roles that damages the well-being of society as a whole:

> when men contend for their freedom, and to be allowed to judge for themselves respecting their own happiness, it be not inconsistent and unjust to subjugate women, even though you firmly believe that you are acting in the manner best calculated to promote their happiness? Who

[17] As retrieved on August 15, 2023, at: https://core.ac.uk/download/pdf/36679668.pdf.

> made man the exclusive judge, if woman partake with him the gift of reason?

Besides the moral and political arguments, Wollstonecraft pointed out an economic aspect against different education for boys and girls: the kind of education provided to girls, aimed at making them seductive to secure good marriages, is a waste of resources that prevents society from becoming wealthier. She anticipated the idea that discrimination is not only a matter of unfairness but also of inefficiency.

> It is acknowledged that [women] spend many of the first years of their lives in acquiring a smattering of accomplishments; meanwhile strength of body and mind are sacrificed to libertine notions of beauty, to the desire of establishing themselves - the only way women can rise in the world - by marriage.

Marriage is seen by Wollstonecraft as the only means for women to attain a social position. She even depicted it as legal prostitution:

> men, in their youth, are prepared for professions, and marriage is not considered as the grand feature in their lives; whilst women, on the contrary, have no other scheme to sharpen their faculties. It is not business, extensive plans, or any of the excursive flights of ambition, that engross their attention; no, their thoughts are not employed in rearing such noble structures. To rise in the world, and have the liberty of running from pleasure to pleasure, they must marry advantageously, and to this object their time is sacrificed, and their persons often legally prostituted.

Marriage is a trap for women who lose their status of free individuals to acquire the status of wives subjected to their husbands. And any subjection inevitably leads to obedience and weakness that harm the relationship with children:

> Obedience required of women in the marriage state comes under this description; the mind, naturally weakened by depending on authority,

> never exerts its own powers, and the obedient wife is thus rendered a weak, indolent mother.

Having grown up in families where girls are more subjected to a state of inferiority than boys, young married women mirror it, and young married men expect their wives to behave in such a way:

> For girls, from various causes, are more kept down by their parents, in every sense of the word, than boys. The duty expected from them is, like all the duties arbitrarily imposed on women, more from a sense of propriety, more out of respect for decorum, than reason; and thus taught slavishly to submit to their parents, they are prepared for the slavery of marriage.

According to Wollstonecraft, if marriage is the institution upon which a society flourishes, then "mankind should all be educated after the same model, or the intercourse of the sexes will never deserve the name of fellowship, nor will women ever fulfill the peculiar duties of their sex until they become enlightened citizens enabled to earn their own subsistence, independent of men".

In her novel, *The Wrongs of Woman, or Maria. A Fragment* (1798),[18] Wollstonecraft presented marriage as a prison: "marriage has bastilled me for life," said the main character. Differently from *A Vindication*, where passions and feelings, which were wrongly considered by society as traits of women's personality, are condemned as opposed to rationality and virtue, in *Maria*, they are celebrated, as well as sexuality. Commonly regarded as a masculine instinct that led to depravity in women, Wollstonecraft presented sexuality as a natural force commonly shared by both genders and as a powerful form of communication between them. In her appreciation of emotions and sexuality, Wollstonecraft distanced herself further from Rousseau (Kelly, 1992).

Wollstonecraft's analysis of marriage inspired many scholars of her time, including socialist activists William Thompson and writer Anna Doyle Wheeler, who presented motherhood as the primary cause of women's social inferiority (Thompson & Wheeler, 1825). Their main

[18] As retrieved on August 18, 2023, at: https://www.gutenberg.org/files/134/134-h/134-h.htm.

target was James Mill's argument that women did not need political representation because their fathers or husbands represented their interests well enough (Mill, 1820). However, unlike Wollstonecraft, who adopted motherhood as a justification for the request for equal education between genders, Thompson and Wheeler perceived that motherhood intrinsically disadvantaged women, at least under capitalism. This is because they thought that capitalists exploit women's free labor as mothers: even in a hypothetical equal society, women who are mothers would be performing uncompensated reproductive labor.

Writer and actress Mary Robinson, aka Anne Frances Randall (1757–1800), also got inspired by Wollstonecraft. In her pamphlet on marriage, *A Letter to the Women of England, on the Injustice of Mental Subordination. With anecdotes* (1799), she defined Wollstonecraft "an illustrious British female whose death has not been sufficiently lamented, but to whose genius posterity will render justice".[19] Randall lamented the condition of married women, who were "mere appendages of domestic life" rather than "the partners, the equal associates of man". She insisted on the prejudices and customs that depicted women as inferior to men. Randall questioned the reader, asking why "Man may enjoy the convivial board, indulge the caprices of his nature; he may desert his home, violate his marriage vows, scoff at the moral laws that unite society, and set even religion at defiance, by oppressing the defenseless; while woman is condemned to bear the drudgery of domestic life, to vegetate in obscurity, to love where she abhors, to honor where she despises, and to obey, while she shudders at subordination".[20] Her answer was the lack of education, which she argued was a tool for men to subject women to their power and condemn them to total dependence on their husbands.

---

[19] As retrieved on August 17, 2023, at: https://romantic-circles.org/editions/robinson/mrletterfrst.htm.

[20] As retrieved on August 16, 2020, at: https://onlinebooks.library.upenn.edu/webbin/book/lookupid?key=olbp27270.

2.3 Economic Ideas as Tools for Women's Emancipation: Sophie de Grouchy, Jane Marcet, and Harriet Martineau

The discussion concerning the link between women's education, economic independence, and the role of marriage became central among women intellectuals of the time, especially in France and Great Britain. They emphasized the need for girls to receive regular education while also advocating for women to attain financial independence, explicitly rejecting the doctrine of the separate spheres and the notion of marriage as the ultimate goal for women.

The popularization of political economy played a pivotal role in this transformation. Specific publications were dedicated to spreading economic knowledge among women, greatly encouraging them to advocate for equal education and, consequently, economic independence. This independence would enable them to access the public sphere by entering the job market and pursuing roles in other public dimensions.

Marie-Louise-Sophie de Grouchy, Marquise de Condorcet (1764–1822), was the first woman to explicitly write about political economy. Influenced by the ideas of Adam Smith, she placed a significant emphasis on the role of sympathy and the social contribution of women to the overall improvement of society. Coming from a wealthy family, she received her education at home, benefiting from her mother's teachings and her brothers' tutors. Influenced by the principles of the French Enlightenment, she also studied Voltaire, Rousseau, Smith,[21] and Paine.[22] Married to Nicolas, Marquis de Condorcet, the couple began hosting a salon in Paris where they welcomed numerous scholars of the time. In 1791, together with her husband, she initiated the journal *Le Républicain*, in which she published under a *nom de plume*, her column *La Vérité*.[23] She never wrote about women's rights, albeit biographers

[21] The *Wealth of Nations* was very popular in France and had a huge impact on Turgot and Condorcet, Sophie's husband (Forget, 2003).

[22] Paine lived in Paris during the French Revolution and became a very good friend of Sophie and Nicolas Condorcet.

[23] Edited by Condorcet, Brissot, Paine, Duchatelet, Dumont, and Grouchy, the magazine lasted for four issues in the spring/summer of 1791 and was devoted to spreading the word of the

agree that she influenced her husband's short piece *On the Admission of Women to the Rights of Citizenship* (1790) regarding women's enfranchisement, which was one of the most important parts of the Gironde's agenda. However, this agenda was abandoned when the group lost its leading role during the Revolution. Alongside other famous French *salonnières* of the time, such as Madame Helvetius, Madame de Stael, and Madame Roland, de Grouchy was a passionate scholar and a prolific writer.

Influenced by Locke's *Some Thoughts Concerning Education* (1693), which is based on the idea that proper education of children is necessary to raise them to be virtuous, de Grouchy shared Wollstonecraft's idea of education as a proper instrument aimed at overcoming desires by adopting the guidance of reason.

During the Revolution, de Grouchy began to work on her commentary on Adam Smith's *The Theory of Moral Sentiments*, which she published in her own name. The book, titled *Letters on Sympathy*, is a collection of eight letters to C***[24]: first drafted between 1791 and 1792, they appeared a few years later (1798) along with her French translation of Smith's work.

By following Adam Smith, she considered the pivotal role of sympathy in building social interactions among individuals and in establishing morality. Nonetheless, she criticized Smith for not delving into the origin of the sentiment of sympathy, which might be rooted in the physical attachment between children and the person who nurtures them, whether it is their biological mother or their nurse.[25]

She was influenced by her brother-in-law Pierre Cabanis' vision. Cabanis, a physician, considered emotions as organic responses to external feedback (Cabanis, 1802). Grouchy was firmly convinced that sympathy arises from a combination of pleasure and pain. Sympathy

Revolution and justifying it to foreigners. Its main aim was to support republicanism against monarchy.

24 C*** might be either her husband, Condorcet, or her brother-in-law and friend, Pierre-George Cabanis, who shared with the couple a deep interest in physiology and its link with individual behavior and social dynamics.

25 Differently from Madame Roland and Mary Wollstonecraft, who pointed out the importance for babies to be physically connected with their mothers.

serves as the starting point for moral development, beginning with the physical attachment of infants and culminating in the dynamics of social behavior that allow societies to develop peacefully. In framing sympathy in this manner, she combined Smith's notion of sympathy, rooted in human psychology, with utilitarianism. More precisely, Grouchy considered sympathy as the ability and inclination to feel others' pain and the desire to alleviate it.

The first letter explains how the author departs from Smith's argument on sympathy as a human disposition. De Grouchy pointed out that an inquiry into the origin of sympathy is necessary to understand the dynamics of human behavior. The physiological nature of sympathy is grounded in a baby's initial skin contact with her nurse, which enables them to discover pleasure. The next two letters present a theory of the development of sympathy as a child grows and begins to adopt rational and strategic behaviors, when different forms of sympathy and emotions develop through interactions with others. *Letters IV* and *V* provide an account of the origins of morality as a product of reason influenced by sympathy. In the final three letters, de Grouchy explores possible political, economic, social, and legal reforms made possible by the French Revolution.

While in de Grouchy's *Letters* there was undoubtedly a feminist vibe that reflected her husband's 1790 paper on women's rights and perhaps even inspired that paper, the *Letters* did not present a feminist agenda. De Grouchy's focus was on humanity, with women explicitly included as equals: the very first teacher of sympathy is the wet-nurse; the most prominent model of a good teacher was Sophie's own mother; mothers and fathers were equally encouraged to participate in a child's education. Nonetheless, women were not given separate consideration. In her discussion of family law, she did not mention reforms that would have specifically affected women.

In her defense of equality, de Grouchy addressed the problems brought about by inequality in status, privileges, and wealth, and how the law contributed to these problems by maintaining privileges (*Letter VIII*, p. 152). She highlighted the disadvantages faced by women who were pressured by societal norms to become wives and mothers when the most common crimes women were accused of and severely punished were infanticide or performing abortions. De Grouchy's discussion against torture and severe punishment was influenced by the writings of the Italian philosopher Cesare Beccaria.[26]

She wrote:

> In order for the fear of a sentence to be effective and beneficial the sentence must not outrage. Its justice must be perceptible to average reason, and it must especially awaken the conscience, at the same time as it punishes its silence and slumber. But this will not be so [...] if a judge can arbitrarily harden or soften a sentence; if there are privileges, hereditary, personal or local which offer a legal loophole, direct or indirect (Letter VIII).[27]

Although de Grouchy did not specifically address women's rights, she advocated for short-term, renewable marriage contracts, clear rights for children born outside of marriage and their mothers, as well as the possibility of divorce.[28]

De Grouchy also argued that a heavily regulated market increased poverty, forcing the poor to remain impoverished or even become poorer because they could not control their exchanges or negotiate their work and production. Like Condorcet and Turgot, Grouchy believed that burdening the market with strict laws constituted a form of domination, and allowing farmers and merchants to determine their own prices would help alleviate poverty in the country. Thus, she can be interpreted as one of the original proponents of commercial republicanism (Bergès, 2018).

De Grouchy's classical liberalism emerged in her *Letters*. She anticipated the famous modern-day distinction between positive and negative

---

26 Beccaria's book *On Crimes and Punishment*, published in 1764, was translated into French that same year and published with a lengthy commentary from Voltaire. Beccaria went to Paris and spent much of 1776 in Madame Helvetius's salon in Auteuil. His influence was no doubt still present some years later when the Marquis de Condorcet, his brother Pierre-George Cabanis, and his future wife, Sophie, also became frequent visitors.

27 As retrieved on August 13, 2023, at: https://www.earlymoderntexts.com/assets/pdfs/degrouchy1798.pdf.

28 Divorce was legalized and made more accessible for a brief period during the French Revolution before it was codified under Napoleon in a way that made it much more difficult to obtain, especially for women.

liberty in her writings (Schliesser, 2017). According to Bergès (2021), De Grouchy's philosophy aligned with the republican tradition by presenting arguments for gender and class equality, while Halldenius (2015, 2019) pointed out that, unlike Wollstonecraft, de Grouchy did not explicitly advocate for equal citizenship rights for women.

In Great Britain, the debate on the connection between women's education, marriage, and economic independence was initiated by Lady Mary Wortley Montagu (1689–1762), who, inspired by James Steuart's book, *An Inquiry into the Principles of Political Economy* (1767), promoted the idea that women should be actively involved in economic matters. This idea was further supported by Priscilla Wakefield (1751–1832), who drew inspiration from Adam Smith's writings (Dimand, 2003) when composing *Reflections on the Present Condition of the Female Sex; with Suggestions for Its Improvement* (Wakefield 1798 [2015]), a book focused on women's education and financial independence.

Jane Haldimand Marcet (1769–1858) and Harriet Martineau (1802–1876) were popularizers of political economy. They both emphasized the influence of gender norms on institutions like marriage, which was often the only way for women to gain access to any kind of resources. However, their economic analyses took place in different genres and focused on different topics.

Marcet's primary goal was to advocate for a free-market education for girls, following classical economists like Smith, Ricardo, and Malthus (Marcet, 1816). In 1833, she authored a collection of stories on economic issues aimed at improving the conditions of the working classes (Marcet, 1833). Her aim was to make political economy accessible to the common people. Her efforts were appreciated by Ricardo, who provided Marcet with advice for a second edition. Prominent figures like Macaulay, McCulloch, Say, and Malthus also praised her books. Similar to Wollstonecraft, Marcet stressed the importance of education as a means to instill high moral standards in the new generations.

She wrote:

> I would endeavour to give the rising generation such an education as would render them not only moral and religious, but industrious, frugal, and provident. In proportion as the mind is informed, we are able to

calculate the consequences of our actions: it is the infant and the savage who live only for the present moment; those whom instruction has taught to think, reflect upon the past and look forward to the future. Education gives rise to prudence, not only by enlarging our understandings, but by softening our feelings, by humanising the heart, and promoting amiable affections.[29]

Marcet specifically included political economy in the new educational agenda: "if a more general knowledge of political economy prevented women from propagating errors respecting it, in the education of their children, no trifling good would ensue."

And she continued:

Political Economy, though so immediately connected with the happiness and improvement of mankind, and the object of so much controversy and speculation among men of knowledge, is not yet become a popular science, and is not generally considered as a study essential to early education. This work, therefore, independently of all its defects, will have to contend against the novelty of the pursuit with young persons of either sex, for the instruction of whom it is especially intended.

Like Marcet, Martineau's commitment was to popularize economic knowledge through narrative. Between 1832 and 1834, she published nine volumes of *Illustrations of Political Economy* (Martineau, 2018) to promote liberal principles through economic storytelling. Martineau's publications provided her with financial independence as well as immense popularity.[30] She insisted on the importance of studying political economy and of extending this subject to everyone.

She wrote:

Can anything more nearly concern all the members of any society than the way in which the necessaries and comforts of life may be best procured and enjoyed by all? Is there anything in any other study (which

[29] As retrieved on August 13, 2023, at: https://oll.libertyfund.org/title/marcet-conversations-on-political-economy.

[30] Martineau's works was praised by James Mill, McCulogh, and John Stuart Mill.

> does not involve this) that can be compared with it in interest and importance? And yet Political Economy has been less studied than perhaps any other science whatever, and not at all by those whom it most concerns—the mass of the people.[31]

In Martineau's volumes, women played the role of either readers of the *Illustrations* or characters within the tales. They were depicted as fundamental elements of the economic process. Furthermore, they were considered as potential economists: "till their day of emancipation arrives, till the customs of society shall allow them the natural rights of men and women—the power of social exertion, and the enjoyment of social independence" (Martineau, 2018). Women were especially important in understanding domestic economy.

The position of Martineau on marriage in her *Illustrations* is well explained by Levy and Peart (2022). As in Malthus's account, Martineau seconded "preventive check" and suggested to delay marriage, in order to decrease child mortality rate (the "positive check"). She wrote: "by bringing no more children into the world than there is a subsistence provided for, society may preserve itself from the miseries of want. In other words, the timely use of the mild preventive check may avert the horrors of any positive check" (Martineau, 2018). In Martineau's view, overpopulation will prevent humankind from attaining its final aim: the greatest happiness of the greatest number.

Martineau published several writings specifically on the condition of women in her time and joined anti-slavery groups in America when she traveled there between 1834 and 1836. During that time, American activists for individual freedom combined abolitionism and the women's rights movement, and Martineau enthusiastically shared their commitment to the emancipation of both Blacks and women (Yates, 1985).

In her essay on marriage, Martineau observed that a "married woman is treated as the inferior party in a compact in which both parties have an equal interest. Any agreement thus formed is imperfect and liable to disturbance, and the danger is great in proportion to the degradation

[31] As retrieved on August 13, 2023, at: https://oll.libertyfund.org/title/martineau-illustrations-of-political-economy-vol-1.

of the supposed weaker party" (Martineau, 1838, 61). She then added that unmarried women who had jobs were often forced into job sectors that were not profitable and were overstocked, reinforcing the idea that marriage was the main goal for women. As a consequence, education for girls was oriented toward getting married and women remained: "unfit for anything when their aim is accomplished as if they had never had any object at all. They are no more equal to the task of education than to that of governing the state; and, if any unexpected turn of adversity befalls them, they have no resource but a convent, or some other charitable provision" (64).

In 1851 Martineau was invited to a Women's Rights Convention in America. As she was unable to attend, she sent the commission a letter where she underlined the necessity to fight for the equality of individuals. In a passage of her letter, here she clearly accused the doctrine of the separate spheres as detrimental for women: she insisted on the fact that women, like men, needed an education "with a view to action", not oriented toward getting married, but aimed to acquire knowledge in "physical science, or law, government, or political economy" in order to let women be doctors and not only nurses, lawyers and not only witnesses, legislators and not only passive citizens, engaged in business and not only consumers (Martineau, 1851, 77).

In her essay *The Woman Question*, Martineau (1855) criticized Wollstonecraft by claiming that the model of education she proposed was insufficient for the effective emancipation of women because it did not take account of the possibility for women to well perform in both the private and public sphere. Martineau wished women to reach a time when they could finally enjoy benefits of both spheres, i.e. to be happy as mothers and wives and to be successful in their profession; this will happen when they finally stop considering the former as the sole possible way to accomplish themselves, and when they will be ever allowed to get a proper education to achieve the latter by having a voice in the public domain.[32]

[32] Some authors considered *Illustrations* as an endorsement of patriarchal ideologies because Martineau accepted the 'masculine' discourses in order to make her ideas accessible to any reader (Roberts, 2022).

Marcet and Martineau represented the first tentative effort to embed political economy as a fundamental part of the ordinary educational system to promote economic knowledge among ordinary people and women (Dalley, 2010; Polkinghorn, 1995). Although they did not specifically write against the traditional marriage as the major reinforcement of the doctrine of the separate spheres, their commitment to extend economic education to everyone represented a significant step forward in the direction of women's independence.

2.4 Harriet Taylor Mill on Marriage and Divorce and Her Influence on John Stuart Mill

During Queen Victoria's reign (1837–1901), the rhetoric of marriage and family as the only condition for women's fulfillment pushed many women activists to propose a significant reform of young women's education. These reforms included the introduction of boarding schools, the training of women teachers, and the gradual access to university education for women (Mallett, 2016a, 2016b).[33] Furthermore, in 1870, the Married Women's Property Act marked a significant change in nineteenth-century British property law. The Act granted British women the right to own and control personal property, dramatically increasing the bargaining power and property holdings of married women (Combs, 2006). This legal shift in married women's property rights facilitated the growing involvement of women in educational investments and made women's education even more desirable.[34]

[33] One major obstacle was unequal access to education. Women were barred from universities, clubs, and scholarly societies involved in the formation of political economy. Their education focused solely on female accomplishments which included foreign languages, literature, and art. While seen as a much-needed preparation for future middle and upper class wives, it had the effect of marginalizing women from public debates (Rostek, 2014, 2019).

[34] As Robb (1992) pointed out, in nineteenth-century England, a significant number of women made substantial investments for income, capital growth, or a share in the family business. Women investors, a group often overlooked by scholars, were particularly active in the stock market (Rutterford & Maltby, 2006).

In those times, Harriet Hardy (1807–1873), later known as Harriet Taylor Mill, wrote her pamphlets on marriage and the education of women (Taylor Mill, 1832/1833; 1851 [1994]; 1998) and she co-authored with her second husband, John Stuart Mill, an essay specifically on marriage and divorce (Taylor Mill & Mill, 1832/1833).[35]

In their coauthored pamphlet, the authors presented the nature of marriage as it should be understood if natural individual rights, equal for everyone regardless of gender, were properly applied to the spouses: a contract between two free and equal individuals, who freely choose to spend a part, or perhaps all, of their lives together in the name of their affection. Unfortunately, as the Mills added, at their time, marriage was understood in a completely different way: not a contract between equals, but rather "a relation between a superior and an inferior, between a protector and a dependent". In fact, married women were forced to lose their properties, which went to their husbands.

They wrote:

> This conclusion is, the absurdity and immorality of a state of society and opinion in which a woman is at all dependent for her social position upon the fact of her being or not being married. Surely it is wrong, wrong in every way, and on every view of morality, even the vulgar view—that there should exist any motives to marriage except the happiness which two persons who love one another feel in associating their existence (Taylor Mill & Mill, 1832/1833, 4).

This procedure was reinforced by the lack of education for girls: uneducated women were not able to take care of themselves and were not allowed to be authentically free. They wrote: "It is not law, but education and custom which make the difference" (ibid.).

Furthermore, they pointed out the immorality of considering women as valuable for the society only if they get married:

> A single woman therefore is felt both by herself and others as a kind of excrescence on the surface of society, having no use or function or office

[35] As retrieved on August 14, 2023, at: https://englishiva1011.pbworks.com/f/MARRDIVR.PDF.

> there. She is not indeed precluded from useful and honorable exertion of various kinds: but a married woman is presumed to be a useful member of society unless there is evidence to the contrary; a single woman must establish what very few either women or men ever do establish, an individual claim (ibid.).

Contrary to what usually happened, they wrote:

> Marriage, on whatever footing it might be placed, would be wholly a matter of choice, not, as for a woman it now is, something approaching to a matter of necessity; something, at least, which every woman is under strong artificial motives to desire, and which if she attain not, her life is considered to be a failure (Taylor Mill & Mill, 1832/1833, 7).

The authors continued to argue that this miserable situation was worsened by the impossibility of divorcing. This situation made: "marriage a lottery and whoever is in a state of mind to calculate chances calmly and value them correctly, is not at all likely to purchase a ticket" (Taylor Mill & Mill, 1832, 8). According to the Mills, an easy way to avoid unhappy marriages would have been the possibility to divorce. However, at their time, divorce was largely accessible only to men, and had to be granted by an Act of Parliament, which was prohibitively expensive.[36]

Specifically, regarding divorce, Taylor Mill and Mill wrote:

> It is not denied by anyone that there are numerous cases in which the happiness of both parties would be greatly promoted by a dissolution of marriage. We will add, that when the social position of the two sexes shall be perfectly equal, a divorce if it be for the happiness of either party, will be for the happiness of both (Taylor Mill & Mill, 1832/1833, 8).

They insisted on the idea that without divorce, women are like slaves:

> When women are merely slaves, to give them a permanent hold upon their masters was a first step towards their evolution. That step is now

[36] It was only in 1857 that the Matrimonial Causes Act allowed women to divorce, albeit with the requirement to prove their husbands had been unfaithful. Furthermore, women had to provide additional faults, such as cruelty, rape and incest.

> complete: and in the progress of civilization, the time has come when women may aspire to something more than merely to find a protector. (...) woman in short is no longer a mere property, but a person who is counted not solely on her husband's or father's account but on her own. She is now ripe for equality. But it is absurd to talk of equality while marriage is an indissoluble tie (Taylor Mill & Mill, 1832/1833, 11).

In the same year (1832), Taylor Mill published a short essay on divorce where she advocated the possibility of obtaining it without requiring any plausible reason and with minimal cost or no expense at all. She insisted on the fact that divorce might be compared to the end of a contract, which should involve a reduction of any possible transaction costs.

She wrote:

> Would not the best plan be divorce which could be attained by any without any reason assigned, and at small expenses, but which could only be finally pronounced after a long period? (...) In the present system of habits and opinions, girls enter into what is called a contract perfectly ignorant of the conditions of it, and that they should be so is considered absolutely essential to their fitness for it! (Taylor Mill, 1832/1833, 13).

Taylor Mill's long essay *The Enfranchisement of Women* (1851) was a manifesto against the doctrine of the separate spheres.[37] Written as a summary of the debate that was occurring in the United States about the possibility of extending suffrage to women, it represented a plea for equality between women and men, encompassing all the arguments that would later be developed by John Stuart Mill in his essays *On Liberty* (1859) and *The Subjection of Women* (1869).[38] Taylor Mill underlined that this movement was "not merely for women, but by them" (Taylor Mill, 1851, 1). Protesters demanded: "1. Education in primary and high schools, universities, medical, legal, and theological institutions. 2. Partnership in the labours and gains, risks and remunerations, of productive industry. 3. A coequal share in the formation and administration of laws

[37] As retrieved on August 14, 2023, at: http://acdc2007.free.fr/harriettaylor1851.pdf.

[38] The debate began at the Convention of Women, which took place in the State of Ohio, in the spring of 1850. Subsequently, more public meetings were held at Worcester in Massachusetts, under the name of "Women's Rights Convention".

—municipal, state, and national—through legislative assemblies, courts, and executive offices" (ibid).

In her essay, Taylor Mill insisted on the principle that civil and political rights derive from natural rights which "acknowledge no sex"; and on the idea that the equality before the law makes women entitled to share responsibilities in the public sphere along with their male fellow citizens.

Taylor Mill wondered how it was possible to speak about 'inalienable' rights (life, liberty, and the pursuit of happiness) when women were forced to alienate two of them in favor of men. She named a social structure as such a 'caste' system:

> far from being expedient, we are firmly convinced that the division of mankind into two castes, one born to rule over the other, is in this case, as in all cases, an unqualified mischief; a source of perversion and demoralization, both to the favoured class and to those at whose expense they are favoured; producing none of the good which it is the custom to ascribe to it, and forming a bar, almost insuperable while it lasts, to any really vital improvement, either in the character or in the social condition of the human race (Taylor Mill, 1851, 97–98).

According to Taylor Mill, a society could prosper only if women were actually as free as men to pursue their ability, skills, capacities, and knowledge: allowing women to enter the public sphere would have increased the completion among individuals and reduced any privilege. She wrote: "We deny the right of any portion of the species to decide for another portion, or any individual for another individual, what is and what is not their proper sphere. The proper sphere for all human beings is the largest and highest which they are able to attain to. What this is, cannot be ascertained, without complete liberty of choice" (Taylor Mill, 1851, 100). And she continued: "if those who assert that the 'proper sphere' for women is the domestic, mean by this that they have not shown themselves qualified for any other, the assertion evinces great ignorance of life and of his story. Women have shown fitness for the highest social functions, exactly in proportion as they have been admitted to them" (Taylor Mill, 1851, 101).

As Taylor Mill claimed, her contemporary men were rent-seekers who monopolized power and wealth by preventing women (and slaves) from flourishing as individuals and reducing their social well-being. She pointed out that the subjection of women in the private sphere violated two natural rights: freedom and private property. In fact, married women were deprived of their liberty and personal assets in favor of their husbands.

Taylor Mill explained that three arguments were adopted to prevent women from getting access to the public sphere: the maternity argument (claiming that public roles are incompatible with raising and taking care of children); the competition argument (stating that public roles of women reduced the value of men's commitment and time spent in their public roles); the personality argument (asserting that public roles changed women's attitude making them less available in taking care of the domestic sphere).

Taylor Mill claimed that the maternity argument was a pretense for the exclusion as it was an argument that could not be applied to childless women. Furthermore, marriage was often chosen by women "because there is no other career open to them, no other occupation for their feelings or their activities" due to the lack of education women faced.

The competition argument was nonsense as competition, provided by women in the public sphere, destroys monopolies of men in the public sphere and monopolies are always a damage for the well-being of the society. Furthermore, even in a scenario where both men and women earn the same amount of salary as men previously earned alone, the final situation would present no income difference but an increase of well-being for women, no longer considered "servants, but partners" (Taylor Mill, 1851, 105).

Finally, the personality argument against the admission of women to the public sphere was rooted in an obsolete vision of the world according to which both the marketplace and the political arena make individuals selfish, violent, and arrogant, therefore not suitable for women.

Given that these three arguments were not solid, Taylor Mill recognized patriarchy as the origin of the subjection of women. She wrote: "why each woman should be a mere appendage to a man, allowed to have no interests of her own, that there may be nothing to compete in her mind with his interests and his pleasure; the only reason which can be given is, that men like it" (Taylor Mill, 1851, 107).

She described patriarchy a system inherited by the past when:

> The wife was part of the furniture of home—of the resting-place to which the man returned from business or pleasure. His occupations were, as they still are, among men; his pleasures and excitements also were, for the most part, among men—among his equals. He was a patriarch and a despot within four walls, and irresponsible power had its effect, greater or less according to his disposition, in rendering him domineering, exacting, self-worshipping, when not capriciously or brutally tyrannical (Taylor Mill, 1851, 109).

According to Taylor Mill, the situation at her time was different, though. On one side, tyranny in the household was no longer acceptable nor was the relegation of women outside the public sphere. On the other side, care, reciprocity, and cooperation became ineludible elements of a society rooted in the ideals and the values of the Enlightenment, the Glorious Revolution, and the American Revolution.

As we can easily imagine, the impact of Taylor Mill's idea of the notion of liberty as well as her fight against the subjection of women had a profound impact on John Stuart Mill, who developed his wife's major arguments in his two books published in 1859 and 1869.[39] It is important to underline that Mill's books are intertwined, albeit they were originally published separately. As Hirschman pointed out, although Mill was more interested in class than in gender, he called for a radical change of patriarchal structures in order to achieve freedom for women. Moller Okin (1979) well explained that Mill had simply applied the principle of classical liberalism to women by pointing out the importance of their education as a tool to improve the society as a whole. He shared with Taylor Mill the notion of marriage as a free contract between free parties, equally educated. Nevertheless, he remained in favor of the traditional division of labor within the family, assuming a trade-off between marriage and career, and considering women more suitable

[39] As retrieved on August 15, 2023, at: https://oll.libertyfund.org/title/mill-on-liberty-and-the-subjection-of-women-1879-ed.

to perform well in the private sphere. Like his wife, Mill promoted education for women and was in favor of their enfranchisement, but he somehow constrained his liberalism within the doctrine of the separate spheres. His main concern was that the entrance of women into the public sphere would have led to the commodification of domestic duties and child-rearing that he evidently feared as a potential way to harm society.

John Stuart Mill's attitude led many feminist scholars to criticize his position which was based on the socio-legal aspects of the subordination of women and not on the cultural aspects which subjugated women. Some scholars claimed that Mill's focus was limited to overcoming legal barriers against women without considering the subjection of women not only by the law, but also by customs and social pressure (Bell, 2001; Gatens, 1991).[40] Furthermore, as McCabe (2015) wrote, Mill's attitude of considering women as the weakest sex led many scholars to ponder the possibility of feminists to abandon classical liberalism (Donner, 1993). This critique did not take account of Mill's own vision of marriage as the perfect form of *philia*, i.e. a friendship between equals that emphasized the value of virtuous and non-instrumental relationships in human life. Conversely, Mill considered the traditional marriage as slavery. He was very aware that economic and social structures of his time compelled individual choices (Shanley, 1981). As noted by Urbinati (1991), some feminists criticized Mill's idea that a negative impact on the well-being of children and the management of the household might occur when married wives and mothers get a position in the job market. Furthermore, feminists criticized Mill's belief that when women choose to get married they specialize in the profession of household management, arguing that this specialization is the natural result of their specific nature.

Nonetheless, this feminist critique does not fully take into account Mill's fight against the subjection of women, which was intrinsically related to the notion of liberty as a natural right. We cannot help

[40] In the secondary literature, there have been several attempts to reconcile Mill's position on working married women and the equality between women and men, as well summarized by Sigot and Beaurain (2009).

but consider *On Liberty* and *The Subjection of Women* as a diptych on freedom and women's emancipation.

Mill (1859) clearly claimed that his subject was Civil or Social Liberty intended as "the nature and limits of the power which can be legitimately exercised by society over the individual" established by a mechanism of constitutional checks and balances and by the right to exercise suffrage (Mill 1859, 5). As he wrote: "the only purpose for which power can be rightfully exercised over any member of a civilized community, against his will, is to prevent harm to others" (ibid, 10). In the private sphere, there is individual freedom and individuals' choices are effects of their conscience, their knowledge and their feeling, which regulate the combination among them. The private sphere cannot be constrained in any way by any political institution as well as by any "despotism of customs".

The relationship between individuals and society must be granted by the principle of non-interference: "the individual is not accountable to society for his actions, in so far as these concern the interests of no person but himself". If individual's actions somehow harm others "the individual is accountable, and may be subjected either to social or to legal punishments" (ibid, 64).[41]

Mill explicitly regarded education for both men and women as the primary instrument aimed at leading individuals to be aware of the nature of both personal freedom and civil liberty: it is the duty of parents to provide this kind of education to children as well as it is the duty of the State to make it possible for its citizens.[42]

---

[41] Mill was aware that there were many situations in which the boundary between the private and public spheres was difficult to define, and there might be circumstances that could lead individuals to harm themselves, which might be prevented by the State. Examples of such situations included fornication and drinking, which cannot be prohibited, but prostitution and alcoholism might be. He addressed these issues by applying cost–benefit analysis to them.

[42] Mill explicitly stated that he was addressing the enforcement of education by the State, not the State's ability to direct that education. He wrote: "A general State education is merely a contrivance for molding people to be exactly like one another, and as the mold in which it casts them is the one that pleases the predominant power in the government, whether that be a monarch, a priesthood, an aristocracy, or the majority of the existing generation, it tends to establish a despotism over the mind, which naturally leads to one over the body" (Mill 1859, 72).

Ten years later, in his *Subjection of Women* (1869), Mill shifted the main points on individual freedom expressed in *On Liberty* specifically on the condition of women of his time in order to promote their political enfranchisement. *The Subjection of Women* explored patriarchy and slavery as expressions of men's power firmly rooted in a legal framework, political structures, and cultural pressure on gender and ethnicity, perpetually reinforcing the inequality of women who were compared to slaves (Folbre, 2009).[43]

According to Mill, women were not only prevented from exercising their individual freedom in the private sphere, and often denied the freedom to follow their own desires and feelings, but they were also constrained in their civil or social liberty by a society that imposed legal barriers to their flourishing and subjected them to social stigma if they did not adhere to social norms. These legal barriers are particularly odious and extremely unfair, as they did not prevent any harm to women whose education was denied in the name of liberticidal principles that relegated them to the private sphere only.

Mill applied the principle of 'perfect equality', which admitted neither power nor privilege for one gender, nor subjection and disability for the other. He claimed that "the inequality of rights between men and women has no other source than the law of the strongest" rather than the rule of law based on the "moral sentiments of mankind." Yet, Mill explained that the subjection of women to men was an effect of the mechanism of the power of the strongest over people who are closer, such as in the relationship between masters and slaves as well as between husbands/fathers and wives/daughters.

Mill also pointed out that the majority of women accepted their subjection and considered it natural. Only recently, he added, especially in the United States, many women activists started to protest against their social condition and to demand education, admission into professions, and political representation.

---

43 The debate on the nature of Mill's contribution in the history of feminism has been broadly analyzed (see Sommers, 1994). Mill's *The Subjection of Women* was reprinted in New York and Philadelphia and translated into many European languages and it paved the way for more radical forms of feminism (Nussbaum, 2010).

The subjection of women, Mill insisted, had played a socio-psychological role: women were enslaved and indoctrinated to cherish their subjection. He wrote:

> [men] have therefore put everything in practice to enslave [women's] minds. The masters of all other slaves rely, for maintaining obedience, on fear; either fear of themselves, or religious fears. The masters of women wanted more than simple obedience, and they turned the whole force of education to affect their purpose (Mill 1869, 88).

Mill insisted on the fact that women have been educated to submission by insisting on their "sentimentalities that it is their nature to live for others; to make complete abnegation of themselves, and to have no life but in their affections". Intellectual, economic, and social independence were not an option in the education of women. Women were supposed to fulfill their lives only by being obedient wives and lovely mothers, receiving all they had as gifts from their male figures, either their fathers or their husbands. This view was outdated and no longer acceptable.

He wrote:

> "The social subordination of women thus stands out an isolated fact in modern social institutions; a solitary breach of what has become their fundamental law; a single relic of an old world of thought and practice exploded in everything else, but retained in the one thing of most universal interest; as if a gigantic dolmen, or a vast temple of Jupiter Olympius, occupied the site of St. Paul's and received daily worship, while the surrounding Christian churches were only resorted to on fasts and festivals" (ibid, 91).

In Mill's opinion, marriage, often seen as the ultimate goal for women, was used as a means to make them servile, and the lack of education served as the primary tool to maintain their complete dependence on men, which he described as "foul rather than fair means". Married women would lose their property and consequently their freedom. The definition of marriage as 'one person in law' favored men while subjecting women to their arbitrary authority. Mill went on to compare the despotism of the head of the family to political despotism, even though he acknowledged that there might be good husbands, just as there could be good kings. Nevertheless, the well-being of the partner is not legally ensured; it ultimately depends on good luck.

Mill argued that marriage should be viewed as a "voluntary association between two people", a "partnership in business" where both partners share control and responsibilities equally:

> The equality of married persons before the law, is not only the sole mode in which that particular relation can be made consistent with justice to both sides, and conducive to the happiness of both, but it is the only means of rendering the daily life of mankind, in any high sense, a school of moral cultivation (ibid, 81).

If marriage is understood in such terms, the family becomes "the real school of the virtues of freedom" and "a school of sympathy in equality" instead of being "a school of despotism and of obedience". According to Mill, the notion of power, which rules the family as well as a society, should be extended to women within families and societies. Nevertheless,

> when a woman marries, it may in general be understood that she makes choice of the management of a household, and the bringing up of a family, as the first call upon her exertions, during as many years of her life as may be required for the purpose; and that she renounces, not all other objects and occupations, but all which are not consistent with the requirements of this (ibid, 110).

This is the passage that has been heavily criticized by some secondary literature and does not align with Taylor Mill's narrative, according to which women are entirely entitled to perform in both the private and public spheres.

The third chapter of *The Subjection of Women* is entirely dedicated to the opportunity for women to obtain their political rights, both as voters and potential candidates. This is based on the principle that "any of the mental differences supposed to exist between women and men are merely the natural result of differences in their education and circumstances, and indicate no radical difference, far less radical inferiority, of nature" (ibid, 113).

Mill concluded his essay by considering whether the consequences of the proposed changes in our customs and institutions would improve the condition of women and society as a whole. According to Mill, the prevalence of justice over injustice would prevent "sex from functioning as a disqualification for privileges and a badge of subjection". Social well-being can only flourish through the enhancement of individual happiness, as denying liberty in the name of power creates a despotic mechanism that leads to unhappiness on one side and fear of losing privileges on the other side.

References

Astell, M. (1697). *A Serious Proposal to the Ladies*. Richard Wilkin at the King's-Head in St. Paul's Church-Yard.

Astell, M. (1700). *Some Reflections Upon Marriage, Occasion'd by the Duke and Dutchess of Mazarine's Case; Which Is Also Consider'd*. Printed for John Nutt, near Stationers-Hall.

Barclay, K., Meek, J., & Thompson, A. (Eds.). (2020). *Courtship, Marriage and Marriage Breakdown*. Routledge.

Beccaria, C. (1764 [2009]). *Dei delitti e delle pene*. English translation: Newman, G. R., & Marongiu, P. (Eds.). *On Crimes and Punishments* (5th ed.). Transactions Publishers.

Bell, J. (2001). J. S. Mill on Wages and Women. A Feminist Critique. *Review of Social Economy, 59*(4), 509–527.

Bergès, S. (2018). What's It Got to Do with the Price of Bread? Condorcet and Grouchy on Freedom and Unreasonable Laws in Commerce. *European Journal of Political Theory, 17*(4), 432–448.

Bergès, S. (2021). Revolution and Republicanism: Women Political Philosophers of Late Eighteenth-Century France and Why They Matter. *Australasian Philosophical Review, 3*(4), 351–370.

Botting, E. (2006). *Family Feuds. Wollstonecraft, Burke, and Rousseau on the Transformation of the Family*. State University of New York Press.

Broad, J. (2015). *The Philosophy of Mary Astell: An Early Modern Theory of Virtue*. Oxford University Press.

Butler, M. (1978). Early Liberal Roots of Feminism: John Locke and the Attack on Patriarchy. *The American Political Science Review*, 72(1), 135–150.

Cabanis, P. G. (1802). *Les Rapports du Physique et du Moral*. Baillère.
Combs, M. B. (2006). *Cui Bono?* The 1870 British Married Women's Property Act, Bargaining Power, and the distribution of Resources Within Marriages. *Feminist Economics, 12*(1–2), 51–83.
Condorcet, N. (1790 [2012]). "Sur l'admission des femmes au droit au cité", *Journal de la Société de 1789*, 3 July 1790, number 5; translated as "On the Emancipation of Women". In S. Lukes & N. Urbinati (Eds.), *Condorcet: Political Writings* (pp. 156–162). Cambridge University Press.
Coontz, S. (2006). *Marriage, a History*. Viking.
Dalley, L. (2010). Domesticating Political Economy: Language, Gender, and Economics in the *Illustrations of Political Economy*. In E. Dzelzainis & C. Kaplan (Eds.), *Harriet Martineau: Authorship, Society and Empire* (pp. 103–117). Manchester University Press.
Defoe, D. (1724). *The Fortunate Mistress, or a History of the Life of Mademoiselle de Beleau Known by the Name of the Lady Roxana*. T. Warner and the Black Boy.
De Gouges, O. (1788). *Pour Les Dames, Ou le Portrait des Femmes. Preface for the Ladies, or the Portrait of Women*. https://www.olympedegouges.eu/docs/ba.Preface-pour-les-dames.pdf
De Gouges, O. (1791). *Déclaration des droits de la femme et de la citoyenne*. https://www.gutenberg.org/cache/epub/53595/pg53595-images.html
De Gouges, O. (1791 [2014]). *Femme reveille-toi! Declaration des droits de la femme et de la citoyenne et autres ecrits* (Martine Reid, Ed.). Gallimard.
De Gournay, M. (1622). *Égalité des Hommes et des Femmes*. Honoré Champion.
De Gournay, M. (1626 [2002]). *The Ladies' Complaint in Apology for the Woman Writing and Other Works* . University of Chicago Press.
De Grouchy, S. (1798). *Théorie des Sentiments Moraux, suivi d'une Dissertation sur l'Origine des Langues, par Adam Smith, traduit de l'Anglais sur la septième et dernière édition, par S. Grouchy, Ve Condorcet. Elle y a joint huit Lettres sur la Sympathie*. Buisson.
De Grouchy, S. (2019). *"Letters on Sympathy": A Critical Engagement with Adam Smith's "The Theory of Moral Sentiments."* Oxford University Press.
Dimand, R. (2003). An Eighteenth-Century English Feminist Response to Political Economy: Priscilla Wakefield's *Reflections* (1798). In R. Dimand & C. Nyland (Eds.), *The Status of Women in Classical Economic Thought* (pp. 194–205). Edward Elgar.
Donner, W. (1993). J.S. Mill's Liberal Feminism. *Philosophical Studies, 69*(2–3), 155–166.

Fenelon, F. (1687). *Traité de l'éducation des filles*. Pierre Aubouin, Pierre Emery et Charles Clouseer.

Folbre, N. (2009). *Greed, Lust, and Gender*. Oxford University Press.

Forget, E. (2003). Cultivating Sympathy: Sophie Condorcet's Letters on Sympathy. In R. Dimand & C. Nyland (Eds.), *The Status of Women in Classical Economic Thought* (pp. 142–161). Edward Elgar.

Frye, M. (1997). Some Reflections on Separatism and Power. In D. Tietjens Meyers (Ed.), *Feminist Social Thought: A Reader* (pp. 406–414). Routledge.

Gatens, M. (1991). *Feminism and Philosophy*. Polity Press.

Godineau, D. (2004). *Citoyennes Tricoteuses. Les femmes du peuple à Paris pendant la Révolution française*. Perrin.

Halifax, G. (1688). *Advice to a Daughter as to Religion, Husband, House, Family and Children, Behaviour and Conversation, Friendship, Censure, Vanity and Affectation, Pride, Diversions*. M. Gillyflower and B. Tooke.

Halldenius, L. (2015). *Mary Wollstonecraft and Feminist Republicanism*. Routledge.

Halldenius, L. (2019). De Grouchy, Wollstonecraft, and Smith on Sympathy, Inequality, and Rights. *Australasian Philosophical Review, 3*(4), 381–391.

Hirschman, N. (2007). *Gender, Class, & Freedom in Modern Political Theory*. Princeton University Press.

Hirschman, N., & McClure, K. (Eds.). (2007). *Feminist Interpretations of John Locke*. The Pennsylvania State University Press.

Hopkins, L., & Norrie, A. (2019). *Women on the Edge in Early Modern Europe*. Amsterdam University Press.

Kelly, G. (1992). *Revolutionary Feminism. The Mind and Career of Mary Wollstonecraft*. Palgrave Macmillan.

Lerner, G. (1986). *The Creation of Patriarchy*. Oxford University Press.

Levy, D., & Peart, S. (2022). Harriet Martineau (1802–1876). In D. Boudreaux & A. Skoble (Eds.), *The Essential Women of Liberty* (pp. 17–29). Fraser Institute.

Locke, J. (1693). *Some Thoughts Concerning Education*. A. and J. Churchill.

Locke, J., & Botting, E. (2009). To Tocqueville and Beyond. In L. Jill & E. Hunt Botting (Eds.), *Feminist interpretations of Alexis de Tocqueville* (pp. 1–18). Pennsylvania State University Press.

Mallett, P. (2016a). *Women, Marriage and the Law in Victorian Society*. https://www.routledgehistoricalresources.com/feminism/essays/women-marriage-and-the-law-in-victorian-society

Mallett, P. (2016b). *Victorian Education and the Women's Movement*. https://www.routledgehistoricalresources.com/feminism/essays/victorian-education-and-the-womens-movement
Marcet, J. (1816). *Conversation on Political Economy*. Longman.
Marcet, J. (1833). *John Hopkins' Notion on Political Economy*. Longman.
Martineau, H. (1838). *On Marriage* (G. Yates, Ed., pp. 58–65). New Rutgers University Press.
Martineau, H. (1851). *Letter to American Women's Rights Convention* (G. Yates, Ed., pp. 74–78). Rutgers University Press.
Martineau, H. (1855). *The Woman Question* (G. Yates, Ed., pp. 81–83). Rutgers University Press.
Martineau, H. (1983 [2018]). *Illustrations of Political Economy.* http://oll.libertyfund.org/titles/martineau-illustrations-of-political-economy-9-vols
McCabe, H. (2015). John Stuart Mill, Utility and the Family: Attacking 'the Citadel of the Enemy.' *Revue internationale de philosophie, 272*, 225–235.
Mill, J. (1820). *Essays on Government*. J. Innes.
Mill, J. S. (1859). *On Liberty*. Parker.
Mill, J. S. (1869). *The Subjection of Women.* Longmans, Green, Reader, and Dyer.
Moller Okin, S. (1979). *Women in the Western Political Thought*. Princeton University Press.
Moore, W. (2009). Love and Marriage in 18th-Century Britain. *Historically Speaking, 10*(3), 8–10.
Nussbaum, M. (2010). Mill's Feminism: Liberal, Radical, and Queer. In G. Varouxakis & P. Kelly (Eds.), *John Stuart Mill: Thought and Influence. The Saint of Rationalism* (pp. 130–145). Routledge.
Nyland, C. (1993). John Locke and the Social Position of Women. *History of Political Economy*, 25 (1), 39–63.
Polkinghorn, B. (1995). Jane Marcet and Harriet Martineau: Motive, Market Experience and Reception of Their Works Popularizing Classical Political Economy. In M.A. Dimand, R. Dimand, and E. Forget, (eds.) *Women of Value: Feminist Essays on the History of Women in Economics* (pp. 71–81). Edward Elgar Publishing.
Poullain de la Barre, F. (1673). *De l'égalité des deux sexes: Discours physique et moral où l'on voit l'importance de se défaire des préjugés*. Jean du Puis.
Poullain de la Barre, F. (1674). *De l'éducation des dames pour la conduite de l'esprit, dans les sciences et dans les moeurs: Entretiens*. Jean du Puis.
Poullain de la Barre, F. (1675). *De l'excellence des hommes, contre l'égalité des sexes*. Jean du Puis.

Reuter, M. (2019). François Poullain de la Barre. In *The Stanford Encyclopedia of Philosophy*. https://plato.stanford.edu/archives/win2019/entries/francois-barre

Richardson, S. (1740). *Pamela; or, Virtue Rewarded*. Rivington.

Robb, G. (1992). *White-Collar Crime in Modern England: Financial Fraud and Business Morality: 1845–1929*. Cambridge University Press.

Roberts, C. (2022). *The Woman and the Hour. Harriet Martineau and Victorian Ideologies*. University of Toronto Press.

Robinson, M. (aka) Randall Anne Frances. (1799). *A Letter to the Women of England, on the Injustice of Mental Subordination. With Anecdotes*. T.N. Longman, and O. Rees.

Rostek, J. (2014). Female Authority and Political Economy: Jane Marcet and Harriet Martineau's Contradictory Strategy in Disseminating Economic Knowledge. In R. Nischik & S. Mergenthal (Eds.), *Anglistentag 2013: Proceedings* (pp. 21–33). WVT.

Rostek, J. (2019). English Women's Economic Thought in the 1970s. In K. Madden & R. Dimand (Eds.), *Routledge Handbook of the History of Women's Economic Thought* (pp. 33–52). London: Routledge.

Rousseau, J. J. (1761). *Julie ou la nouvelle Héloïse* [Julie or The New Heloise]. Marc Michael Rey.

Rousseau, J. J. (1762a). *Émile ou de l'éducation* [Emile or On Education]. Lean Neaulme.

Rousseau, J. J. (1762b). *Du Contrat Social; ou, Principes du droit politique* [The Social Contract, or Principles of Political Right]. Marc Michael Rey.

Rutterford, J., & Maltby, J. (2006). The Widow, the Clergyman, and the Reckless: Women Investors in England: 1830–1914. *Feminist Economics, 12*(1), 111–138.

Schliesser, E. (2017). Sophie de Grouchy, The Tradition(s) of Two Liberties, and the Missing Mother(s) of Liberalism. In J. Broad & K. Detiefsen (Eds.), *Women and Liberty, 1600–1800: Philosophical Essays* (pp. 109–122). Oxford University Press.

Shanley, M. (1981). Marital Slavery and Friendship: John Stuart Mill's The Subjection of Women. *Political Theory, 9*(2), 229–247.

Sigot, N., & Beaurain, C. (2009). John Stuart Mill and the Employment of Married Women: Reconciling Utility and Justice. *Journal of the History of Economic Thought, 31*(3), 281–304.

Smith, A. (1759 [2002]). *The Theory of Moral Sentiments*. Cambridge University Press.

Smith, A. (1776 [1981]). *An Inquiry into the Nature and Causes of the Wealth of Nations*, reprinted in *The Glasgow Edition of the Works and Correspondence of Adam Smith* (R. H. Campbell, A. S. Skinner, & W. B. Todd, Eds.). Liberty Fund.

Sommers, C. H. (1994). *How Stole Feminism? How Women Have Betrayed Women.* Simon and Schuster.

Taylor Mill, H. (1832/1833 [1970]). On Marriage. *In Collected Works of John Stuart Mill*, (pp. 373–377). The University of Chicago Press.

Taylor Mill, H. & Mill, J. (1832/1833 [1970]) *Essays on Sex Equality*. In *Collected Works of John Stuart Mill*, (pp. 35–49). The University of Chicago Press.

Taylor Mill, H. (1851 [1994]). *Enfranchisement of Women.* Originally published (anonymously) in: *Westminster and Foreign Quarterly Review.* In A. Rossi (Ed.), *Essays on Sex Equality* (pp. 93–121). The University of Chicago Press.

Taylor Mill, H. (1998). *The Complete Works of Harriet Taylor Mill*. Indiana University Press.

Thompson, W., & Wheeler, A. (1825). *Appeal of One Half the Human Race, Women, Against the Pretension of the Other Half, Men, to Retain Them in Political, and thence in Civil and Domestic, Slavery*. Longman, Hurst, Rees, Orme, Brown and Green.

Todd, J. (2002). *Mary Wollstonecraft: A Revolutionary Life*. Columbia University Press.

Tomaselli, S. (2021). *Wollstonecraft: Philosophy, Passion, and Politics*. Princeton University Press.

Urbinati, N. (1991). John Stuart Mill on Androgyny and Ideal Marriage. *Political Theory, 19*(4), 626–648.

Wakefield, P. (1798 [2015]). *Reflections on the Present Condition of the Female Sex, with Suggestions for Its Improvement*. Cambridge University Press.

Webb, S. (2020). Philosophy as a Feminist Spirituality and Critical Practice for Mary Astell. *Metaphilosophy, 51*(2–3), 280–302.

Wollstonecraft, M. (1787). *Thoughts on the Education of Daughters*. Woodstock Books.

Wollstonecraft, M. (1790 & 1792 [1992]). *A Vindication of the Rights of Men, a Vindication of the Rights of Woman*. Oxford University Press.

Yalom, M. (2001). *A History of the Wife*. HarperCollins Publisher.

Yates, G. (1985). Introduction. In *Harriet Martineau on Women*. Rutgers University Press.

3

Women and the Job Market in Victorian England and Progressive America

The doctrine of the separate spheres was seriously questioned in the late nineteenth century, when middle and upper-class women, who were used to perfom their role of wives and mothers in the domestic sphere, entered the workforce. This phenomenon was primarily the result of the struggle for secondary education for girls and women at that time. Differently from them, lower-class women had always used to work in the domestic sphere either as servants or as workers, sometimes runners, of small home-based businnesses.

Some historians argue that industrialization and the subsequent separation of workplace and home exacerbated women's withdrawal from the public sphere because the separation of the two spheres made them no longer able to combine motherhood with working in their small family-based firms that gradually disappeared. Elsewhere, it is suggested that small home-based businesses persisted through the nineteenth century, making it possible for lower-class women to take care of their families and to perform in business as they did in the past. Other historians argue that middle and upper-class businesswomen outsourced their domestic duties to other women such as residential servants in order to devote themselves to their business in the marketplace (Aston & Bishop, 2020).

G. Becchio, *The Doctrine of the Separate Spheres in Political Economy and Economics*, Palgrave Studies in Classical Liberalism,
https://doi.org/10.1007/978-3-031-51262-9_3

Historians who moved beyond the doctrine of the separate spheres emphasized intersections and liminal spaces. During the Second Industrial Revolution, some women ran their business among their community, going beyond the domestic sphere but still not far from home; certain women became bankers and successful merchants, particularly in major American cities like New York[1] (Lofland, 1998). Nonetheless, businesswomen were typically limited to obtaining only moderate credit and were discouraged from making significant investments. Their accumulation of wealth often faced stigma and was devalued in the mainstream press. As Aston and Bishop (2020) argued, men and women were not different in their entrepreneurial ambition or in their abilities, rather they faced different gendered external forces. Especially married women were subjected to legal constraints; as a result, many women in business resorted to adopt a male persona, using the names of their husbands or sons (Becchio, 2020).[2]

As a matter of fact, despite the growing gender competition in the labor market, gender disparities persisted regardless of class: female workers continued to receive lower salaries, they remained segregated in gender-specific sectors, and business opportunities were often more challenging for women than for men. Additionally, only when girls gained equal access to academic education as boys (in late nineteenth-early twentieth century), an important effect on the transformation of women's roles in society occurred: middle-class educated women began to find employment in various sectors traditionally dominated by men. This marked the beginning of a vibrant, albeit lengthy, process of women's emancipation, which involved a renegotiation and reconstruction of gender ideology (Yohn, 2006).

[1] Sisters Victoria Claflin Woodhull (1838–1927) and Tennessee Claflin (1844–1923) opened a Wall Street Brokerage firm. Hetty Green (1834–1916), nicknamed the 'Witch of Wall Street', was a successful financier.

[2] The phenomenon of female entrepreneurship, which emerged in nineteenth century, is also somehow related to the doctrine of the separate spheres. Some recent literature had shown that, regardless of national and international framework, religion, custom, and so forth, businesswomen, intended as someone who finds opportunities in the market, takes risks, makes money, and creates a living for their family, constantly emerged (Aston & Bishop, 2020; Craig, 2016; Davidhoff & Hall, 2002).

Occupational segregation and the gender pay gap were justified by the doctrine of the separate spheres, which was grounded in the perceived inherent differences between men and women. As we know, according to this doctrine, women were seen as naturally oriented toward marriage and motherhood, with their commitment to the job market assumed to cease upon marriage. Consequently, investing in education that would enable women to secure better-paying jobs was considered a waste of resources, especially because women's skills were deemed to be of lower quantity and quality compared to those of men. The existing disparity between men and women in terms of high-profile performance, which was widely accepted, further justified the practice of differential wages. In addition to labor market segregation and the gender pay gap, there was a divergence in the targeting of consumption based on gender. Gender marketing, primarily centered around an idealized middle-class housewife responsible for purchasing all the necessary items for her family and easy to manipulate, began to emerge and reinforced the rhetoric of the division of roles between genders in the private and public spheres (Sivulka, 2009). Finally, in the United States, during the Progressive era a significant increase in college-educated women occurred, albeit it was almost impossible for a woman of the time to have a family along with a career: seventy-five percent of all women who earned doctoral degrees between 1877 and 1924 remained single.

3.1 Women at Work: The Economic Challenges of the Time

Traditionally, lower-class women were typically engaged in one of three primary occupations: working on farms, laboring in factories, or providing their services to upper-middle-class households. During the Middle Age, food and crafts produced in farms and small villages were sold by women at local marketplaces. Moreover, there were female guilds where both single and married women could work independently of their husbands. Women in guilds had same rights and duties as men, albeit they often had to meet additional conditions such as proving their chastity and adhering to a specific dress code. In some cases, widowed women were permitted to continue their husbands' guild memberships if they were capable of sustaining their businesses. However, the situation was more challenging for married women, often under the control of their husbands, making it difficult for them to become involved in a guild. Conversely, single women found it relatively easier to join a guild.[3] The inclusion of women as guild members increased the opportunities for them to access formal education and develop important skills: members of guilds were encouraged to acquire skills such as writing, reading, and arithmetic.

Outside of the guilds, women might be employed as unskilled laborers in farms and they were frequently chosen over men for such positions because they could be paid lower wages.[4] There are historical records of women engaging in trade in various European cities, including Italian, French, German, and Eastern European regions. In the thirteenth century, for instance, women accounted for 21% of those involved in trade contracts. Additionally, women contributed 14% of the capital in seafaring ventures during that period (Crowston, 2008).

Household production was prevalent actively involving women. Within the household, families would supply their own materials, produce finished goods, primarily for local markets, and often combine these activities with farming. Home-based work, such as garment making, hosiery production, and shoemaking, persisted throughout the nineteenth century.

Some historians contend that, as modern times progressed, women's positions in business deteriorated: with the decline of guilds and the

---

[3] Major jobs done by women in the medieval period included: brewer, laundress, barrel and crate maker, soap boiler, candle maker, book binder, doll painter, butcher, keeper of town keys, tax collector, shepherd, musician, rope maker, banker, money lender, inn keeper, spice seller, pie seller, wool trader, wine merchant, steel merchant, copper importer, currency exchanger, pawn shop owner, lake and river fisherwoman, baker, oil presser, builder, mason, plasterer, cartwright, wood turner, clay and lime worker, glazier, ore miner, silver miner, book illuminator, scribe, teacher, office manager, clerk, court assessor, customs officer, porter, tower guard, prison caretaker, surgeon, and midwife.

[4] For example, in Wurzburg, between 1428 and 1449, there were records of 323 female building site workers, paid 7.7 pfennings a day, and 13 male building site workers, paid 11.6 pfennings a day.

expansion of the domestic market, women were sometimes exploited within family businesses (Burnette, 2008).[5]

As Craig (2016) pointed out, in the early modern era, women were engaged in the job market as employees and in business as freelances, although many scholars of the time, such as Sombart (1909), dismissed the idea that women could excel in jobs requiring exceptional skills and creativity.[6] Nonetheless, the majority of women were often omitted from statistical records and they were ghettoized to specific sectors such as dressmaking and millinery: "early modern society was patriarchal. Women's inferiority was taken for granted and justified. Self-exclusion was a common phenomenon. However, self-employed business was often the only way for poor women to eke out a living" (Craig, 2016, 83).

During the Industrial Revolution, significant changes occurred for women in the marketplace. The first Census of England and Wales, published in 1841, revealed that female labor-force participation was low, with 40% of employed women working in domestic service.[7] The Occupational Distribution in the following Census (1851) revealed a significant disparity, with the total number of men employed being three times that of women (6,545,000 versus 2,832,000). Additionally, the percentage of unemployed women was notably high, at 83.3%, in contrast to the 30.2% unemployment rate for men. In the nineteenth century, the number of women employed especially in the textile sector increased, while live-in servants were often unpaid occupations (Mitchell, 1962, 60).

While new technologies were expected to disrupt men's monopoly in sectors requiring physical strength, they had a twofold effect that reinforced the gender division of labor. On one hand, machinery often

[5] Ivy Pinchbeck (1930) claimed that women benefited from having more time to devote to their homes and families. Davidoff and Hall (1987) saw women withdrew from work as a negative result of gender discrimination. Similarly, Horrell and Humphries (1995) believed that declining demand for female workers caused the female exodus from the workplace.

[6] Sombart blamed middle-class women for pressuring their husbands to provide them with luxuries, which he believed reinforced in men the spirit of capitalism.

[7] Though economic historians have identified some flaws in the Census, such as the omission of many employed individuals, particularly those working on farms where women were often considered family members (Higgs, 1987). For an overview of the Victorian and Edwardian censuses of England and Wales as a problematic source for studying the work of women, see Higgs and Wilkinson (2016).

necessitated unskilled workers, a category associated with women, while men supervised the processes, perpetuating the traditional subordination of women from the household into the factories. On the other hand, in regions where a high number of female workers were employed, there was less inclination to invest in new technologies.

Although female workers earned their own salary and began to challenge power relations in the private sphere, women remained marginalized in specific low-paying jobs, such as domestic work, childcare, nursing, water fetching, and clothing production, all of which marginalized women further. Job market segregation reinforced the distance between the household and civil society, accentuating the notion of the double spheres. As Craig questioned: "the separate sphere ideology thus become a paradigm—a framework used by historians to make sense of empirical data. But did businesswomen really disappear from the stage—or merely from the historians' radar screen, obscured by thick fogs of normative discourse?" (Craig, 2016, 96).

The doctrine of the separate spheres was reinforced by married women's self-constraint. Indeed, there was a striking difference between the number of unmarried and married women who entered the job market: the 1911 census in Great Britain revealed that sixty-nine percent of unmarried women worked compared to only nine per-cent of married women. The 'cult of domesticity', which centered on a family model with a male breadwinner with a dependent wife and children, played a pivotal role in discouraging women from pursuing a career. Furthermore, pressure from unions or labor organizations pushed women to think in terms of a 'family wage' rather than individuals' liberty to choose whether or not to join the workforce.

Many British socialist thinkers as well as American economists of the Progressive era advocated for state intervention to regulate industrial production and to protect female workers.[8] Nonetheless, state regulation of women's work in factories led to the proliferation of the 'sweating system', also known as the 'cottage industry': this system involved providing materials to workers and compensating them based on the

[8] Goldin (1991) considered protection legislation either as a genuine attempt to ensure women's health in workplaces or as a means to reinforce the self-interest of male workers, especially those involved in unions.

number of pieces they assembled either in their homes or in small workshops (sweatshops).[9] The primary sector where this system was prevalent was the garment industry: usually a male supervisor, the *sweater*, oversaw the predominantly female and child workforce engaged in long shifts (typically lasting between fifteen and eighteen hours per day) while receiving a very low wage, and facing precarious sanitary conditions.[10] To make things worse, families of working women often lived in sweatshops.

Factories organized work accordingly to gender too with men typically performing the supervisory roles and positions categorized as 'skilled', while women were relegated to unskilled tasks. Moreover, women were consistently paid less than men. This phenomenon dramatically increased during the period of immigration waves (see this Chapter, paragraph 4).

Women workers' low standards in workplaces as well as their low wages were analyzed early on. In 1887, Ida Van Etten, the first Secretary of the Working Women's Society of New York,[11] wrote an article to challenge the view of statistician Carrol D. Wright who justified the existing conditions of women workers by considering them "the very weakest and most dependent of all the people". Van Etten lamented the "prevailing state of public ignorance regarding the evils of working women's condition" and advocated for "justice, not charity" for women workers. She pointed out that, at the current rate of wages, women were unable to save any money or engage in any activity requiring even a small amount of capital. Differently for men, who even "at the lowest round of the industrial ladder (...) can look forward to the pleasures of a comfortable home, of educating his children, and enjoying a competency in his old

[9] In Great Britain, the sweating system first appeared in early nineteenth century and was banned by law in 1909. In the United States, it began during the Civil War, when women and children were employed in making uniforms for soldiers (Domosh & Seager, 2001).

[10] The term sweatshop was coined by Charles Kingsley (1850).

[11] The Working Women's Association (WWA) was founded in New York City on September 17, 1868, in the offices of *The Revolution*, a women's rights newspaper established earlier by Elizabeth Cady Stanton and Susan B. Anthony. Its purpose was to create "an association of working-women which might act for the interests of its members, in the same manner as the associations of working-men now regulate the wages, etc. of those belonging to them" (Flexner, 1959).

age, for the working woman there exists no such plans or hopes" (Van Etten, 1887, 315).

The competition between men and women in the job market led to a twofold debate among economists of the time. First, it prompted a discussion on the economic consequences of women entering the workforce, including the consideration of implementing legal restrictions on women's employment, such as limiting the number of hours they could work.[12] Second, it raised the issue of wage differentiation between male and female workers as a means to promote men's careers and discourage women from pursuing their ambitions[13] (Bodichon 1857; Bosanquet, 1902, 1906).

3.2 Debates Among Economists: Gender Discrimination in Employment and Pay

Many economists of the time argued that the influx of female workers into the job market would lead to a decrease in the average salary for both men and women. They contended that when the earnings of men and women were combined, it would not significantly impact the family's income. Consequently, the presence of women, especially if married, in the labor force resulted in being useless for the well-being of their families.

As a matter of fact, these economists used this argument to promote the doctrine of separate spheres in a subtle manner, aiming to reinforce restrictions on women's participation in the job market. Their main point was about the fact that working women would have been distracted from their main task, i.e. taking care of their families and households. Since the family was considered the foundation of social well-being, this shift was viewed as potentially detrimental to society as a whole. Some women

---

[12] In 1848, women's workhours were regulated at ten hours/day; in the following decades, a wider discussion on factory legislation took place.

[13] On average, there was no gender wage gap for teenagers. Beginning at age 16, a large gender wage gap emerged; at age 30, female workers in factories earned only one-third as much as men; annual earnings of married women averaged only about 28% of their husband's earnings (Mitchell, 1962).

shared this view too. Figures like Helen Dendy Bosanquet (1860–1925) supported women's education as a means to enhance the well-being of society; she advocated for women's access to the labor force; she struggled against any government limitation on female employment and against programs based on State's charity; she promoted equal pay between men and women (Akkerman, 1998; Groenegewen, 2000). Nevertheless, Bosanquet limited female employment to unmarried women and in her writings on family and household, she clearly stated that married women should primarily consider themselves good wives (Bosanquet, 1902, 1906).

Differently from Bosanquet, the non-academic economist Millicent Fawcett (1847–1929) did not distinguish between married and unmarried women (Becchio, 2020; Pujol, 1992; Pujol & Seitz, 2000). She particularly insisted on the importance of women's education, challenging the primary tendency of parents to view investments in education as valuable only for their sons, while considering daughters as destined for marriage without any need for any specific higher education.

On the opposite side, economists who were in favor of women's participation in the job market fought against the doctrine of the separate spheres: they insisted on the idea that integrating women into the labor force would enhance overall social well-being. They argued that human progress should not be hindered by prejudices and traditions rooted in gender stereotypes. These stereotypes had relegated women's aspiration to the private sphere while simultaneously reinforcing men's power in the public sphere. Furthermore, they pointed out the need to challenge men to equally share responsibilities in the private sphere.

The debate involved many outstanding economists and scholars of the time, such as William Jevons, Alfred Marshall, John Stuart Mill, Francis Edgeworth, Karl Pearson, Arthur Pigou, Sidney Webb, William Smart, Beatrice Webb, Eleanor Rathbone, Ada Heather-Bigg, and Millcent Fawcett in England as well as Henry Seager, Richard Ely, Matthew B. Hammond, Mary Van Kleeck, Sophonisba Breckenridge, Charles Person, and John Commons in the United States (Groenewegen, 1994; Leonard, 2005a, 2005b; Madden & Dimand, 2019).

William Jevons (1883) made a distinction between married and unmarried women as well as between women working in factories and those working as domestics. He proposed the differentiation of workhours and workplaces according to class, race, and gender and he recommended the complete exclusion of mothers from factories arguing that their primary duty was to care for the family and eventually to help their husbands with an extra-mural job (Peart, 1996).

Like Jevons, Alfred Marshall held a conservative view of the modern conception of women's role: he argued that women had different mental attitudes that made them unsuitable for theoretical works and less valuable professionals. Furthermore, he believed that the traditional family was crucially vital for social development and emphasized the role of women as wives and mothers being more significant than their presence in the labor force (Groenewegen, 1995). In his *Principles* (1890), Marshall opposed the employment of married women and adopted the notion of a family wage that should be eventually subsidized by the State if the husbands' wage was not enough to cover it. He also promoted a reform of educational system to improve the supply of skilled labor force. Marshall's perspective on social investments in human capital included women, but he saw their employment as detrimental because it reduced the time they could spend on childbearing and, consequently, on increasing human capital for the improvement of society. Instead of encouraging women to be more competitive in the labor market, Marshall believed that they should be educated to contribute more effectively to the human capital investment in their children. Hence, he regarded women's lower wages as an incentive for them to stay at home.

Marshall's account of family's economic behavior aligns with the Victorian model of the separate spheres. According to Marshall, an ideal family should be based on responsible parenting, a gendered division of labor between husbands and wives, and a combination of familial and state investment in children's education that reinforced the gendered division of labor between sexes (Bankovsky, 2018, 2020). Motherhood was seen by Marshall as a women's duty, while fatherhood was underrated as men got rewarded in the marketplace (Pujol, 1984). Hence, he was in favor of the extension of the Factory Acts, aimed at restricting the employment of children and women in factories as well as advocating for subsistence wages for women and family wages for men. In Marshall's view, women should devote all their time and energy to the development of their children and household management, being this their *natural* duty (Gouverneur, 2023). Family, as conceived by Marshall, was a production input of the national industrial system rather than an agent of consumption. Hence, he endorsed home management education for girls and technical education for boys.

Later, Arthur Cecil Pigou (1920) introduced the notion of wages based on marginal productivity rather than subsistence requirements. According to him, the common notion that women were paid less than men because their salaries supported only themselves while men's salaries supported the whole family was flawed. Nevertheless, Pigou still justified lower pay for women ('unfair wages'): he drew from Marshall's ideas to develop a general national human capital investment policy that primarily focused on men's skills, as he believed women were primarily engaged in nonmarket reproductive work. In two articles published in the *Economic Journal*, Francis Ysidro Edgeworth (1922, 1923) seemed to promote an enlargement of the job opportunities for women, but he also questioned women's abilities and justified unequal wages (Pujol, 1992).

Against Jevons and Marshall, John Stuart Mill blamed any factory legislation which limited women, seeing it as a reflection of the traditional idea of women being subjected to men. In his *Principles* (1848), he insisted on granting women full access to workplaces and asserted that there could be no justification for sacrificing women's freedom to participate in the workforce for the sake of social utility.

In the *Economic Journal*, Ada Heather-Bigg (1855–1944) denounced men's attitude to oppose women's employment as an attempt to protect their dominant status:

> It is clear that something else moves [men] than 'mere dread that maternal and household duties may be neglected. Analyzing carefully, we find that what they object to is the wage-earning not the work of wives. Home-work enables a married woman to become joint earner with her husband, and they profess to fear that facilities in this direction may lead to the gradual substitution of the wife for the husband as bread-winner (...). It is indisputable that women of the working classes always have been joint earners with their husbands. At no time in the world's history has the

> man's labour alone sufficed for the maintenance of his wife and children. (…) Though women did not earn wages for all the multifarious occupations which 'looking after the home' formerly involved, it is clear they did as much of the necessary work of the world as they do now. If, then, the fallacy that there is a limited amount of work to be obtained, and that the more the women take the less the men get, be supposed true, it is certain that female labour competed as much with male labour heretofore as now. The only difference was that each woman took an infinitesimal share of a great many different kinds of work (…) So long as the wife must contribute her quota to family maintenance, it is distinctly advisable that she should be allowed to do this in the way she herself finds least irksome (Heather-Bigg, 1894, 55–58).

The debate on the consequence of women's entry into the labor force was intertwined with discussions about equal pay.

Sidney Webb (1891) categorized women workers into four groups: manual laborers, routine mental workers, artistic workers, and intellectual workers. In the case of the latter two groups, gender had little influence on determining wages. However, for routine mental workers, Webb found that women consistently earned less than men. He argued that the gender wage gap was a consequence of women's labor being generally inferior in terms of both quantity and quality. Webb believed that this disparity was even more pronounced in the United States compared to England, and cited available data of the time that showed evidence across various leading industries employing manual labor. This wage disparity persisted even in industries like textiles. Furthermore, in cases where women earned more than men, the difference in their favor was much smaller than the difference in favor of men in the opposite scenario. Finally, while women's wages were relatively closer to men's in certain industries, particularly in weaving, it was undeniable that men's wages remained superior.

Lately, Beatrice and Sidney Webb reinforced Sidney's earlier conclusions:

> we are so accustomed in the middle class to see men and women engaged in identical work, as teachers, journalists, authors, painters, sculptors, comedians, singers, musicians, medical practitioners, clerks or what not,

> that we almost inevitably assume the same state of things to exist in manual labor and manufacturing industry. But this is very far from being the case (Webb & Webb, 1898, 94).

Many prominent economists in both England and the United States shared Webb's viewpoint, suggesting that the lower wages paid to women were partially justified by the perceived inferiority of women's work.[14] American labor economist Matthew B. Hammond (1868–1933) summed up Webb's argument as follows. In the majority of trades and industries, men and women do not compete for the same work, with the only exception of garments industry. In cases where piece-rate payment is used, women's wages are equal to men's, despite women typically are less productive due to their shorter working hours. However, women's natural disadvantage in terms of productivity is exacerbated by societal custom. Women's lower standard of living and their partial dependence on their husbands prevent them from obtaining what Hammond referred to as their "true economic wages". Hammond wrote: "it must be repeated that these conclusions apply only to manual work. Doubtless they are in a degree applicable also to the higher callings; but here woman's inferiority is usually less, and the influence of custom, of the standard of living and of the irregular and temporary character of her employment is much greater" (Hammond, 1900, 535).

Scottish economist William Smart (1853–1915), who was mainly influenced by the notion of subjective value, as developed by the Austrian school of economics, explained women's lower wages compared to men by attributing this wage disparity to the marginal productivity theory of wages (Smart, 1892).[15] He summarized the possible explanations of the gender pay gap as follows: a matter of supply and demand; an effect of women not being breadwinners; a result of women having a lower standard of living compared to men; a consequence of women's performance at work being inferior to that of men; and the fact that products made by women are generally less valuable in the market. Therefore, he analyzed each of them.

---

[14] Among them, William Smart, John A. Hobson, and Carroll D. Wright (Hammond, 1900).

[15] As retrieved on August 22, 2023 at: https://www.gutenberg.org/cache/epub/52959/pg52959-images.html.

According to Smart, the adoption of the supply–demand explanation was flawed because it only holds in perfect competition which is never the case. The argument that women are not breadwinners is questionable too, as it assumes that the wage-earning unit is the family, "an old-time idea which, however beautiful and desirable, is a little out of place in the conditions to which the factory system has brought us" (Smart, 1892, 11). The standard of living argument does not apply broadly to women's wages because women's standards of living differ from men's in terms of items rather than costs, and there is no uniformity in women's standards across different social classes. The argument that women's work is inferior is due to factors like their limited availability to work extra hours and specific legislation that restricted their working hours. Finally, the argument about commodities made by women being cheap goods is weak because the value of a product is determined by consumer demand, which depends on its marginal utility, and while it may be true that lower wages led to lower prices, the reverse causation does not necessarily happen.

Based on his analysis, Smart concluded that the difference of wages between men and women was not primarily a matter of efficiency, but rather "a question of difference of wage between two non-competing groups, and of groups where the levels of wage are determined by a different law" (Smart, 1892, 20). Hence, two more aspects needed to be addressed: the segregation of women in certain sectors of the labor market and the wage difference between skilled female labor and unskilled male labor.

Smart provided a common answer to both the issues: according to him, women lose competitive advantages because they are "physically weaker; subject to little ailments which make them less regular in attendance; more liable to distraction of purpose; perhaps worse educated; and, probably, more slipshod in their methods" (Smart, 1892, 20).

Millicent Fawcett wrote several articles on gender labor gap and gender wage gap (Fawcett, 1892; 1917; 1918a, 1918b). According to Fawcett, women's lower performance in labor was due to two main factors: the peculiar way the labor market relegated women to low-wage jobs by creating *de facto* occupational segregation (Fawcett, 1892); the role of trade unions in perpetuating gender wage disparities. Moreover, some trade unions had policies that excluded or marginalized women, further limiting their access to better-paying jobs (Fawcett, 1917).

Besides Fawcett, Beatrice Webb and Eleanor Rathbone were other major women scholars and economists involved in the debate. They shared a critical attitude toward equal pay. Contrary to Fawcett's voices for equal pay, Beatrice Webb believed that equal pay posed a threat to the working class' standard of living. Instead, she promoted state regulation of the sweating system (Webb, 1896). Eleanor Rathbone argued that equal pay would have led women's exclusion from skilled jobs. Therefore, she proposed a differentiated wage system and a form of state subsidy for motherhood, which implicitly reinforced the stereotype of women's role in society as mothers (Rathbone, 1917). Neither Webb nor Rathbone fully endorsed equal pay for equal work, as they considered it irrelevant for the majority of women who were confined in separate jobs and were struggling for a minimum wage and improved working conditions. Rather both Webb and Rathbone invited women to join trade unions' general agenda of social reforms[16]. Although Webb mitigated her position against equal pay, after World War I, like Rathbone she considered motherhood as the primary task for women. Especially, Rathbone insisted on the undervaluation of domestic labor and child-rearing. She wrote: "Women in the workplace are birds of passage, marriage and the bearing and rearing of children are their permanent occupations" (1917, 65).

In the United States, economists of the Progressive Era tended to discourage women's participation in the labor-force. The main reasons behind this attitude were to protect what was considered the biologically weaker sex from the dangers of working in the marketplace; to prevent working women from resorting to prostitution; to shield male heads of households from the economic competition with women; to ensure that women could better fulfill their eugenic duties as 'mothers of

[16] As Pujol rightly pointed out, the differences between Fawcett, Rathbone, and Webb depended on their political orientation: Fawcett insisted on classical liberal feminist principle of equal rights; Rathbone, although "politically unaligned", was close to "welfare socialism"; Webb, a founder of Fabianism, subordinated gender to class (Pujol, 1992, 91). Fawcett was against any form of protectionism, as she championed classical liberalism. Rathbone saw the formula as a "trap" set by the trade union movement to decrease women's employment (Chassonnery-Zaïgouche, 2019).

the race'. These arguments took on various forms: paternalistic concerns about women's health, moralistic appeals to women's virtue, the advocacy of 'family wage' to protect men from competition with working women, the promotion of the virtues of motherhood, and the support for eugenic principles aimed at enhancing the overall health of the population (Leonard, 2005a).

Reformers of the Progressive Era attempted to explain women's wages by attributing them to women's consumption preferences.[17] Columbia economist Henry R. Seager (1870–1930) argued that women's willingness to accept low wages was connected to their "natural" subordination. Influenced by the Austrian school theory of value, Seager considered wages, like any other price, determined by consumption: since women were dependent on their husbands or fathers, they were paid lower wages compared to men, who were viewed as the primary breadwinners of the family (Seager, 1913).

Progressive Era welfare activists, both male and female, tended to endorse Seager's family-wage argument. For instance, Person (1915) insisted on the notion of the family as "the true social unit": he believed that the salaries of working women and girls were subsidiary source of their families. Furthermore, the temporary nature of women's works implied inefficiency which contributed to lower wages. This wage disparity for women was seen as a result of intense competition among low-skilled workers and the increasing population pressure, both of which were exacerbated by the large-scale immigration to the United States during that period.

There were a few detractors of the family-wage argument, including Florence Kelley and Sophonisba Breckenridge (Gordon, 1992). Florence Kelley pointed out that the American tradition of men supporting their families was rapidly changing due to the influence of immigration and the growing number of married women immigrants from southeastern European nations, who provided a source of cheap female labor (Kelley, 1912).

[17] Theresa McMahon's (1925) contrasted the "American Standard of living" with the "immigrant," and the "feminine" standards of living.

Breckinridge was a staunch opponent of the protective legislation: she believed that it aimed to reduce women's competition in the job market as well as their salaries. She viewed such legislation as a constraint on women rather than as a form of protection. She believed that this legislation was rooted in outdated notions. She wrote:

> The survival in present-day notions of the mediaeval idea that where unsuitable conditions of intercourse between the sexes exist it is the women whose presence is the disturbing factor. While this legislation may 'protect' women workers against certain forms of brutality and greed on the part of employers, and while it may 'protect' some women against the competition of others of lower standards and seemingly greater need, it is still to be borne in mind that the object of such control is the protection of the physical well-being of the community by setting a limit to the exploitation of the improvident, unworkmanlike, unorganized women, who are yet the mothers, actual or prospective, of the coming generation. The effectiveness with which this power of control is assumed and exercised is one standard by which the community must judge itself and be judged of others (Breckinridge, 1906, 108–109).

After World War I, Breckinridge wrote a lengthy article against the family-wage argument (Breckinridge, 1923). She challenged the idea that men's salaries depended on family needs while women's pay was estimated on individual's requirements. She pointed out that men were also paid on an individual basis, but the absence of protective legislation in their case gave them greater bargaining power. Breckinridge argued that minimum-wage law and wage-scales legislation, which were applied exclusively to women, were established on the needs of a single woman without considering the possibility that female workers might be responsible for supporting other family members.

Breckinridge analyzed the stance of British economists of the time on equal pay. She pointed out that Beatrice Webb had proposed a specific occupational rate for all workers rather than advocating for gender-equal pay. Webb also had promoted the idea of a national minimum wage that applied to all workers regardless of gender. She had emphasized the importance of eliminating all "sex exclusions" and opening up all positions and professions to qualified individuals without regard to gender.

While Rathbone and Fawcett converged on defining "equal pay for equal work a claim to secure for women a fair field of competition with men, their work being accepted or rejected on its merits", Edgeworth "embodie[d] in his definition of equal work the idea of equal freedom in the choice of work and that equal freedom to prepare for work by acquiring skill, on which Mrs. Webb laid such emphasis" (Breckinridge, 1923, 525–526).

Breckinridge insisted on considering equal pay as a demand for fair treatment against discrimination targeting women workers, especially if married. She wrote:

> the demand for an equal wage when resolved into its constituent elements proves rather to be a demand for freedom (1) to select one's employment in accordance with one's capacities, (2) to be equipped to do the job selected in a way and after a standard determined by an objective analysis, and (3) to be so remunerated as to be able to render one's own most efficient service without constituting one's self a menace to a standard of life already built up by other workers (Breckinridge, 1923, 543).

Breckinridge's colleague and coauthor, Edith Abbott, accused most economists of the time of using the family-wage argument to support restrictions on women's employment and unequal pay.[18] She wrote:

> contrary to contemporary popular opinion, women were not displacing men in factories (…) ongoing labor shifts and adjustments [were] not to sort of Gresham's law in which cheap women's labor drove out men's (...) Instead these changes were attributed to factors such as immigration, workplace monopolization by men's union, and technological innovation. Furthermore, the notion of supplementary wages, which is usually complementary to the notion of family wage, is determined not by the bargaining power of the man, but often by the helplessness of the woman

[18] The collaboration between Breckinridge and Abbott was long lasting: in 1927, they founded the journal *Social Service Review* to promote social work research in academic and to strengthen the welfare agenda in politics. They presented urban environment, rather than the family, as the source of major social problems (Breckinridge & Abbott, 1912).

> and of the minor children who have become the apparent collectors of their own wages (Abbott, 1910, 2).[19]

She was particularly focused on addressing the gender pay gap, by adopting Mitchell's classification of wage earners (Mitchell, 1908), not based on industries or occupations, but according to the rates of wages received.[20] Against Webb's theory that women were paid poorly due to their inefficiency resulting from a lower skill profile, Abbott emphasized different factors: women often faced restriction of opportunities for proper training and education, which hindered their ability to acquire higher-paying skills; custom and traditions often dictated that women should accept a 'lower standard of life', which influenced their wages; women assumed that they would eventually leave the workforce after marriage, resulting in shorter working lives; there was a persistent lack of organization among women; women faced occupational segregation in lower-skilled jobs and the consequent oversupply of labor within those sectors.

Abbott particularly criticized custom and traditions as significant barriers to achieving gender pay equity:

> Unfortunately the employment of women was not considered on its own merits, it met condemnation instead of encouragement. It has become something of a public habit to speak of the women who work in factories today as if they were invaders threatening to take over work which belongs to men by custom and prior right of occupation (Abbott, 1910, 322).

Clara Collet, a colleague and coauthor of both Breckinridge and Abbott, authored the book *Educated Working Women* (1902), a collection of her previous writings that were specifically targeted against the doctrine of the separate spheres adopted to criticize middle-class women workers who were supposed to perform their social function in the private sphere.

---

19 As retrieved on August 23, 2023 at: https://historyofeconomicthought.mcmaster.ca/abbott/WomenIndustry.pdf.

20 She arranged wage earners in five groups, those who received from 25 to 99 cents a day; from \$1 to \$1.49; from \$1.50 to \$1.99; from \$2 to \$2.49; from \$2.50 and over. Data revealed that the majority of women were not merely in the lowest group but in the lowest half of the lowest group.

Overall, she criticized the educational system of the time in the United States, which was geared toward training girls exclusively in domestic labor with the assumption that they would eventually get married.

In conclusion, as Leonard (2005a) pointed out, American progressives adopted a paternalistic vision: they preferred to advocate legal protection for women rather than acknowledge that women's wages were unfairly low. Additionally, many American progressives shared a chauvinistic attitude, attempting to shield men from the economic competition with women. This was often justified using eugenic arguments aimed at protecting the race from women's participation in the labor force. Women's labor legislation in the United States further reinforced the doctrine of the separate spheres by emphasizing motherhood as the most important role for women as both individuals and social agents. For instance, a reduction of working hours for women was deemed necessary in order to prevent any harm to family life and the reproductive health of women (Goldmark, 1912).[21]

Motherhood as the primary role for women was encouraged and reinforced by two main arguments: family wage and concerns about social vice. Family-wage proponents believed that society was built upon households led by a male breadwinner and emphasized the importance of women as mothers (Kelley, 1912, 1914). Hence, women were seen as contributors to a family's income rather than as individuals capable of independent living. As a result, advocates of the family wage considered wages as payments intended to cover a consumption standard, rather than compensation for the value of a worker's marginal product. Moreover, women were often deemed unemployable and subject to exclusionary labor legislation, which was reinforced through various justifications: paternalistic efforts to protect women from the risks of

[21] In 1908, the case *Muller v. Oregon* inaugurated women's labor legislation in the United States. In 1912, the State of Massachusetts passed the first act providing a minimum wage for women while establishing a commission to study industrial conditions and set wage rates. By 1919, minimum wage laws were applied in fifteen states, including DC. After the First World War, things changed: in 1923 the District of Columbia minimum wage law was declared unconstitutional. The decision was later reinforced by the final decision of the United States Supreme Court, which highlighted a conflict between the principles of protection and liberty and claiming for the abolition of labor legislation, which made women less competitive than men when entering the job market.

market labor, moralistic concerns about preventing temptations like prostitution (see Sect. 4.3), support for family wages to shield male breadwinners from economic competition from women, and maternalistic ideals that aimed to confine women to their roles as mothers, specifically as 'mothers of the race' (Leonard, 2005a).

Regardless of the specific arguments put forth, the justifications for banning or restricting women's labor were based on the doctrine of the separate spheres, which excluded women from the public sphere (as wage workers) and promoted subsidies aimed at encouraging them to remain at home. Progressive reformers highly praised motherhood, with even feminist Charlotte Perkins Gilman considering women primarily as mothers and then as workers (see next paragraph).

Richard T. Ely passionately wrote about the necessity of female labor legislation, including regulations on working hours and, in some cases, the complete prohibition of night shifts, especially for married women. He wrote:

> No woman desires to work twelve and thirteen hours daily in a factory; and contracts for such toil are involuntary in substance even if voluntary in form. A tenth labour day for women, such as has been passed in Massachusetts and sustained by the Supreme Court of that state, does not deprive 'Mary Holmes' of liberty-it affords her liberty. It does not restrict her right to work; it enlarges that right; for it conserves her health and strength and lengthens out the period of profitable work. If she is a mother, it also enlarges the freedom of her children and adds to their efficiency by giving her at least some shreds of time and strength for her family (Ely, 1908, 141).

Ely strongly criticized Mill's insistence on gender equality and his view that the subjection of women was primarily due to the legal conditions of marriage and the denial of suffrage. He denied the possibility for women to protect themselves adequately in labor contracts without a special protective legislation. He wrote: "The reasons for [woman's] economic disabilities are as profound as her sex differences and must be reckoned with in any realistic legislation. This is the verdict of the world's civilization" (Ely, 1908, 143).

On the opposite side, the National Woman's Party (NWP), founded in 1916, regarded female labor legislation as another form of sex discrimination, ultimately inimical to women's interests.[22] When members of NWP, such as Alice Paul and Maud Younger, proposed the first Equal Rights Amendment (ERA), many progressive reformers defined it 'stupid' (Kelley, 1921). When economist John R. Commons became president of the National Consumers League (1923), he struggled against the Equal Rights Amendment, and leading progressives discouraged women from fighting for equal pay, being them among the strongest supporters of the doctrine of the separate spheres.

3.3 Women and the Economy: Crossing the Boundaries of the Private Sphere

In 1910, labor economist Helen Sumner summarized the situation of women workers in the United States at that time. She categorized women's work into five groups: unpaid labor, independent gainful labor, domestic service, wage labor in manufacturing industries, and wage labor in trade and transportation. The manufacturing industries generally represented working-class employment, while trade and transportation industries were typically associated with middle-class employment. She pointed out that phenomena such as industrialization and urbanism had dramatically changed women's position in the labor market as well as their overall status: unpaid home-working women became paid factory workers, while both independent home workers and wage-earning home workers were employed in factories and workshops, which were gradually transformed in sweatshops.[23]

The passage from home work, either paid or unpaid, to factories, was a central point in questioning the legitimacy of the doctrine of the separate spheres: differently from many reformers of her time, Sumner

---

[22] New York's prohibition of night work by women, for example, had led to the dismissal of thousands of women workers. This event led to foundation of the Women's League for Equal Opportunity in 1915 (Baker, 1925: 425–26).

[23] As reported by Sumner, in 1900, only one-fifth of all females over 16 years old were breadwinners.

did not blame this passage because "the entire history of women's work shows that their wage labor under the domestic system has almost inevitably been under worse conditions of hours, wage and general sanitation than their wage labor under the factory system" (Sumner, 1910, 12). Furthermore, she added, the number of businesswomen and female professionals had significantly increased as well as salaries in domestic service, manufacturing, and trade and transportation sectors.

The introduction of machinery, artificial power, and division of labor created opportunities for women in new industries. However, women continued to be employed in unskilled and poorly paid occupations that did not directly compete with men. According to Sumner, not only custom and prejudices but also factors like lack of training and ambition as well as a general sense of irresponsibility made women workers to accept subordination in the market labor. Especially the lack of training and ambition—Sumner continued—created a vicious circle for women: they were aware that well-paid positions were rarely available to them, leading them to a loss of self-confidence and a reluctance to invest in training. According to Sumner, before the industrial revolution, women did not perceive any trade-off between marriage and work, as they actively worked in household. However, the industrial system, with its machinery and division of labor, disconnected work from marriage, leading to new challenges for women in the workforce: "there grew up a hybrid class of women workers in whose lives there is contradiction and internal if not external discord. Their work no longer fits in with their ideals and has lost its charm" (Sumner, 1910, 15). Moreover, Sumner continued, women's wages were consistently lower than men's and women often had to endure excessively long working hours, especially during times of economic depression and panic. Instead of protecting women workers, custom and practices as well as legislation exploited them. To address these issues, trade unions organized strikes, industrial education programs focused on apprenticeships and business colleges, and promoted state legislation aimed to improve conditions for women workers. However, Sumner concluded, their situation remained characterized by long hours, overwork, precarious labor conditions, miserably low wages, lower standards of living, and dependence on men's charity, such as fathers, brothers, and husbands. She also emphasized that women's resources were often wasted when directed solely toward motherhood.

Questioning the role of motherhood as the main purpose of women was a central issue in challenging the doctrine of the separate spheres. This challenge was particularly significant when economic independence was presented as the primary means to overcome traditional gender roles and create a society where individuals were equally free.

Abbott (1910) pointed out that the phenomenon of professional women striving to realize a new ideal of economic independence, which takes them out of their home and makes them engaged in new and varied occupations, was a recent phenomenon that involved middle-class and upper-class women, while women of the working classes were always been expected to be self-supporting. Collet seconded Abbott and insisted on the revolutionary aspect of middle-class women who shifted from the private sphere to the public sphere by entering the labor force in competition with men and providing self-supporting jobs.

As previously mentioned, Collet analyzed the costs and benefits of this new figure of female middle-class worker in several writings collected in her 1910 book. She scrutinized the elements that could promote a girl's career, by pointing out that usually parents take it for granted that their daughters will be married. Nonetheless, she continued, middle-class girls had finally begun to consider marriage as a potential choice rather than a destiny. They also started to think about earning an adequate income: "If she has any public spirit, she will not undersell her poorer competitors, and will see no reason why she should not be paid the full worth of her services; she will be glad to know that her services are really worth her living" (Collet, 1890 [1910]).[24] Collet noticed that usually middle-class girls became teachers which remained a poorly paid job, albeit it payed better than most other work done by women, with no real chance to build up a career. Collet underlined that those who pursued an intellectual career faced several social barriers that made achieving economic independence difficult. She insisted on the fact that thinking in terms of competition instead of in terms of cooperation between men and

[24] As retrieved on August 23, 2023 at: https://www.gutenberg.org/files/68623/68623-h/68623-h.htm.

women in professional sectors or managerial positions was a common mistake. In fact, men and women can bring different problem-solving approaches to the table, and working together can lead to faster and more efficient problem-solving processes. Therefore, occupational segregation, which protected men's privileged position in the market, was detrimental for social well-being.

In an essay dated 1898 [1910], Collet pointed out that middle-class women's salaries should be raised to a level sufficient to maintain their current and future standard of living by considering that a financially independent woman might enjoy recreation, including traveling, holidays and amusement, which require a greater expenditure of money than a purely domestic life demands. Two years later, Collet wrote about the enormous change faced by middle-class women in the previous twenty-five years:

> No middle-class woman educated in the high schools is unable to earn a living if she wants; parents started to recognized that their daughters should be fitted to be self-supporting; girls tend to think about a possible professional career and regard marriage as a possibility which may someday call them away from the path they are pursuing, but which should not be allowed to interfere with their plans in the meantime (Collet, 1900 [1910], 138).

Teaching and nursing professions, which encompassed the majority of educated women, made great advances. Women began to consider their jobs as a means and not an end: a means to fulfill their expectation of an interesting life. Collet wrote:

> here lies the great difference between men and women in the labour market. All that the average man demands is that his work should be honest and remunerative. It need not be interesting, or elevating, or heroic. Most women, on the other hand, who look forward to a long working career must have an occupation to which they can give both heart and mind. (...) What [men] earn is of more importance than what they do (...) generally speaking, the women who earn the highest incomes are the women who have chosen their work for the work's sake (Collet, 1900 [1910], 141).

As Collet wrote, this new woman, economically independent and cherishing life, was often unpopular, because she had the ability to dismantle gender barriers and prejudices and this, after all, means progress for women and for the race. Like many other progressive reformers, Collet paradoxically embraced the desire for racial purity: on one side, they were open-minded and progressive on gender matters, on the other side, they embraced eugenics intertwined with racist ideologies.

Some authors considered this combination of feminism and eugenics an effect of nativism rather than nationalism. Nativists intentionally ignored the fact that native people in America were not white Anglo-Saxons but Indigenous American (or Indians). As it is well-known, nativists justified their position by dating the birth of the American nation back to the Eighteenth century when former British colonies got their independence and the Founding Fathers devoted themselves to building the United States of America as a nation (Athey, 2000). Nevertheless, if nativists grounded eugenics and racial purity on a political (and military) event carried out in the name of the nation, they inevitably switched from nativism to nationalism. Supporters of eugenics were concerned about the possibility that some genes might cause low intelligence or immoral, criminal, or antisocial behavior.[25]

Although eugenics was overtly criticized,[26] during the Progressive Era, between 1890 and 1930, many feminists supported eugenic laws on sterilization. Among them were the National Federation of Women's Clubs, the Women's Christian Temperance Union, the National League of Women Voters, and a variety of state and local feminist organizations (Ziegler, 2008). The involvement of feminist reformers in the eugenics movement can been regarded as consistent with their support of social control (Willrich, 1998) or simply as a form of racism (Gordon, 2002).

Eugenic feminists argued that the decline of the race could be prevented only if women were granted greater political, social, sexual,

[25] In 1896, Connecticut passed a law requiring medical exams before issuing marriage licenses. In 1907 Indiana passed the first compulsory sterilization law. Supporters included Theodore Roosevelt, W. E. B. Du Bois, Margaret Sanger, and many more (see Leonard, 2016).

[26] In 1913, a referendum authorizing sterilization failed in Oregon and Nebraska's governor vetoed a eugenics bill. Some state courts declared forced sterilization laws unconstitutional.

and economic equality.[27] As mentioned, feminist reformers's involvement in eugenics might be explained by considering what feminists had in common with eugenics movements the call to legal reform, such as birth control, based on racial assumptions. Nonetheless, eugenics and feminism of the time split up in two cases: on one side, feminists reformers rejected eugenic laws that included women in the category of 'defective' in case of lack of femininity; on the other side, mainstream eugenics rejected some feminist promotion of free love and economic independence for women.[28]

The combination of feminism and eugenics was advocated by Charlotte Perkins Gilman (1860–1935): she played a pivotal role in showing that a 'new woman', or better said a new image of a woman not constrained within the private sphere, was possible, albeit she doubled down gender emancipation with her support of eugenics. By the time of the publication of her book *Women and Economics* (1898), mainstream eugenics and feminism did not get along well: feminists deployed eugenicists who usually opposed higher education and professional employment for women as well as eugenic sterilization laws that imposed to control women's sexual behavior. Nonetheless, in her book, Perkins Gilman presented the androcentric culture as a form of power that had made women servants, harming both women and the Anglo-Saxon race. She argued that relegating women to the private sphere made the race weak and put it in danger. Later, she explicitly embraced the eugenics position. Between 1908 and 1916, she published some radical eugenic articles in her journal, *The Forerunner*. She combined her own version of eugenics with feminist stances by suggesting that the eugenic salvation of the race required legal reforms, such as birth control, as well as better opportunities for women in professional employment and higher education.

In 1908, without mentioning the trauma of slavery, she defined African-Americans as a race inferior to Caucasians "whose present status

[27] For an analysis of the relationship between feminism and eugenics movement of the time see Makepeace (2009).

[28] Eugenic feminism declined gradually throughout the 1940s especially when American policy of sterilization was associated with Nazi policy as well as when eugenics was questioned by new genetic studies (Ziegler, 2008).

is to us a social injury."[29] Conversely, against the vision of women's inferiority, she pointed out the effects of a long tradition of subjection. Given that "the African race, with the advantage of contact with our more advanced stage of evolution, has made more progress in a few generations than any other race has ever done in the same time, except the Japanese", Perkins Gilman suggested a form of enlistment, i.e. segregation, until the level of civilization between the two 'races' would be achieved. By the early 1920s, Gilman was routinely advocating for eugenic causes, particularly for laws against interracial mixing, in major American magazines. Her essay entitled "Sex and Race Progress" (Perkins Gilman, 1929) argued that male sexual indulgence as well as social pressure on women to be virtuous, stupid, and weak damaged the race.[30]

The tension between feminism and eugenics in Perkins Gilman is particularly impressive if we consider that she came from a family whose paternal line counted in the Beecher clan, a family of abolitionists which included sisters Harriet, author of *Uncle Tom's Cabin*, Catharine, promoter of women's education and founder of her own school, and Isabella, a leader of the suffragist movement.

Perkins Gilman was not a trained economist, but rather a journalist and writer, economic arguments were constantly presented in her writings which were mainly published in the popular press. She argued that the doctrine of the separate spheres perpetually subjugated women in their roles as wives and mothers, and she insisted on the financial autonomy and independence of women who were still confined in their roles as wives and mothers.

Between 1894 and 1897, Perkins Gilman spent several months at Hull House in Chicago, where she worked with Jane Addams[31] The two

---

[29] As retrieved on August 25, 2023 at: https://www.journals.uchicago.edu/doi/pdf/10.1086/211645.

[30] Scholarship on Charlotte Perkins Gilman and eugenics is divided. Some scholars minimized Gilman's association with eugenics (Hill, 1980; Lane 1990); some others considered her position clearly biased by racism (Scharnhorst 2000).

[31] In 1889, Jane Addams, along with Ellen Gates Starr, the Hull-House, founded the most famous social settlement located in Chicago. Social settlements began in the 1880s in London in response to problems created by urbanization, industrialization, and immigration. Settlement houses typically attracted educated, native born, middle-class and upper-middle class women and men, known as "residents," to live (settle) in poor urban neighborhoods. The residents

writers and activists mainly discussed the economic relationship between men and women and the education of children (Grimm, 1997; McCrary, 2018). Spending time with Addams at the Hull House was fundamental in writing *Women and Economics* (Perkins Gilman, 1898) as well as her following fictional utopian novels (Perkins Gilman, 1911, 1915, 1916).

In *Women and Economics,* Perkins Gilman argued that women were subjugated in their roles as wives and mothers and insisted on the necessity of female economic independence for the improvement of marriage and the family. She lamented that "the economic status of the human race in any nation, at any time, is governed mainly by the activities of the male: the female obtains her share in the racial advance only through him."[32] And she added:

> We are the only animal species in which the female depends on the male for food, the only animal species in which the sex-relation is also an economic relation. With us an entire sex lives in a relation of economic dependence upon the other sex, and the economic relation is combined with the sex-relation. The economic status of the human female is relative to the sex-relation (Perkins Gilman, 1898, 5).

According to Perkins Gilman, woman's sole economic control came through the power of sex attraction either in marriage or in prostitution—"the open market of vice"— and this fact made "us sick with horror" (ibid, 63). Men control the demand, women the supply; and mothers prepare their children to perpetuate the sexual-economic relation in terms of such. She defined patriarchy as a permanent sexual-economic relation which affects everyone in the world and lasted since forever: "[patriarchy] began in primeval savagery. It exists in all nations. Each boy and girl is born into it, trained into it, and has to live in it" (ibid, 79). This sexual-economic relation perpetually harmed the society

of HullHouse offered classes, such as English, cooking, sewing, and technical skills, to new immigrants. The residents paid rent and contributed to the activities and services that the Settlement was committed to providing to the community. Among services there were a nursery and a kindergarten, a public kitchen, public baths, and a playground.

[32] As retrieved on Augusts 24, 2023 at: https://www.gutenberg.org/cache/epub/57913/pg57913-images.html.

as a whole while social well-being must be grounded in economic relations based on equality rather than on power. Furthermore, public goods are often sacrificed in the name of the family. Finally, and this is the most peculiar explanation provided by Perkins Gilman, market exchange, which is supposed to be rooted in economic cooperation, had been ruled by sex-competition among males in the process of selecting the females and among females in the process of getting well getting selected for marriage in order to achieve economic protection that actually became economic and social dependence.

Perkins Gilman believed that the sexual-economic system was an effect of individualism and selfishness; while society should be led by cooperation provided by "race energy, not sex-energy". Race-energy, Perkins Gilman explained, got its peak only when everyone, regardless of gender, was allowed to be creative in performing several tasks and was not confined to sex-energy, as women traditionally were. Nonetheless, Perking Gilman was not a detractor of individualism in the name of the social corpus, *à la* Rousseau. Quite the opposite: she promoted women's freedom as a consequence of the application of the principle of 'equality before the law' that led to democracy:

> Democracy means, requires, is, individual liberty. While the sexual-economic relation makes the family the center of industrial activity, no higher collectivity than we have to-day is possible. But, as women become free, economic, social factors, so becomes possible the full social combination of individuals in collective industry. With such freedom, such independence, such wider union, becomes possible also a union between man and woman such as the world has long dreamed of in vain (ibid, 145).

In *Human Work,* she wrote: "a democracy for men and a patriarchate for women is a brain-splitting anachronism".[33] And she added that when women finally become "free economic agents" the society will be improved in "health and happiness", being social benefits not only a matter of the economy but also of ethics (Perkins Gilman 1904, 345).

[33] As retrieved on August 24, 2023 at: https://www.gutenberg.org/cache/epub/64098/pg64098-images.html.

Hence, the economic independence of women will increase the moral level of society as a whole.

Perkins Gilman insisted on the fact that institutions have been shaped around male dominance, which implied a subjection of women constrained into the domestic sphere that perpetuated traditional gender roles. Furthermore, she promoted an equal division of homework between men and women and self-determination of women in their professional activities (Allen, 2009; Becchio, 2020).[34]

She wrote:

> although it must be admitted that men make and distribute the wealth of the world, yet women earn their share of it as wives. This assumes either that the husband is in the position of employer and the wife as employee, or that marriage is a 'partnership', and the wife an equal factor with the husband in producing wealth (Perkins Gilman, 1898, 10).

Perkins Gilman aimed to eliminate gender discrepancies within society by promoting the idea of a 'new woman' able to challenge traditional female roles in societal structures that were built upon gender stereotypes rooted in androcentrism. Perkins Gilman's 'new woman' was envisioned as well-informed and well-educated, assertive, confident, and influential as well as compassionate, nurturing, and sensitive. Education, for Perkins Gilman, was the most effective way to transform society. She scrutinized education in terms of gender-economic discrepancy and she criticized the degree of competition in schools, which perpetuated the patriarchal culture and reinforced the cult of domesticity for girls. She argued that a reevaluation of social values and attitudes toward women, as well as their roles within the economy and society, should be a primary societal goal. Unlike the existing androcentric society grounded on male-dominated culture, a reevaluation of social values and attitudes toward women and their role within the economy and society should be the most important social aim. In fact, the liberation of women was contingent upon their education and economic independence.

---

34 As Martin claimed, Perkins Gilman's ideas were fundamental in the tradition of female writers aiming to transform society by educating other women and advocating for a more democratic system (Martin, 1985).

Women and Economics represented a turning point in public opinion in the United States about the social role of women and the urgency to free society from the cultural gendered stereotypes that traditionally ruled both private and public spheres (Allen, 2009). In 1899, one year after the publication of Perkins Gilman's book, Thorsten Veblen echoed some of the arguments made by Perkins Gilman in order to describe the social and economic status of women of his time.[35]

In *Human Work* (1904), Perkins Gilman revisited the tension between individual self-improvement and social constraints: she pointed out that social progress has always been promoted by individuals when system sets them free. Conversely, the masses, oriented by prejudices and stereotypes, tend to resist change and slow down progress. Perkins Gilman believed that this principle should also be applied to the emancipation of women. She wrote: "in more recent times we can see as plainly how the advance of women, their fuller education and general development, a most important step in social evolution, has been as earnestly opposed by the great majority of persons, acting under the dominance of long-held lines of hereditary ideas and superstitions" (Perkins Gilman, 1904, 25).[36] When society finally eliminates sexual-economic discrimination among genders, women could contribute as producers of social well-being rather than being confined to roles as social consumers, parasites of men who had monopolized the supply side of the economic exchange: "when women no longer make their living out of their loving, the prostitute, and that more successful specialist, the mercenary wife, will leave the world" (ibid, 371).

---

[35] Thorsten Veblen (1899) used the same argument a year later, when he insisted on the fact that women have become a tool for improving their husband's class status (Becchio, 2020). Veblen wrote: "Where the fighting class is in the position of dominance and prescriptive legitimacy, the canons of conduct are shaped chiefly by the common sense of the body of fighting men. (…) The discipline of predatory life makes for an attitude of mastery on the part of the able-bodied men in all their relations with the weaker members of the group, and especially in their relations with the women. (…) All the women in the group will share in the class repression and depreciation that belongs to them as women, but the status of women taken from hostile groups has an additional feature. Such a woman not only belongs to a subservient and low class, but she also stands in a special relation to her captor. She is a trophy of the raid, and therefore an evidence of exploit, and on this ground, it is to her captor's interest to maintain a peculiarly obvious relation of mastery toward her" (Veblen, 1899, 506–507).

[36] As retrieved on August 24, 2023 at: https://www.gutenberg.org/cache/epub/64098/pg64098-images.html.

In her *The Man-Made World, or Our Androcentric Culture* (Perkins Gilman 1914), she criticized the masculine ideology of the separate spheres which affected women, who acquired a "masculine mind", identifying themselves solely as economically dependent on men (see Chapter 4). In this passage, she presented the first feminist critique of the notion of the economic agent intended as a male competitive and selfish actor:

> Our current teachings in the infant science of Political Economy are naively masculine. They assume as unquestionable that 'the economic man' will never do anything unless he has to; will only do it to escape pain or attain pleasure; and will, inevitably, take all he can get, and do all he can to outwit, overcome, and if necessary destroy his antagonist. Thus the Economic Man. But how about the Economic Woman? To the androcentric mind she does not exist. Women are females, and that's all; their working abilities are limited to personal service (Perkins Gilman, 1914, 77).

In this passage, Perkins Gilman anticipated feminist economics' critique of androcentrism of neoclassical economics (See Chapter 6).

After the publication of her major nonfiction books, Perkins Gilman presented the concept of 'new woman' in several female utopian novels (Perkins Gilman, 1911, 1915, 1916) where she rephrased her gynocentric theory in fiction, describing a utopian world where the cultural ideal of manliness was overtaken and replaced by femaleness (De Simone, 1995; Nadkarni, 2014; Robertson, 2018).

Herland (1915) is Perkins Gilman's most famous utopian novel.[37] In this book, she presented an all-female society where women lived

---

[37] The story is about a scientific expedition carried on by three men, Terry, a chauvinist playboy, Jeff, an emotional doctor, and Vandyck, a sociologist who played the role of the narrator. Their journey is aimed to reach a place where rumors said there is an all-female community. Actually they arrived there and got acquainted with what had happened two thousand years earlier, when a volcanic eruption killed the majority of the men, while the survivors, who tried to violently seize the power, were tamed by a revolt of women. As times passed, the women of *Herland* discovered that they might get pregnant via parthenogenesis and they began to give birth to five girls at a time. Inhabitants of *Herland* are vegetarian; they work out every day; they do not wear any corset; they self-sustain the community. The debate between women of *Herland* and the three male explorers about notions such as gender, sex, womanhood, and manhood allows the reader to understand the author's vision of a 'new society'.

perfectly happily without competing for mating, being free from any form of gender stereotype and from any subjection: "the women of *Herland* have no fear of men. Why should they have? They are not timid in any sense. They are not weak".[38] Moreover, Perkins Gilman made a trailblazing distinction between sex and gender, by pointing out the social and cultural aspect of the latter that determined the subjection of women.

Through the voice of the narrator, one of the three explorer who discovered *Herland*, she explained:

> When we say *men, man, manly, manhood*, and all the other masculine derivatives, we have in the background of our minds a huge vague crowded picture of the world and all its activities (…) And when we say *women*, we think *female*—the sex. But to these women, in the unbroken sweep of this two-thousand-year-old feminine civilization, the word *woman* called up all that big background, so far as they had gone in social development; and the word *man* meant to them only *male*—the sex (Perkins Gilman, 1915, 137).

This epiphany gave the narrator "a queer feeling" (ibid, 141). Women of *Herland* were not subjected to the doctrine of the separate spheres. As the narrator explained, the domestic sphere was not "their place". Moreover, Perkins Gilman insisted on the fact that if men were properly educated to individual freedom and equality, they could join a society without a rigid separation of spheres and without adhering to gender stereotypes. Actually the novel ended with one of the three explorers who decided to stay there along with her pregnant wife symbolizing the potential for a 'new society' to evolve if a 'new woman' had indeed emerged.

[38] As retrieved on August 24, 2023, at: https://www.gutenberg.org/files/32/32-h/32-h.htm.

3.4 Women and Immigration in the Progressive Era: Sex and Race Intersected

During the Second industrial revolution and the Progressive Era, between 1880 and 1910, labor migration from Europe to the United States has been estimated at about twenty million individuals. Unlike the first wave of immigrants who arrived in the country during the mid-nineteenth century from England, Germany, Ireland, and Scandinavia, the vast majority of new immigrants were from Austria, Hungary, Italy, and Russia. They met the requirement of being 'free white persons' as established by the 'Naturalization Act' (1790).[39] Champions of nativism and eugenics, such as Prescott Hall, founded the Immigration Restriction League (1894): its aim was to prevent immigrants from southern and eastern Europe due to a belief that they were racially inferior to western and northern Europeans (Lee, 2019; Petit, 2010). Immigration legislation was justified on the principle that the labor force should discard unfit workers, labeled 'parasites,' 'unemployable', 'low-wage races', and 'industrial residuum'.[40]

Immigration led to rapid urbanization: higher wages in factory jobs attracted immigrants into the cities: by 1900, thirty million people (30% of the population) lived in urban contexts. Department stores, chain stores, and shopping centers beneficiated the emergent middle-class; while immigrants were faced with overcrowding, inadequate housing, and low-quality conditions of work. Moreover, their wages provided little more than subsistence living. Within the cities, enclaves of immigrants created tight-knit communities based on their common culture.

---

39 The Congress established that only white, male, property owners could naturalize and acquire the status of citizens after two years of residency. This law produced the legal category of 'aliens ineligible for citizenship' which largely affected Asian immigrants especially after the Chinese Exclusion Act (1882), a ten year ban on Chinese laborers immigrating to the United States. In the early 1890s, the literacy test was proposed and went through several effective laws.

40 Scholars of the time divided 'races' into: Nordic, White, Caucasian, and Anglo-Saxon without any biological basis, which in fact does not exist, by making difficult to classify groups of immigrants, who may be white but not Anglo-Saxons and so forth. In the end, being white overlapped with being European (Bateman, 2003).

While men initially represented the majority, at the beginning of the twentieth century German and Irish immigrant women exceeded men.[41] Immigrants from southern and eastern Europe and China were mainly established in the East Coast or in Midwest. They were largely employed in unskilled sectors as workers in factories or as domestic servants. Besides domestic work, women immigrants primarily worked in all branches of the textile, food processing, and tobacco industries while men immigrants worked in the steel and mechanics industries, mining, and construction. Many women started micro businesses like laundries, sewing, or performing piece work at home.

The economic role of immigrant women has been often neglected. Nevertheless, their labor, whether as employers or as supporters of family businesses, played a central role in making America's prosperity happen. Furthermore, migration and urbanization led to a considerable transformation of the public and private spheres: the integration of immigrants was made possible through the recruitment of women, who were sometimes former migrants themselves, at the transit infrastructures and at border posts at arrival. Women immigrants were expected to build new communities and simultaneously maintain the culture of their home.

The connection between gender and immigration may be summed up as a double-bind of being both women and foreigners. This intersectionality is central in the process of understanding their agency and voice in making America their new home and in grappling with the ideals of American womanhood. The interrelation of class and gender in female immigration is another fundamental element of this historical process. Immigrant women were usually poor and early nineteenth-century female charity workers attributed their poverty to the low level of morality of the immigrants themselves. Charities, mainly led by local middle-class women reformers, believed it was their patriotic duty to teach immigrant women morality, i.e. Anglo-American values, in order to prevent any social conflict.

[41] On January 1, 1892, Ellis Island was opened and registered the first female immigrant, an Irish girl, named Annie Moore (Mercurio, 2008).

By adopting this principle, the settlement house movement arose. Modeled after Hull House in Chicago, many settlements were opened.[42] Their ultimate goal was to offer programs for immigrants aimed to integrate them into a nation-building program, based on social consensus between locals and immigrants. Usually, settlement houses were managed completely by women. The Americanization programs were intended to embed the culture of immigrants into American culture and values as the only way to achieve and maintain social harmony: immigrants should be educated and Americans should be protected. Hence, a special focus was directed to female new-comers who were expected to make the Americanization possible.

American reformer Mary Gibson wrote: "teachers attempted to convince foreign-born wives themselves to attend classes in English, civics, and domestic science or home economics. The classes were held at local schools or in neighborhood homes, while later some were moved to small houses equipped with American-style furniture and household equipment" (Gullet, 1995, 75).

Immigrant women were essential in maintaining their culture which for many reformers put the American society in danger. Left by themselves, immigrant women were seen as a threat: they were isolated and unable to feel at home, often in conflict with their children, who were growing up by adopting American values. Reformers were worried that the double-sided, generational, and cultural clash, between mothers and children could have led to juvenile delinquency and social disorder.

Some historians pointed out that personal ambition and the rhetoric of self-made improvement played a major role in the assimilation of immigrants: reformers believed that once immigrants de-emphasized group cooperation in favor of their own individual material interests the economy of the country would be strengthened and the immigrant standard of living would be improved (Gullett, 1995). The rise of home economics as a domestic science (see Chap. 5.1) was part of this Americanization program specifically aimed to transform immigrant women from unskilled workers into household managers.

---

[42] Among them, the University Settlement in New York City, the College Settlement in Los Angeles, and the San Francisco Settlement (Fink, 1997).

Immigrant women partially accepted this process. On one side, they often joined facilities provided by settlement houses, especially English classes or some welfare service such as kindergartens or basic medical care. On the other side, they struggled to keep their culture up by hanging out with their fellow immigrants with whom they often shared the feeling of being forced to Americanization rather than to be welcomed in a pluralistic national consensus.[43]

In 1913, the minimum-wage legislation passed in nine states, affecting the female labor force and especially women immigrants whose salary was usually below the approved level. Economists, such as Persons (1915) explained that reasons must be found in the following elements: the fact that the majority of women workers are young, and therefore inexperienced, especially among immigrants; the temporary nature of their commitment, which usually ends when they get married; the nature of their salaries as a subsidiary source of family income; women's immobility due to their commitment to family that usually leads them to work less and to quit jobs in case their husbands get a promotion or need to move from a city to another. Persons suggested to raise the legal age of entering employment and to limit the number of the newly immigrants, especially women, whose combination of age, sex, and race made them the most unskilled workers in the job market, by suggesting them to keep their role within the private sphere and avoid to furtherly overcrowding the market. Person's position was shared by many famous scholars and economists of the time.

As historians (Freeden, 1979; Furner, 1975; Jacobson, 1998; Saxton, 1990) and historians of economics (Bateman, 2003; Cherry, 1976, 1980; Leonard, 2003, 2005a, 2005b, 2016; Ramstad & Starkey, 1995) have intensively described, race is a fundamental tool for understanding the history of immigration in the United States, and this racial stigmatization had a double impact on immigrant women, subjecting them to both gender and racial biases.

Economists of the time emphasized the race of immigrants rather than their number or their socio-cultural status. The first president of

[43] Many states (California, Idaho, Utah) passed coercive Americanization legislation, such as classes compulsory for immigrants.

the American Economic Association, Francis Amasa Walker, was against immigration, arguing that newly arrived individuals lowered the salaries and, consequently, the income of "Nordic" laborers' as well as their reproduction rates which directly depended on income (Bateman, 2003). Walker explained a 'race suicide' theory, based on the lower fertility of the Americans, who were considered a superior race, but unable to maintain their demographic rate and surpassed by immigrants from southern Italy, Hungary, Austria, and Russia (Walker, 1891, 1892). Walker clearly failed to consider the decline of the local population as a response to urbanization, higher living standards, and a postponed age of marriage.

Yale economist Irving Fisher, who co-founded the American Eugenics Society (1926) and served as its first president, seconded Walker's ideas. In his presidential address to the Eugenics Research Association (Fisher, 1921), he declared:

> I should, as an economist, be inclined to the view that unrestricted immigration . . . is economically advantageous to the country as a whole (...). But the core of the problem of immigration is one of race and eugenics; [and] the problem of the Anglo-Saxon racial stock [is] being overwhelmed by racially inferior defectives, delinquents and dependents (as in Leonard, 2005a, 2005b, 209).

In his pamphlet *Eugenics* Fisher defined eugenics "as an application of modern science to improve the human race" (Fisher, 1913, 2) as well as "the hygiene of future generations" (ibid, 17) and "the essential foundation of ethics in the future" (ibid, 19). He presented a series of possible genetic combinations between 'human breeds' as potentially harmful for the well-being of the society as a whole, such as the rise of feebleminded, and he suggested prohibiting marriages among some groups as well as sterilization. The major target of Fisher and his proposals was immigrants, whom were blamed for being carriers of 'race degeneration'. He urged for their genetic control and promoted anti-immigration laws (Cot, 2005).

Like Fisher, other economists of the time, such as Ross, Patten, Fetter, and Farnam embraced eugenics on a racial basis grounded on the notion of 'fitness' applied to sex and class: women and lower-class people were commonly regarded as biologically inferior. Patten, Fetter, and Farnam advocated eugenics as the substitution of social for natural selection of the fittest. Ross (1901) theorized that the "native" Anglo-Saxons were biologically well-adapted to rural and traditional life, while the racially inferior immigrants, especially Southern Europeans, Slavs, Asiatics, and Jews, were better adapted to the new emerging urban context thus they would outbreed the superior Anglo-Saxon race (Leonard, 2003, 2005a).

John R. Commons based his argument on ethnicity and environment rather than on eugenics and race. In his *Races and Immigrants* (1907), he argued that wage competition lowered wages and selected for the unfit races as they required a lower standard of life.[44] Lower standards of life, according to Commons, put democracy in danger.

He wrote:

> the peasants of Catholic Europe, who constitute the bulk of our immigration of the past thirty years, have become almost a distinct race, drained of those superior qualities which are the foundation of democratic institutions. If in America our boasted freedom from the evils of social classes fails to be vindicated in the future, the reasons will be found in the immigration of races and classes incompetent to share in our democratic opportunities. (Commons, 1907, 12)[45]

---

[44] Retrieved on August 28, 2023, at: https://www.gutenberg.org/files/34028/34028-h/34028-h.htm.

[45] Commons described immigration waves during the nineteenth century by comparing numbers and movements of imports of merchandise per capita of the population. First immigrants were German and Irish, then Brits and Scandinavians arrived. At the end of the century, Italian immigration became noticeable: Commons considered Italian immigration to be different from that of other groups, as it was not primarily driven by the oppressions of a dominant race in their home country, unlike Russian, Slavic, and Austrian-Hungarian immigrants. Instead, Italian immigration was seen as a response to the economic and political conditions in a recently united Italy. Commons suggested that Italian immigration might be temporary and aimed at generating revenue for the mother country. Furthermore, he made a distinction between immigrants from Northern and Southern Italy: "[the former] is an educated, skilled artisan, coming from a manufacturing section and largely from the cities. He is Teutonic in blood and appearance. The South Italian is an illiterate peasant from the great landed estates, with wages less than one-third his northern compatriot. He descends with less mixture from the ancient inhabitants of Italy. Unhappily for us, the North Italians do not come to the United States in considerable numbers, but they betake themselves to Argentina, Uruguay, and Brazil in about the same numbers as the South Italians come to us" (Commons, 1907, 78).

Although Commons shared the anxiety of President Theodore Roosevelt, who strongly invited women to recognize that "the greatest thing for any woman is to be a good wife and mother" in order to avoid any alarm for the future of the nation, Commons claimed that the suicide-rate theory was not due to immigrants, rather it was the result of personal decisions, such as postponing the age of marriage, limiting the number of births after marriage, and an increase in the proportion of unmarried people. The solution, according to Commons, was education and prosperity for all immigrants, in order to lower their birth rate as well.

Commons' solution implies two disturbing aspects: the persistence of the racial argument and gender discrimination.

The racial argument persisted when he wrote:

> We speak of superior and inferior races, and this is well enough, but care should be taken to distinguish between inferiority and backwardness—between that superiority which is the original endowment of race and that which results from the education and training which we call civilization. While there are superior and inferior races, there are primitive, mediæval, and modern civilizations, and there are certain mental qualities required for produced by these different grades of civilization. (Commons, 1907, 211)

Gender discrimination persisted when he invited women to cover their principal social role of being wives and mothers.

The idea that some immigrant groups, along with Blacks, were perceived as the cause of social and economic problems, coupled with the eugenic suggestion that the state should plan human breeding to reduce the proportion of the unfit, attracted the majority of the scholars of the time, including women scholars, who were not immune by racial eugenics. Besides Perkins Gilman's position (see the previous paragraph), Margaret Sanger.[46] Sanger embraced eugenics, although she was very progressive when she initiated the birth control movement in the United

[46] In early 1910s, Sanger initiated a sex education column titled "What Every Girl Should Know" for *The Call*, a socialist newspaper, and in 1914 founded a monthly magazine, *The Woman Rebel*: both featured birth control information and openly opposed the Comstock Act, a federal law passed in 1873 that prohibited contraceptives. On October 16, 1916, Sanger opened America's first birth control clinic in the Brownsville district of Brooklyn (Sanger 1916).

States, by publishing *Family Limitation* (Sanger 1914), an appeal to women's right to enjoy their sexuality and to take the responsibility for family planning, including choosing abortion. Birth control was in fact a way to regulate the number of immigrants who "come in hordes, have brought with them their ignorance of hygiene and modern ways of living and they are handicapped by religious superstitions" (Sanger, 1920, 36). She insisted on the role that immigrant mothers could play in encouraging their children to become integrated into the Americanization process:

> If we are to develop in America a new race with a racial soul, we must keep the birth rate within the scope of our ability to understand as well as to educate. We must not encourage reproduction beyond our capacity to assimilate our numbers so as to make the coming generation into such physically fit, mentally capable, socially alert individuals as are the ideal of a democracy. (…) We must set motherhood free. We must give the foreign and submerged mother knowledge that will enable her to prevent bringing to birth children she does not want. We know that in each of these submerged and semisubmerged elements of the population there are rich factors of racial culture. Motherhood is the channel through which these cultures flow. Motherhood, when free to choose the father, free to choose the time and the number of children who shall result from the union, automatically works in wondrous ways. It refuses to bring forth weaklings; refuses to bring forth slaves; refuses to bear children who must live under the conditions described. It withholds the unfit, brings forth the fit; brings few children into homes where there is not sufficient to provide for them. Instinctively it avoids all those things which multiply racial handicaps. Under such circumstances we can hope that the "melting pot" will refine. We shall see that it will save the precious metals of racial culture, fused into an amalgam of physical perfection, mental strength and spiritual progress. Such an American race, containing the best of all racial elements, could give to the world a vision and a leadership beyond our present imagination (Sanger, 1920, 31–32).[47]

[47] As retrieved on August 28, 2023 at: https://www.gutenberg.org/cache/epub/8660/pg8660.html.

Going against the prevailing opinions, economist Emily Green Balch actively opposed the racial and eugenics arguments. Balch was an expert in labor immigration and had spent her sabbatical year (1904/05) in the Balkans, where she analyzed the economic conditions of Slavic people within the Hapsburg Empire. Upon returning home, she continued her work on Slavic immigration in the United States (Balch, 1910a). Prior to Balch, Ida Van Etten (1893) had defended Russian Jewish immigrants who were arriving in New York. She pointed out their education, willingness to work, and desire to integrate, as well as their tendency to organize in trade unions and advocate for improved working conditions. Van Etten argued that their way of life and work would not decrease competition for jobs in certain trades, but would actually benefit workers and overall social well-being.

Balch emphasized that it was immigration status, rather than race, that presented a challenge for immigrant women. She noted that immigrant women often had a lower quality of education, a characteristic they shared with lower-class American girls of the time.[48] Hence, she promoted the urgency of educating women to become skilled professionals and workers as well as potential wives and mothers. She believed that if immigrant women were provided with education, they could contribute to preventing the degeneration of American society (Balch, 1910b).[49]

---

[48] Balch studied economics and sociology at the University of Chicago in the 1890s. She was the first recipient of the European Fellowships, and she spent 1895/96 in Berlin, where she was a student of Adolph Wagner and Gustav Schmoller. She taught history of socialism, labor economics and the economic role of women at Wellesley, invited by Katherine Coman (they had met during their journey from Germany back to the United States). A fervent socialist, she was very active in promoting pacifism during the First World War and interwar. She was a Nobel Peace laureate in 1946 for her activities with the Women's International Committee for Permanent Peace, later named the Women's International League for Peace and Freedom (Redmond, 2016).

[49] According to Balch, this kind of education will fit the six types of modern women: "single professionals (evidence of self-exclusion from marriage was common in medicine, law, architecture, art and business); educated married professionals able to combine motherhood and a very elastic profession in terms of time; educated married professionals, who choose to quit their job for their full-time motherhood, but who have the chance to get back into workforce when children are grown up; unmarried women of leisure, [who] make the most disposable force in our society. Some of them, the spenders, live purely parasitic lives, absorbing the services of others and consuming social wealth without rendering any return; married women who devoted

Against the alarmism about immigrants, especially from the south-east of Europe, she denied that the new immigrants were racially inferior and pointed out the importance of immigration for American prosperity. Balch fought against any form of restriction of immigration and against the literacy test, proposed by Commons and Fisher. She also insisted on the environmental effect on immigrants and their children and on the importance of knowing their cultural background in order to make them able to develop an intricate blend of old and new elements. Furthermore, she was against the idea that immigration reduced American wages by showing data on the real wages of unskilled labor, which had been rising from 1840 to 1900. Balch also disputed Commons' claim that immigrants undermined union organizations by showing their involvement in strikes and unionism (Balch, 1912).

Summing up, the role of immigrant women during the Progressive Era, a period marked by massive immigration to the United States, was fundamental for economic development and social cohesion. American middle-class women directed settlement houses, women's clubs, and social movements advocating for compulsory public education, regulation of sweatshop labor, and public sanitation. Immigrant women played a pivotal role in the process of Americanization. Both groups shared a 'maternalistic' perspective, viewing motherhood not only as a primary natural role for women but also as a social responsibility. The welfare of mothers and children became a public policy issue. This combination created new and viable spaces for women to operate outside the private sphere. Women's involvement in positive social change reinforced the movement for women's suffrage and encouraged other public debates aimed at leaving behind the doctrine of the separate spheres (see Chapter 4).

The interconnection between native Americans and immigrants in urban environment, along with the increasing numbers of middle and working-class women in the labor force, reshaped the ideology of the separate spheres and made the emergence of the 'new woman' possible (see Chapter 4.2).

---

themselves to family and housekeeping no matter about education; working-class women no matter about their marital status" (Balch, 1910b, 64).

Before the process of industrialization and urbanization, the stereotypical American woman lived in small towns. She was typically white, middle-class, Protestant, native-born, married, slightly better educated than her mother, and likely to have fewer children. She rarely appeared in the public sphere, confining herself to the private one and reinforcing the 'cult of true womanhood', which portrayed women as domestic and submissive figures whose primary goal was to raise their children. Women who were active in public life usually belonged to women's associations advocating for reforms, education, and suffrage.

Industrialization provided the impetus for middle-class women to enter the public sphere. Industrialization created jobs outside the home for an increasing number of women, including married women, while the poor living conditions of immigrants in urban contexts led to numerous social issues that middle-class women were determined to address by fostering a sense of community that transcended the boundaries of the domestic sphere (Cordery, 2007).

The redefinition of the boundaries of the separate spheres was not a voluntary movement though. Industrialization required female workers, whose numbers dramatically increased from fifteen percent in 1870 to twenty-one percent in 1900. The typical female worker was young, urban, single, and either an immigrant or the daughter of immigrants, living at home with her family. Her work was often considered temporary until marriage, as working outside the home was seen as unfit for motherhood. However, many married women worked to support their families. Self-employed women were consistent exceptions. As explained in this chapter, women's wages were consistently lower than those of men, based on the principle of the family wage. In rural areas, the situation was different: women's labor in fields and barns was crucial for the family's survival. For instance, Native American women, untouched by industrialization, immigration, and urbanization, used to share nearly equal status with men within their communities.

References

Abbott, E. (1910). *Women in Industry: A Study in American Economic History*. D. Appleton and Company.
Akkerman, T. (1998). Liberalism and Feminism in Late Nineteenth Century Britain. In T. Akkerman T. & S. Stuurman (dds.) *Perspectives on Feminist Political Thought in European History: From the Middle age to The Present*, (pp. 168–185). Routledge.
Allen, J. (2009). *The Feminism of Charlotte Perkins Gilman: Sexualities, Histories, Progressivism*. The University of Chicago Press.
Aston, J., & Bishop, C. (2020). Discovering the Global Perspective. In J. Aston & C. Bishop (Eds.), *Female Entrepreneurs in the Long Nineteenth Century. A Global Perspective* (pp. 1–31). Palgrave Macmillan.
Athey, S. (2000). Eugenic Feminisms in Late Nineteenth-Century America: Reading Race in Victoria Woodhull, Frances Willard, Anna Julia Cooper and Ida B. Wells. *Genders*. Available at https://www.colorado.edu/gendersarchive1998-2013/2000/06/01/eugenic-feminisms-late-nineteenth-century-america-reading-race-victoria-woodhull-frances
Baker, E. (1925). *Protective Labor Legislation: With Special Reference to Women in the State of New York*. Columbia University.
Balch, E. (1910a). *Our Slavic Fellow Citizens*. Charities Publication Committee.
Balch, E. (1910b). The Education and Efficiency of Women. *Annals of the Academy of Political Science, 1*(1), 61–71.
Balch, E. (1912). Restriction of Immigration: Discussion. *American Economic Review, 2*(1), 63–66.
Bankovsky, M. (2018). Alfred Marshall's Household Economics: The Role of the Family in Cultivating an Ethical Capitalism. *Cambridge Journal of Economics, 43*(1), 249–267.
Bankovsky, M. (2020). A History of Early Household Economics: Improving the Family's Contribution to Industrial Production and Rationalizing Family Consumption. *Oxford Economic Papers, 72*(4), 1–21.
Bateman, B. (2003). Race, Intellectual History, and American Economics: A Prolegomenon to the Past. *History of Political Economy, 35*(4), 713–730.
Becchio, G. (2020). *A History of Feminist and Gender Economics*. Routledge.
Bodichon, B. (1857). *Women and Work*. Bosworth and Harrison.
Bosanquet, H. (1902). *The Strength of the People. A Study on Women's Wage*. Macmillan.

Bosanquet, H. (1906). *The Family*. Macmillan.
Breckenridge, S. (1906). Legislative Control of Women's Work. *Journal of Political Economy, 14*(2), 107–109.
Breckenridge, S. (1923). The Home Responsibilities of Women Workers and the 'Equal Wage.' *Journal of Political Economy, 31*(4), 521–543.
Breckenridge, S., & Abbott, E. (1912). *The Delinquent Child and the Home*. Russell Sage Foundation.
Burnette, J. (2008). Women Workers in the British Industrial Revolution. In R. Whaples (Ed.), *EH.Net Encyclopedia*. Available at http://eh.net/encyclopedia/women-workers-in-the-british-industrial-revolution/
Chassonnery-Zaïgouche, C. (2019). Is Equal Pay Worth It? In K. Madden & R. Dimand (Eds.), *Routledge Handbook of the History of Women's Economic Thought* (pp. 129–149). Routledge.
Cherry, R. (1976). Racial Thought and the Early Economics Profession. *Review of Social Economy, 34*, 147–162.
Cherry, R. (1980). Biology, Sociology, and Economics—An Historical Analysis. *Review of Social Economy, 38*, 141–154.
Collet, C. (1890 [1910]). The Economic Position of Educated Working Women. In C. Collet. *Educated Working Women*, (pp. - 26). P.S. King and Sons.
Collet, C. (1898 [1910]). The Expenditure of Middle-Class Working Women. In C. Collet. *Educated Working Women*, (pp. 66–89). P.S. King and Sons.
Collet (1900 [1910]). Through Fifty Years: The Economic Progress of Women. In C. Collet. *Educated Working Women*, (pp. 134–143). P.S. King and Sons.
Commons, J. R. (1907). *Races and Immigrants in America*. Chautauqua Press.
Cordery, S. (2007). *The Gilded Age: Essays on the Origins of Modern America*. Rowman & Littlefield Publishers.
Cot, A. (2005). Breed out the Unfit and Breed in the Fit: Irving Fisher, Economics, and the Science of Heredity. *The American Journal of Economics and Sociology, 64*(3), 793–826.
Craig, B. (2016). *Women and Business Since 1500. Invisible Presence in Europe and North America?* Palgrave Macmillan.
Crowston, C. (2008). Women, Gender, and Guilds in Early Modern Europe: An Overview of Recent Research. *International Review of Social History, 53*(16), 19–44.
Davidoff, L., & Hall, C. (1987). *Family Fortunes: Men and Women of the English Middle Class, 1780–1850*. University of Chicago Press.
Davidhoff, L. & Hall, C. (2002). *Family Fortunes: Men and Women of the English Middle Class 1780–1850*. Routledge.

De Simone, D. (1995). Charlotte Perkins Gilman and the Feminization of Education. *WILLA, 4*, 13–17.
Domosh, M., & Seager, J. (2001). *Putting Women in Place*. Guilford Press.
Edgeworth, F. Y. (1922). Equal Pay for Men and Women for Equal Work. *The Economic Journal*, 32(128), 431–457.
Edgeworth, F. Y. (1923). Women's Wages in Relation to Economic Welfare. *Economic Journal, 33*(132), 487–495.
Ely, R.T. (1908). Economic Theory and Labor Legislation. *American Economic Association Quarterly, 3rd Series, 9*(1), 124–153.
Fawcett, M. G. (1892). Mr. Sidney Webb's Article on Women's Wage. *The Economic Journal*, 2(5), 173–176.
Fawcett, M. G. (1917). The Position of Women in Economic Life. In W. H. Dawson (ed.). After-War Problems, (pp. 191–215). Allen & Unwin.
Fawcett, M. G. (1918a). Equal Pay for Equal Work. *The Economic Journal*, 28(109), 1–6.
Fawcett, M. G. (1918b). Equal Pay for Equal Value. *The Economic Journal*, 114(18), 387–390.
Fink, L. (1997). *Progressive Intellectuals and the Dilemmas of Democratic Commitment*. Harvard University Press.
Fisher, I. (1913). *Eugenics*. Good Health Publishing.
Fisher, I. (1921). Impending Problems of Eugenics. *Scientific Monthly, 13*(3), 214–231.
Flexner, E. (1959). *Century of Struggle*. Harvard University Press.
Freeden, M. (1979). Eugenics and Progressive Thought: A Study in Ideological Affinity. *Historical Journal, 22*(3), 645–671.
Furner, M. (1975). *Advocacy and Objectivity: A Crisis in the Professionalization of American Social Science, 1865–1905*. University Press of Kentucky.
Goldmark, J. (1912). *Fatigue and Efficiency: A Study in Industry*. Charities Publication Committee.
Goldin, C. (1991). *Understanding the Gender Gap: An Economic History of American Women*. Oxford University Press.
Gordon, L. (1992). Social Insurance and Public Assistance: The Influence of Gender in Welfare Thought in the United States, 1890–1935. *American Historical Review, 97*(1), 19–54.
Gordon, L. (2002). *The Moral Property of Women: A History of Birth Control Politics in America*. University of Illinois Press.
Gouverneur, V. (2023). Families and Women in Alfred Marshall's Analysis of Well-Being and Progress. *History of Political Economy, 55*(5), 799–830.

Grimm, R. T. (1997). Forerunners for a Domestic Revolution: Jane Addams, Charlotte Perkins Gilman, and the Ideology of Childhood, 1900–1916. *Illinois Historical Journal, 90*(1), 47–64.

Groenewegen, P. (1994). *Feminism and Political Economy in Victorian England*. Edward Elgar.

Groenewegen, P. (1995). *A Soaring Eagle: Alfred Marshall 1842–1924*. Edward Elgar.

Groenegewen, P. (2000). "Helen Dendy Bosanquet". In R. Dimand, M.A. Dimand and E. Forget (eds.). *A Biographical Dictionary of Women Economists* (pp. 60–65). Edward Elgar.

Gullett, G. (1995). Women Progressives and the Politics of Americanization in California, 1915–1920. *Pacific Historical Review., 64*(1), 71–94.

Hammond, M. B. (1900). Women's Wages in Manual Work. *Political Science Quarterly, 15*(3), 508–535.

Heather-Bigg, A. (1894). The Wife's Contribution to Family Income. *The Economic Journal*, 4(13), 51–58.

Higgs, E. (1987). Domestic Service and Household Production. In A. John (Ed.), *Unequal Opportunities*. Basil Blackwell.

Higgs, E., & Wilkinson, A. (2016). Women, Occupations and Work in the Victorian Censuses Revisited. *History Workshop Journal, 81*(1), 17–38.

Hill, M. A. (1980). *Charlotte Perkins Gilman: The Making of a Radical Feminist, 1860–1896*. Temple University Press.

Horrell, S., & Humphries, J. (1995). Women's Labour Force Participation and the Transition to the Male-Breadwinner Family, 1790–1865. *Economic History Review., 48*, 89–117.

Jacobson, M. (1998). *Whiteness of a Different Color: European Immigrants and the Alchemy of Race*. Harvard University Press.

Jevons, W. S. (1883). Married Women in Factories. In Jevons W. S. *Methods of Social Reform and Other Papers*, (pp. 101–114). Macmillan and Co.

Kelley, F. (1912). Minimum-Wage Laws. *Journal of Political Economy, 20*(10), 999–1010.

Kelley, F. (1914). *Industry in Relation to the Family, Health, Education, Morality*. Longmans Green.

Kelley, F. (1921, March 5). "The New Women's Party." Survey. Rpt. In S. Lipshultz (Ed.), *Social Feminism, Labor Politics, and the Supreme Court of the 1920s* (pp. 199–200). Routledge.

Kingsley, C. (1850). *Cheap Clothes and Nasty*. W. Pickering.

Lane, A. J. (1990). *To Herland and Beyond: The Life and Work of Charlotte Perkins Gilman*. Pantheon.

Lee, E. (2019). *America for Americans: A History of Xenophobia in the United States*. Basic Books.
Leonard, T. (2003). "More Merciful and Not Less Effective": Eugenics and American Economics in the Progressive Era. *History of Political Economy, 35*(4), 687–712.
Leonard, T. (2005a). Protecting Family and Race. The Progressive Case for Regulating Women's Work. *American Journal of Economics and Sociology, 64*(3), 757–791.
Leonard, T. (2005b). Eugenics and Economics in the Progressive Era. *Journal of Economic Perspectives, 19*(4), 207–224.
Leonard, T. (2016). *Illiberal Reformers: Race, Eugenics and American Economics in the Progressive Era*. Princeton University Press.
Lofland, L. (1998). *The Public Realm: Exploring the City's Quintessential Social Territory*. Aldine de Gruyter.
Madden, K., & Dimand, R. (2019). *Routledge Handbook of the History of Women's Economic Thought*. Routledge.
Makepeace, C. (2009). To What Extent was the Relationship Between Feminists and the Eugenics Movement a 'Marriage of Convenience' in the Interwar Years? *Journal of International Women's Studies, 11*(3), 66–80.
Marshall, A. (1890). *Principles of Economics*. Macmillan.
Martin, J. (1985). *Reclaiming a Conversation: The Ideal of the Educated Woman*. Yale University Press.
McCrary, L. (2018). From Hull-House to Herland: Engaged and Extended Care in Jane Addams and Charlotte Perkins Gilman. *Politics & Gender, 15*(1), 1–21.
Mercurio, M. (2008). Welcome Home Annie: Rethinking Ellis Island and Annie Moore in the Classroom. *Social Education, 72*(4), 203–206.
McMahon, T. (1925). *Social and Economic Standards of Living*. DC Heath.
Mill, J. S. (1848). *Principles of Political Economy*. Parker.
Mitchell, C. W. (1908). *Gold Prices and Wages Under the Greenback Standard*. University of California Press.
Mitchell, B. R. (1962). *Abstract of British Historical Statistics*. Cambridge University Press.
Nadkarni, A. (2014). *Eugenic Feminism: Reproductive Nationalism in the United States and India*. University of Minnesota Press.
Peart, S. (1996). *The Economics of W.S. Jevons*. Routledge.
Perkins Gilman, C. (1898). *Women and Economics: A Study of the Economic Relation Between Men and Women as a Factor in Social Evolution*. Small, Maynard & Co.

Perkins Gilman, C. (1904). *Human Work*. McLur, Phillip & Co.
Perkins Gilman, C. (1911). *Moving the Mountain. Serialized in The Forerunner*, Vol. 4.
Perkins Gilman, C. (1914). *The Man-Made World, or Our Androcentric Culture*. Charlton Company.
Perkins Gilman, C. (1915). *Herland*. Pantheon Book.
Perkins Gilman, C. (1916). *With Her in Our Land*. Charlton.
Perkins Gilman, C. (1929). *Sex and Race Progress*. Macaulay Company.
Persons, C. E. (1915). Women's Work and Wages in the United States. *Quarterly Journal of Economics, 29*(2), 201–234.
Petit, J. (2010). *The Men and Women We Want: Gender, Race, and the Progressive Era Literacy Test Debate*. Boydell and Brewer, University of Rochester Press.
Pigou, A. C. (1920). *The Economics of Welfare*. Macmillan & Co.
Pinchbeck, I. (1930). *Women Workers and the Industrial Revolution, 1750–1850*. Routledge.
Pujol, M. (1984). Gender and class in Marshall's Principles of Economics. *Cambridge Journal of Economics, 8*(3), 217–234.
Pujol, M. (1992). *Feminism and Anti-Feminism in Early Economic Thought*. Edward Elgar.
Pujol, M., & Seitz, J. (2000). Millicent Garrett Fawcett. In R. Dimand, M. A. Dimand, & E. Forget (Eds.), *A Biographical Dictionary of Women Economists* (pp. 156–161). Edward Elgar.
Ramstad, Y., & Starkey, J. (1995). The Racial Theories of John R. Commons. *Research in the History of Economic Thought and Methodology, 13*, 1–74.
Rathbone, E. (1917). The Remuneration of Women's Services. *Economic Journal, 27*(105), 55–68.
Redmond, J. (2016). Journeys Toward a Gentleman's Education: International Fellowships and Bryn Mawr College Students, 1900–1930. In L. Panayotidis & P. Stortz, *Women in Higher Education, 1850–1970 International Perspective* (pp. 145–163). Routledge.
Robertson, M. (2018). *The Last Utopians: Four Late Nineteenth-Century Visionaries and Their Legacy*. Princeton University Press.
Ross, E. A. (1901). The Causes of Race Superiority. *Annals of the American Academy of Political and Social Science, 18*(1), 67–89.
Sanger, M. (1914). *Family Limitation*. Margaret Sanger Publishing.
Sanger, M. (1916). *What Every Girl Should Know*. Max N. Maisel.
Sanger, M. (1920). *Woman and the New Race*. Truth Publishing.
Saxton, A. (1990). *The Rise and Fall of the White Republic: Class Politics and Mass Culture in Nineteenth Century America*. Verso.

Scharnhorst, G. (2000). Historicizing Gilman: A Bibliographer's View. In C. Golden & J. Schneider Zangrando (Eds.), *The Mixed Legacy of Charlotte Perkins Gilman* (pp. 65–73). University of Delaware Press.
Seager, H. R. (1913). The Minimum Wage as Part of a Program for Social Reform. *Annals of the American Academy of Political and Social Science, 48*(July), 3–12.
Sivulka, J. (2009). *Ad Women: How They Impact What We Need, Want, and Buy.*
Smart, W. (1892). *Women's Wages.* James Maclehose.
Sombart, W. (1909). Warum gibt es in den Vereinigten Staaten keinen Sozialismus? [engl. Trans.: Socialism and the Social Movement in the 19th Century]. Mohr.
Sumner, H. (1910). The Historical Development of Women's Work in the United States. *Proceedings of the Academy of Political Science in the City of New York, 1*(1), 11–26.
Van Etten, I. (1887). Working Women. *The North American, 144*(364), 312–315.
Van Etten, I. (1893). Russian Jews as Desirable Immigrants. *Forum, 15*, 172–182.
Veblen, T. (1899). The Barbarian Status of Women. *American Journal of Sociology, 4*(4), 503–514.
Walker, F. A. (1891). Immigration and Degradation. *The Forum*, 643–644.
Walker, F. A. (1892). Immigration. *The Yale Review, I*, 131–135.
Webb, B. (1896). *Women and the Factory Acts.* The Fabian Society.
Webb, B. (1920). *Men's and Women's Wages: Should They Be Equal?* The Fabian Society.
Webb, S. (1891). Alleged Differences in Wages Paid to Women and Men for Similar Work. *Economic Journal*, 1($), 369–358.
Webb, S., & Webb, B. (1898). *Problem of Modern Industry.* Longmans.
Willrich, M. (1998). The Two Percent Solution: Eugenic Jurisprudence and the Socialization of American Law, 1900–1930. *Law and History Review, 16*(1), 63–111.
Yohn, S. (2006). Crippled Capitalists: The Inscription of Economic Dependence and the Challenge of Female Entrepreneurship in Nineteenth-Century America. *Feminist Economics, 12*(1–2), 85–109.
Ziegler, M. (2008). Eugenic Feminism: Mental Hygiene, the Women's Movement, and the Campaign for Eugenic Legal Reform, 1900–1935. *Harvard Journal of Law and Gender, 31*, 211–235.

4

Women's New Path Toward the Public Sphere

In her letter to Congressmen, dated March 1776, before the Declaration was written, the future First Lady Abigail Adams (1744–1818) wrote:

> Remember the Ladies, and be more generous and favorable to them than your ancestors. Do not put such unlimited power into the hands of the Husbands. Remember all Men would be tyrants if they could. If particular care and attention is not paid to the Ladies we are determined to foment a Rebellion, and will not hold ourselves bound by any Laws in which we have no voice, or Representation.[1]

Adams was inviting the representatives of the new nation, supposed to be founded on individual freedom, to remove those formal and substantial obstacles which had traditionally prevented women from entering the public sphere on equal terms with men. Only a century later, during the Progressive Era, a lively debate on how to make women's emancipation from the domestic sphere possible occurred in the United States.

---

[1] As retrieved on August 30, 2023 at: https://www.masshist.org/digitaladams/archive/doc?id=L17760331aa#:~:text=%2D%2D%20I%20long%20to%20hear,the%20hands%20of%20the%20Husbands.

G. Becchio, *The Doctrine of the Separate Spheres in Political Economy and Economics*, Palgrave Studies in Classical Liberalism,
https://doi.org/10.1007/978-3-031-51262-9_4

This chapter scrutinizes three topics that were central in the debate: women's suffrage, marriage and family, and prostitution. A further paragraph deals with the intersection of gender and ethnicity being focused on how this fight for women's access to the public sphere affected Black American women, who found themselves in a dual minority status due to both their gender and ethnicity. Consequently, they had to contend with both misogyny and racism. The debate among scholars and economists of the time around these topics was fundamental to understand in what terms the doctrine of the separate spheres was challenged by opening up the gate of the public sphere to the new woman, who exercised social and economic control over their own lives, college educated, professionally trained, self-supporting, living apart from their family, and independent from male control.[2] By 1900, the concept of new woman had almost replaced the notion of women embedded in the cult of domesticity, which was based on the ideal of True Womanhood. Fundamental to the story of the transition from True Womanhood to the new woman was the importance of networking among professional women (Bordin, 1993).

Since the 1880s, an increasing number of women's clubs began 'municipal housekeeping': women were engaged in political activity and in educational programs, such as parent education, vacation schools, visiting nurses, libraries, and in public health, lobbying for regulation of the water and milk supply, drug legislation, sanitary garbage-disposal legislation, public baths, and laundries. Many women fought to close brothels and supported scientific studies on prostitution and venereal diseases. Women's associations sponsored legislation to regulate dance halls, playgrounds, gymnasiums, concert halls, and working girls' clubs, often intended as means to promote assimilation among immigrants. Separate female institutions boosted women's self-esteem; turned them into experts; introduced them to a wider world; put them at ease in public places; provided them with invigorating and supportive circles of friends and coworkers. For many women, club work became their career (Scott, 1991). Women, black and white as well as native-born and immigrant, learned to voice their demands: most

[2] The term New Woman was popularized by Henry James in order to characterize American expats living in Europe: as wealthy and independent women living on their own (Ledger, 1997).

late-nineteenth-century women ventured beyond their domestic sphere under the banner of moral superiority, engaging in a full spectrum of political activities.

The debate around women's political enfranchisement was primarily analyzed by adopting the economic argument based on the opportunity cost of granting the vote to women. On one side, economists and suffragists who supported the economic argument in favor of female suffrage tried to explain that the benefits of women's enfranchisement would outweigh the costs. On the other side, economists and opponents of women's suffrage, known as Remonstrants or Antis, who also employed the economic argument, explained that the costs of women's enfranchisement would outweigh the benefits. They argued that women's political involvement would divert their energy and time from their primary task of caring for their families. Through this line of reasoning, Antis reinforced the doctrine of the separate spheres.

The debate concerning the role of women within their marriage and families was a direct consequence of women entering the job market: economists questioned how family dynamics would be affected by this change and what the consequence would be for society as a whole. This topic was fundamentally linked to the idea that society is grounded on family dynamics and not on individual agency. Families, responsible for guiding children's development into adulthood, instill values that are subsequently reflected in society as a whole. Traditional families were based on marriages and the customary division of roles, wherein men were assigned to the public sphere and women to the private sphere. Assuming, as has always been the case, that power is concentrated in the public sphere traditionally controlled by men, and further assuming, as has also always been the case, that laws, rules, and social norms originating from the public sphere are explicitly established and enforced by the male-controlled public sphere, it follows that the private sphere dedicated to women has always been completely controlled by the public one. Therefore, men have held power over women. This simplified explanation encapsulates the dynamics of patriarchy, which was challenged by the entrance of women in the public sphere.

The shift of women's role toward the public sphere was mainly criticized by economists and other scholars of the time who were worried that the prosperity and well-being of society would collapse as a consequence of the inevitable new changes in family dynamics. The paternalistic approach emphasized the role of men as guardians of women, who were expected to be shielded from the perils of the public sphere. It also underscored the centrality of the family as the primary social agent, whose equilibrium was reached by and maintained through the traditional division of roles between the sexes. The maternalistic approach, mainly developed by female scholars, insisted on the sacred role of motherhood as the ultimate goal for every woman and celebrated the domestic sphere as the heart of society. Both approaches rejected the dissolution of the doctrine of the separate spheres and blamed the rise of women's role in the public sphere, which was intended either as a moral perversion that destroys the harmony of the family or as an inefficient outcome that disrupts the social equilibrium.

Either way, whether overt or covert, chauvinism, bigotry, sexism, and patriarchy played a fundamental role among supporters of the separate spheres.

Finally, economists and reformers of the time engaged in a debate on the nature of prostitution that was hosted in academic journals as well as in more general publications. Prostitution mixed the boundaries between private and public spheres, intertwining issues such as sex work with the low wages of female workers. Some considered prostitution as an efficient economic exchange of sexual performance provided by women and demanded by men. Others considered prostitution as a consequence of a social and economic imbalance in the labor market and within families, particularly among lower-classes (Jordan & Sharp, 2003). The primary arguments in the debate on prostitution revolved around the moral judgment of prostitutes and their economic and social backgrounds.

4.1 The Economic Debate on Women's Suffrage

In the United States, public debates over women's enfranchisement reached their peak during the Progressive Era, albeit the struggle of women to fully gain the right to vote did not materialize until August 18, 1920, when the Tennessee House of Representatives voted to ratify the Nineteenth Amendment to the Constitution, which forbade discrimination at the ballot box 'on account of sex'.[3] Achieving this milestone required a nearly eighty-year struggle, which began around the 1830s, when female abolitionists started to analyze all constraints placed on minorities based on both race and gender (DuBois, 1987).

The battle for suffrage was part of a broader program of reforms that took place between the 1840s and the 1850s. This program aimed to address various issues, including the abolition of child custody laws favoring fathers, the denial of equal education opportunities for women, and the prohibition against women speaking in public.

The argument put forth by the first generation of suffragists (Lucy Stone, Elizabeth Cady Stanton, Susan B. Anthony) was centered on eliminating barriers at the state level that prevented married women from controlling their earnings and accessing state universities. After the foundation (1869) of the National Woman Suffrage Association (led by Stanton and Anthony) and its rival American Woman Suffrage Association (led by Stone and Harper), the debate expanded to include the enfranchisement of black women (Baker, 2002). Stanton and Anthony implemented a 'New York strategy': as the wives of politicians from both parties, they engaged in lobbying efforts to promote legislative measures for both abolitionism and women's enfranchisement. Furthermore, by emphasizing the role of motherhood in the political and public arena, suffragists were able to unite a larger number of activists.

It was challenging to establish a united front in support of women's suffrage. During the Seneca Fall Convention (1848), the resolution

[3] It's worth noting that several states and territories had recognized women's suffrage rights before 1920. These included Wyoming, Utah, Colorado, Idaho, Washington, California, Oregon, Montana, Arizona, Kansas, Alaska, Illinois, North Dakota, Indiana, Nebraska, Michigan, Arkansas, New York, South Dakota, and Oklahoma.

encouraging women's suffrage was the only one that did not receive unanimous approval from the assembly (Buhle & Buhle, 2005). Elizabeth Cady Stanton and the abolitionist Frederick Douglass argued for the importance of women's equal participation in the electoral process. However, many attendees, including radical thinkers like Lucretia Mott, expressed concern that women's suffrage was too morally questionable to be included in the movement's agenda, which was much more focused on the economic rights of women, especially married women.[4]

Beginning in the mid-nineteenth century, several generations of woman's suffrage supporters embarked on this challenging campaign, which also involved political actions such as lobbying parliament and collecting signatures for petitions, all aimed at achieving what was then considered a radical change of the Constitution. After the Civil War, women's suffrage became intertwined with the unresolved political status of former slaves. In 1868, the Fourteenth Amendment was ratified, granting citizenship to all 'male' individuals 'born or naturalized in the United States', including formerly enslaved people, with the exclusion of 'Indians not taxed'. Two years later, in 1870, the Fifteenth Amendment was enacted granting citizens the right to vote regardless of 'race, color, or previous condition of servitude'. Once again, gender was not included in these provisions (Dubois & Dumenil, 2005).

The debate over female suffrage was multifaceted and based on arguments regarding fundamental rights and overall principles with the aim of promoting the "Evolution of a New Woman" (as in Pattern, 1914). It led to drastic changes in traditional gender-based relationships and social institutions, most notably the family: "by focusing on the public sphere, and particularly on citizenship, suffragists demanded for women a kind of power and a connection with the social order not based on the institution of the family and their subordination within it" (DuBois, 1975, 64). Eugenic feminists of the time asserted that women were the bearers of the next generation of the race and therefore had the legal right to vote and politically advocate for interests related to themselves, their children, and the overall well-being of the race as a whole.

[4] Furthermore, given that the electorate was established by states rather than through a federal procedure, women's rights activists believed that achieving women's suffrage required a state by state battle.

In response to these arguments, antisuffragists endeavored to reinforce the patriarchal vision of society. They sometimes invoked the values of small-town America, where the family was considered the rightful unit of civil government, and men were seen as representatives and protectors of women in political matters. The enfranchisement of women, they insisted, would contribute to the dissolution of the family, altering the character and structure of households and the balance of powers within it. Furthermore, Antis considered that women did not need to vote since they were already represented by their husbands, fathers, brothers, and so forth. They viewed women's suffrage as a threat to both themselves and the country and embraced the doctrine of the separate spheres as a reflection of natural law. This argument was especially pursued by champions of the 'cult of domesticity', i.e. the idea that women were responsible for preserving the family's integrity and public health, and their only sphere of influence was the home (see Sect. 4.2 and Sect. 5.1). An emblematic example was Catharine Beecher: although she was a pioneer of women's education intended as a rigorous and professional training in child rearing and home economics, she firmly opposed women's suffrage. She viewed it "not as a privilege conferred but as an act of oppression, forcing them to assume the responsibilities of a man, for which they are not, and cannot, be qualified" (Beecher, 1872, 8).

In 1914, during the lively debate over women's suffrage in the United States, suffragist and historian George Elliott Howard wrote:

> Educated women are not shunning marriage or maternity; but they are declining to view matrimony as a profession, as their sole vocation, or to become merely childbearing animals. Let us not worry about the destiny of college women. It is simply wrong wedlock which they are avoiding. They are declining longer to accept marriage as a sort of purchase contract in which the woman barters her sex-capital to the man in exchange for a life-support (Howard, 1914, 33).

A turning point in the debate was marked by the introduction of a new argument that partially shifted the debate from a moral standpoint—namely, the idea that women and men are equal before the law, toward an analysis of cost–benefit of the female vote and on its potential impact on resource distribution. Many economists and social reformers, including women economists of the time, were no exception. It is hardly surprising given that a large part of the debate centered on the economic consequences of extending suffrage as well as on the legal and economic status of women as individuals and as members of families. They played an active role on both sides of the contention as representatives of a new elite who had established their *bona fides* as scientific experts, they attended public meetings, delivered speeches, and published various pamphlets, leaflets, newspapers, and journals articles outlining the reasons and justifications for either granting or denying women's suffrage (Becchio & Fiorito, 2023).

Richard T. Ely opposed women's suffrage. In 1907, he framed the issue in terms of 'women's biological inferiority', which he used to argue against granting them the right to vote, contending that their needs were adequately represented by men at the ballot box (Ely, 1908). Later, during the heated campaign for the 1912 Wisconsin referendum on women's suffrage, he shifted the argument to the consequences of voting for working women. He claimed that providing them with the right to vote would not improve their conditions that were determined by their 'inferior economic value in the world's labor market'. This economic value, he argued, increased significantly for married women subjected to family-wage conditions, a concept that Ely did not even question (Ely, 1912).

Harvard economist Thomas Nixon Carver was the strongest supporter of the separate spheres and a vehement Antisuffragist. He wrote *Women Suffrage from a Neutral Point of View* (1918), an appeal to return to the notion of family as the basic unit of society, based on harmony, against the individualistic theory, based on conflicts. He explained that if we follow the former, woman suffrage is a 'superfluity', while if we follow the latter, it is a necessity. Needless to say, Carver sympathized with the familistic theory against 'rabid suffragists' who forget the primary role of women as mothers.[5] Furthermore, Carver raised the issue of the physical weakness of women, which contrasted with the notion of government as

[5] Carver's support of the notion of the family as the constituent unit of society led him to look with favor at the enfranchisement of widows, who served as heads of families. He also supported the disfranchisement of bachelors.

a 'masculine affair', and pointed out that the majority of women did not care about the ballot. The familistic argument was previously adopted by Cornell economist Jeremiah W. Jenks who, while serving as president of the American Economic Association (1907), insisted on the notion of 'social efficiency' prevailing over individual rights, including a woman's enfranchisement.[6]

Economists who supported women's suffrage, particularly Columbia faculty members, clustered around the New York Men's League for Woman Suffrage, which was established in 1909, and its monthly organ, *The Woman Voter*.[7] Some of them advocated for an increase of women's salaries, especially in public employments, as an outcome of women's suffrage (Chaddock, 1911; Seager, 1914). Others, however, did not establish a direct connection between suffrage and the reduction of the gender pay gap. They instead emphasized political arguments in favor of suffrage as an ineludible step toward a more well-defined democratic process (Agger, 1911; Beard, 1914; Mitchell, 1915; Mussey, 1912).

On February 11, 1915, economist Wesley Mitchell, who was in favor of women's suffrage, delivered a speech at the Woman Political Union in New York, praising the doctrine of the separate spheres that had led to a gendered division of labor within households, with men responsible for production and women in charge of consumption, based on their skills and inclinations. According to Mitchell, the complementarity between the two spheres and the two genders was instrumental in supporting women's suffrage which would make women 'better citizens' and 'more interesting wives, and wiser mothers' (Mitchell, 1915).

Outside the Columbia University group, economists who supported woman suffrage included Herbert J. Davenport, Simon Patten, Charles Beard, W.E.B. Du Bois, Albert B. Wolfe, and Irving Fisher.

Inspired by Thorsten Veblen, Davenport described the confinement of women to the role of conspicuous consumers of male wealth and blamed the division of roles typical of the separate spheres. He defined himself

[6] Other notable Antisuffragist economists of the time were Charles J. Bullock, a public finance expert from Harvard, Yale's Arthur T. Hadley and Henry W. Farnam (Becchio & Fiorito, 2023).

[7] *The Woman Voter* was edited by Mary R. Beard, Charles Beard's wife (Rosenberg, 2004). The journal hosted the column "The Antis Answered" where leading reformers of the time answered to objections raised by the antisuffragists.

as a ‘feminist’ who deplored the existing situation and called for not only suffrage but also equality of opportunity and economic independence: “so there should be other functions in life for a woman than merely to be a mother” (Davenport, 1916).

Patten shared Davenport’s critique of the separate spheres and of the notion of the family wage (Pattern, 1914, 1919). Unlike Ely or Carver, he pointed out that women’s enfranchisement would enhance social harmony.

Mitchell, Davenport, and Seager supported women’s enfranchisement albeit they largely adhered to the prevailing doctrine of separate spheres. “Men constantly speak of the city’s housekeeping,” wrote Seager in the *Woman Voter* (1911, 8), “but seem to forget that women are the natural housekeepers.” Davenport still considered motherhood as women’s ‘primary responsibility’ and, in complaining about the ‘sterility’ of the ‘parasitic woman’, he affirmed that “it is in the name of motherhood” that we ask for the ballot (Davenport, 1916). Even Patten, arguably the most egalitarian among the progressive reformers, viewed woman suffrage more as a means to foster a new sense of ‘harmony’ within the family under modern industrial conditions than as a path to achieve political equality between the sexes. Beard went a step further and, in his address delivered in 1906, he added a notable eugenic dimension to his pro-suffrage stance: “since intellectual and physical powers are increased through activity and since we inherit from our mothers as well as our fathers, it is legitimate to expect that the “increase of race power will be accelerated by widening the sphere of woman’s activity: by becoming more human and less feminine she will add to the power of the race” (Beard, 1914, 497).[8]

W.E.B. Du Bois authored several editorials published in *The Crisis*, the official organ of the National Association for the Advancement of Colored People, in which he emphasized the complementarity of Black Americans and women’s rights as two dimensions of the same egalitarian principle (Du Bois, 1912a, 1912b). Moreover, he pointed out that woman suffrage would weaken, rather than strengthen, white supremacy

[8] Beard was not an isolated case: other social reformers praised the biological virtues of women’s suffrage (Popenoe & Johnson, 1918).

in the country. Like Du Bois, Wolfe (1913) emphasized the common ground between woman suffrage and the suffrage of Black Americans.

Fisher wrote about women's rights between 1913 and 1920. Initially, he defined himself 'a very mild suffragist' and considered women's enfranchisement 'not a right but an expedient' (Fisher, 1913). Nonetheless, he blamed antisuffragists for adopting the anti-responsibility argument, in which they argued that most women considered suffrage as a way to distract them from their role as wives and mothers. He drew a parallel with the argument adopted by many slaves against their enfranchisement. Furthermore, he admitted that women's suffrage might help in finding a solution to social problems related to education, health, and alcohol. Fisher's advocacy for women's suffrage became stronger in the following years: he firmly supported women's suffrage in a *New York Times* article (Fisher, 1916). In 1918, in a letter to the editor of *the New York Evening Post*, he wrote: "by virtue of our Constitution all men have been placed on an equal footing; equal privileges have been extended to both. Then, why not equality among women?" (Fisher, 1918, 24).

As mentioned earlier, many women economists of the time endorsed women's suffrage. Like the majority of their male colleagues, women academic economists were 'scientists of society' committed to proposing policy measures for a more efficient and equitable society (Fitzpatrick, 1990). Henceforth, they often engaged in public debates about concrete possibilities for improving social well-being. Women's suffrage was certainly a central argument within their agenda. Furthermore, their gender and their lived experiences as women at that time made their arguments relevant either when they adopted a moral argument related to the dignity of individuals or when they supported female suffrage by presenting economic arguments favoring potential reforms, such as the introduction of some labor legislation aimed at reducing gender wage or gender labor inequality.

The most influential group of women economists who joined the debate gathered around Marion Talbot, Dean of Women at the University of Chicago, and included Frances Kellor, Edith Abbott, and Sophonisba Breckinridge. Suffragist women economists were also very active at Wellesley, where Katharine Coman, Helen Sumner, and Emily Green Balch were particularly devoted to the cause. In New York at Columbia,

Katharine Bement Davis and Emilie Hutchinson were also involved (DuBois, 1968; Fitzpatrick, 1990). It is easy to find an immediate connection between these clusters of women economists and their male academic counterparts in the same institutions, especially when we consider the case of Columbia. The profile of their commitment to the cause was different, though: some were inclined to adopt a moral argument emphasizing the equality of individuals regardless of their gender; others were more focused on the direct connection between political representation and wage legislation; while some presented a more economical reasoning rooted in the economic analysis of women's suffrage.

Kellor and Davis were fervent suffragists and activists: they intensively organized campaigns and political rallies and were very active in shaping the political agenda that ultimately led to the passage of the Nineteenth Amendment. Davis, in particular, was one of the most multifaceted women among social reformers during the Progressive Era. Despite her leadership in the women's suffrage movement, she aligned herself with eugenicists (Deegan, 2003; Fitzpatrick, 1990). In 1914, she served as Vice-President of the National American Woman Suffrage Association, and in 1916, she joined the Republican Party's presidential campaign for Charles Evans Hughes. Davis emphasized the necessity for women to vote as a means to expand social and 'industrial justice'.

The notion of industrial justice combined the argument for the equality of the sexes with the urgency of social reforms. It was linked with the discrimination faced by women, especially female blue-collar workers, within workplaces, irrespective of their abilities and skills, as explained by Jane Addams:

> In certain respects, the insistence of women for political expression, which characterizes the opening years of the twentieth century, bears an analogy to their industrial experiences in the early part of the nineteenth century, when the textile industries were taken out of private houses and organized as factory enterprises (Addams, 1914, 3).

Kellor led the Progressive Party's National Service Committee and became a key player in Theodore Roosevelt's presidential campaign. In an undated manuscript, written after the end of 1917 (as the war is mentioned) but prior to the approval of the Nineteenth Amendment, Kellor insisted on the urgency of promoting not only women's suffrage but also active participation by women in public affairs. She argued that without such active involvement, the right to vote would be rendered meaningless:

> It was, of course, natural to assume that the vote being won, the greater part of the work was done: but if so, this judgment showed little real understanding of that highly sensitized masculine organization called the political machine. (Kellor, undated, [presumably 1917] 6).

Kellor's argument encompassed a comprehensive social reform agenda that extended beyond political enfranchisement to include the cultural development of women. In fact, both Davis and Kellor used the moral argument of the equality of the sexes before the law as well as the argument that considered woman's ballot as a tool to improve social legislation, in line with the Progressive platform.

The urgency for affirmative action related to the extension of female suffrage was particularly crucial in the case of Black American women, who faced a double-marginalization. The metaphor of slavery to describe the conditions of many married women played a pivotal role in raising public awareness of the connection between abolitionism and women's suffrage. Although a large number of Black American women suffragists were active members of the National American Woman Suffrage Association (NAWSA), in the 1890s, exclusivism and racism emerged within the movement and led some Black American women to leave NASWA and establish the National Association of Colored Women (Jones, 2020). The official rationale behind exclusivism was the pretense to give votes only to educated women, by arguing that a vote by an illiterate woman was a waste of resources and a cost for the system. As many Black American women were illiterate, they were implicitly excluded from the suffrage extension. The fight against this within-gender-based discrimination compelled Black American women suffragists to promote suffrage as the only means to secure education for the entire Black American community. Henceforth, much like Du Bois, they mostly insisted on the moral argument of the equality of all individuals regardless of color or sex.

Whatever the argument that women economists adopted in the lengthy debate on women's political enfranchisement, their contributions were essential to the cause of women's suffrage: albeit the ideological rhetoric played a significant role in shaping public opinion, the economic analysis of women's ballot was indeed an essential aspect in the reconstruction of the debate that unfolded among economists and social reformers of the time.

The introduction of the economic argument to endorse women's suffrage represented a significant moment in the history of the debate on women's enfranchisement. Interestingly, as mentioned, that argument was adopted not only by Suffragists but also, paradoxically, by the Antis.

The Antis' positions were mainly based on two principles: the preservation of separate spheres as the most ethical as well as rational way to organize society (Howard, 1982; Marshall, 1986), and the rejection of the compelling argument that the woman's ballot would actually reduce the gender wage gap (Kirkby, 1987). In fact, the correlation between lower wages for earning women and their political enfranchisement was the main focus of the debate until the First World War, when the discussion shifted toward the broader social role of women in more general terms.

Whilethe doctrine of separate spheres simultaneously provided an ideological and economic justification grounded on the complementarity of a male public dimension and a female private one, the strict economic analysis whether in favor or against women's suffrage overlooked the ideological dimension and yielded a much more solid rationale for the two opposite positions. The ideological aspect of the doctrine rejected the extension of suffrage for women, arguing that women should remain free to best perform their natural role, i.e. to be good wives and mothers. The economic analysis of women's suffrage was much more focused on the notion of suffrage not intended as an end in itself but as a means to an end, namely, the enhancement of social well-being. Nonetheless, these two dimensions—ideological and economic—were intertwined.

Antis adopted the doctrine of separate spheres as a traditional application of the theory of comparative advantage to the division of roles between men and women. Furthermore, when Antis pointed out that the ballot would require an amount of information that would force women to neglect their duties as wives and mothers, potentially harming family dynamics, they were appealing to the perceived trade-off between the time spent by women within the household (taking care of it and its members) and the time they spent outside the household (by engaging in political matters). Finally, when Antis insisted that a woman ballot would be ineffective in increasing social well-being, being that women were allegedly too ignorant to use the vote wisely, they were applying the concept of opportunity cost to the expansion of suffrage. It is worth noting that the above-mentioned antisuffragist arguments sound legit only if we consider the family, rather than the individual, as the basis of human society.

The supremacy of families over individuals was commonly asserted by the Antis in their public speeches. For instance, an article in the *Chicago Tribune* (Corbin, 1909) reported a debate between suffragists and anti-suffragists on this specific point. Mrs. Corbin, an antisuffragist, presented to the Senate her reasons for opposing the extension of suffrage, echoing arguments made by Ely and Carver. She argued that men and women stood on unequal terms precisely in order to protect the structure of families, which had served as the foundation of society and the nation:

> Thus at the outset of their mature experience men and women stand upon terms of an inequality which neither nature herself, nor legislation, nor statecraft can remove. The best that civilization ever has been able to do is to compensate women for this excess of sacrifice and burden bearing in maternity by absolving them from such forms of labor and responsibility as are inconsistent with their peculiar physique; such as military and jury duty and those political duties which lie so distinctly outside of her natural and seemly labors in the home and society; and giving her, besides, certain legal rights of protection which men neither claim nor enjoy (Corbin, 1909, 1).

Suffragists, including Jane Addams and Marion Talbot, replied to Corbin's argument by pointing out the evidence that the family functions as a well-balanced unit precisely because men and women share common goals and purposes within their partnership, along with a shared commitment to the improvement of society and the nation. As a result, the suffragists contended that the woman ballot would not harm social and national well-being; rather, it would strengthen the implicit agreement between men and women for the sake of the nation. Furthermore, they argued that women would not be compelled to vote: those who were fine with the *status quo* and comfortable with their husbands' votes would not be forced to visit the ballot box.

Helen Sumner conducted a field investigation in Colorado (1906–1907) where woman suffrage had been granted in 1893. Her report, published in 1909, was among the earliest publications that presented the economic argument correlated with women's suffrage. She rightly pointed out that the idea, commonly shared by suffragists, that women's suffrage would lead to equal pay was somehow problematic for several reasons. First, there was no evidence that in the states where woman suffrage had been granted, equal pay had been a result of political enfranchisement rather than of trade unionism. Second, she rightly pointed out that talking about equal pay was different from talking about the gender wage gap: while the former could potentially be addressed through specific legislation, the latter depended on the gender labor gap which is a direct result of part-time jobs versus full-time jobs, extra hours, and so forth. Furthermore, she wrote that there was no evidence that the political enfranchisement of women would lead to a radical shift in women workers' division of their time between work and household responsibilities. Third, even in public-sector jobs, such as public school teachers or postal service employees, where salaries were set by law, women were often underrepresented in higher positions, and the extension of woman ballot was not directly related to this phenomenon, which today is referred to as the 'glass ceiling'.

Sumner's arguments regarding the limited influence of extending women's suffrage on equal pay were partially adopted by some anti-suffragists too, like Minnie Bronson, a well-known Anti who served as General Secretary for the National Association Opposed to Woman Suffrage (NAOWS), based in New York City. In 1912, Bronson published a pamphlet aimed at dismantling the idea that woman suffrage "would lead to a fairer treatment of women in industry and to better law for their protection" (Bronson, 1912, 3). According to Bronson, this idea was fallacious and rested on a false premise. A few weeks later, Edith Abbott and Sophonisba Breckinridge (1912)deconstructed Bronson's argument point-by-point in order to present woman suffrage as the 'surest method' for the protection of female workers.

Bronson's initial argument centered on the thesis that the steadily increasing number of women workers would be enough to compel politicians to ensure that protective legislation adequately addressed issues concerning women workers. Consequently, she contended that extending suffrage to women would incur an unnecessary cost for society:

> Reference to the laws governing the labor of women shows that our law makers, far from enacting laws which discriminate against the wage-earning woman, are constantly enacting new and better laws for her protection; that these laws are constantly improved, not because women have the ballot, or want it, but because women are entering more and more into the industrial life of our country (Bronson, 1912, 4).

Abbott and Breckinridge replied that there was no trade-off between woman ballot and protective legislation. The inclusion of the former does not preclude the latter; in fact, the combination of both would undoubtedly improve the conditions of women in the industrial sector:

> In the first place, suffragists do not claim that the working woman's only redress is through the ballot; they do say and believe that the ballot is the swiftest and most direct means of bringing about such reforms as are demanded; but, since they are denied the ballot, these same women are devoting a disproportionately large measure of time and strength in trying to bring about these reforms in other ways (Abbott & Breckinridge, 1912, 168).

Therefore, denying the ballot to female workers would be far costlier than granting it to them. Bronson continued by pointing out that suffragists often connect the lack of woman ballot with the increasing number of strikes, which might be drastically reduced once protesters gain the ballot. To counter this thesis, Bronson claimed that during the Shirt

Waist Strike, which occurred in New York (November 1909–February 1910), more than 40 percent of strikers were men and around forty-two percent of women were either underage or immigrants without citizenship. Hence, according to Bronson, there was no evidence that woman suffrage would reduce strikes. Abbott and Breckinridge replied that Bronson's argument was flawed: they pointed out that the strikers were not protesting in support of suffrage; rather they were demonstrating to improve their conditions as industrial workers. Furthermore, they affirmed that history had clearly shown that when workmen gained the right to vote, the conditions of all working men had improved. In a similar vein, they believed that once suffrage was granted to women, it would likely result in better conditions for female workers.

Bronson's third argument against women's suffrage involved a comparison of protective legislation in states where suffrage had already been granted with protective legislation in non-suffrage States. According to Bronson, there was evidence that better protective legislation had been enacted in non-suffrage States: she listed a series of specific restrictions for women workers, such as the limitation on the number of hours women could be employed and the prohibition of employing women at night. Abbott and Breckinridge replied that Bronson overlooked the fact that even in non-suffrage states, suffragists had played a pivotal role in making such protective legislation possible, since both protective legislation and the ballot were nonnegotiable aims for them.

Another argument against suffrage raised by Bronson centered on the issue of equal pay for equal work. She cited the wages of teachers as an example, emphasizing that it was false, as suffragists claimed, that in Massachusetts, the average pay of a female teacher was only one-third of that of her male colleagues. She argued that this gender wage gap was not due to discrimination that suffrage might eliminate, rather to the fact that male teachers were typically employed in high schools, colleges, or as principals and supervisors, while women teachers were more commonly hired in primary schools and kindergartens. Nonetheless, Bronson claimed that the lower wages of women teachers and workers were determined by the law of supply and demand: namely, the market demanded women teachers for junior positions and men teachers for positions which required greater responsibility. As she wrote:

> It is true that few women are found in the highest-paid positions of a teaching force, but this is due to other causes than political. In four hundred and seventy-five colleges of various grades and attendance in the United States only eight have women presidents, yet it will scarcely be claimed that this is due to woman's political status. (…) It is not denied that female teachers do not in the majority of cases receive the same pay as men for the work of equal grade; but here the law of supply and demand is paramount (Bronson, 1912, 7–8).

It is worthy to note that on this specific point Bronson made a point as pink ghettoes, the glass ceiling, and the gender wage gap are still present today after a century of women's suffrage.

In their rejoinder, Abbott and Breckinridge replied that there was no need to "enter upon a long discussion of the outworn doctrine of the inflexibility and almost sacred character of supply and demand" (Abbott & Breckinridge, 1912, 172). They drew attention to the inadequacy of labor legislation and stressed that while the ballot might not be the sole means for achieving social reforms, it certainly contributed to reducing the demand for child labor and improving the conditions and overall social well-being of women workers.

The connection among women's suffrage, social welfare and gender wage gap were recurring themes in Abbot's writings as well as in many other women economists of the time, like the economist and suffragist Emilie Hutchinson, who in an article published in 1914 emphasized that woman's suffrage was not solely a matter of justice but also a crucial issue for social welfare:

> By virtue of their new standing in the community, women assume an equal responsibility with men for both good and bad legislation. They become co-partners in the success or failure that accompanies legislative experiments, made presumably for their benefit (Hutchinson, 1914, 108).

In 1914, Breckinridge wrote an article about the connection between women's political enfranchisement and gender wage equality. She considered biases against the capacity of women to perform as well as men do as extra-economic factors that disrupted the equilibrium price of labor and harmed social well-being. She wrote:

> Whatever influence leads to decisions based on social, historical, accidental considerations rather than on considerations of efficiency, competence, industrial capacity operates through non-economical causes and acts to the advantage of men and to the disadvantage of women, while influences bringing about decisions based on considerations of capacity and efficiency operate to the advantage of women (Breckinridge, 1914, 124–5).

Hence, woman ballot would lead to affirmative action aimed at achieving necessary social reforms to bring women to the same degree of skill or occupational capacity as men, such as investments in technical and professional schools that would open up new positions for female workers. Protective labor legislation, Breckinridge continued, was primarily useful for weaker workers who struggled to compete effectively in the job market.

In summary, certain prominent antisuffragists among the leading economists of the period viewed women's enfranchisement as dangerous due to the perceived potential to disrupt the dynamics of the home. This argument was a common thread among antisuffragist women of the time too. Regardless of their political affiliations (Ely being a pro-labor progressive and Carver a staunch conservative), they shared the fear that female participation in political life could undermine the family, which they regarded as the cornerstone of society.

Though many renowned economists were in favor of woman suffrage. Women economists played a major role in supporting woman ballot by adopting, like their male counterparts, a multifaceted approach: some, such as Kellor, Davis, and Talbot, emphasized the moral argument of the equality of the sexes before the law; others, like Breckinridge and Abbott, applied economic arguments to advocate for women's enfranchisement; likewise, Hutchinson and Sumner insisted on the correlation between women's suffrage and protectitive legislation aimed at ensuring special conditions for women workers and achieving wage equality.

Even within the pro-suffrage camp, the Progressive Era reform movement was not immune to the ambiguities and contradictions that marked much of its impetus. For some of the male figures mentioned earlier, extending voting rights to women was desirable more on utilitarian grounds than on strictly egalitarian ones. They believed it was intended to strengthen social bonds rather than to increase the social or political power of women. As Columbia University's historian James Harvey Robinson claimed (1914), woman suffrage was a "matter of expediency," and not of individual rights. This tendency to prioritize the common good over individual rights, particularly women's rights, in this case, was a commonly shared perspective.

4.2 From 'True Womanhood' to the 'New Woman': The Evolution of the Marriage Debate

During the nineteenth century, the debate over marriage and divorce assumed a central place in public discourse and it was intertwined with the ongoing debates over the notion of the new woman. On one side, marriage represented the social institution that granted the doctrine of separate spheres to flourish (Kerber, 1988). On the other side, women's rights activists, utopians, abolitionists, and free lovers perceived marriage as hierarchical, based on the power of husbands over wives, and coercive, based on legislation of the time which imposed *de iure* men's power over women within the institution of marriage (Faulkner, 2019).

Men were expected to play the role of the movers, the doers, the actors, providers for and protectors of the family, strongly committed to their career, and social status; being the sole breadwinners, they ruled the public sphere and behave as patriarchs within their household.[9]

Women, especially those belonging to the upper and middle class, were expected to be dependent on a man, initially as daughters and later as wives, and their personal fulfillment as individuals and social agents was evaluated based on their performance within the private sphere.

[9] By 1852, *The Ladies Counsellor* described the ideal middle-class self-made man as energetic, self-denying, benevolent, cultivated, ambitious, and religious (Hansen, 1994). Nevertheless, writings aimed to criticize the idealization of married men were often published. For instance, Charles Lambs (1811) sarcastically wrote about "the infirmities of Married People", mainly based on 'lack of love' being marriage a man's monopoly over women (as retrieved on August 31, 2023 at: < http://essays.quotidiana.org/lamb/bachelors_complaint_of_the_b/).

Motherhood was the supreme goal of a virtuous woman. The cult of true womanhood was built on the idea that women should be both perfect and obedient wives while also embodying the ideal of a nurturing mother capable of imparting traditional family values in the upbringing of their sons and daughters. As Gerda Lerner (1986) pointed out, the cult of true womanhood was reinforced by social studies of the time that sought to universalize it by tracing its origins back to antiquity and portraying it as the natural role for women. As she noted: "it is no accident that the slogan 'woman's place is in the home' took on a certain aggressiveness and shrillness at the time when increasing numbers of poorer women *left* their homes to become factory workers" (Lerner, 1969, 12).

As previously mentioned, cultural biases about the holiness of motherhood as well as social pressure to get well-married significantly influenced the education of girls. These biases were further reinforced by legislation intended to subjugate women within the private sphere. For instance, in the United Kingdom, prior to the enactment of the 1882 Married Property Act, when a woman got married her wealth was transferred to her husband who controlled her income too. The Matrimonial Causes Act (1857) entitled only husbands to divorce on the grounds of adultery, not vice versa, and once divorced, the custody of children was given to their father. The situation was the same in other European countries as well as in the United States (Menchi & Eisenach, 2016).

In 1839, some U.S. states initiated to enact Married Women's Property Acts.[10] These legal acts marked the initial shift toward considering marriage as a contract between spouses rather than as a transition of women from paternal subjection to marital dependency. Later, legislation on divorce was introduced as well.[11] Although the process in the

[10] The first American law that permitted a woman any control over land was issued in Connecticut in 1808. In 1848, the Married Women's Property Act was issued by New York State: it allowed women to own and control personal property as well as to dispose issues and profits, without making them subjected to the disposal of their husbands. Between the 1870s and 1880s, the Parliament of the United Kingdom passed the two Married Women's Property Acts, which allowed married women to be the legal owners of the money they earned and to inherit property (1870), and it recognized husbands and wives as two separate legal entities (1882).

[11] In 1857, in the United Kingdom, divorce was finally allowed by the Matrimonial Causes Act. Although the Act did not treat women and men equally, being women forced to provide unquestionable proofs in order to file a divorce, the Act freed marriage from the millennial

West took many decades, legal recognition of women's property rights altered the relationship between spouses in terms of household decisions (Moehling & Thomasson, 2020).

As usually happens, social norms and legal rules do not always progress in sync. Sometimes, new social norms drive legislative changes, and at other times, legislation precedes the acceptance of new social norms, while traditional habits may persist, especially in the private sphere. This was evident in the condition of married women. Around the 1870 and 1880s, Anne Brown Adams, a daughter of the abolitionist John Brown, wrote to a friend:

> The struggle for a married woman's rights will be a longer and a harder fought battle than any other that the world has [ever] known. Men have been taught that they are absolute monarchs in their families, (even in a republican country,) ever since the world began, and that to kill a wife by inches, is not murder, women are taught from infancy that to betray [by look or word] or even to mention to an intimate friend the secrets of their married life, is worse than disgraceful. Therein lies the power of the man, He knows that no matter what he does, the woman will keep silent as the grave (…) Women are taught that their only hope of heaven, is to 'endure to the end'. That it is a religious duty to 'submit themselves to their husbands in all things,' I know a man who tells his wife 'I own you, I have got a deed (marriage license and certificate) to you and got it recorded, I have a right to do what I please to you'. And the law of a Christian land says she shall submit, to indecencies that would make a respectable devil blush for shame, Man, who is said to have been created in the image of God, is the lowest animal in the world, and the most cruel. It shatters my faith in the goodness of God, so much that it makes me tremble for my own reason, at times.[12]

---

ecclesiastical power and made it secular (Kha, 2021). Nonetheless, in many countries, divorce was influenced and regulated by religious authorities, whose role is still very important today even in secular societies. Smith (2003) explains that the religious behavior of a given country influences divorce rates in Europe, along with the easing of divorce laws and the rising economic status of women.

[12] As retrieved on August 31, 2023 at: https://www.gilderlehrman.org/sites/default/files/inline-pdfs/T-03007_53.pdf.

The debate on marriage and the family among economists of the time must include a reference to Friedrich Engels' book (1884 [1972]). Drawing from the principles of historical materialism, which emphasize the reproduction of means of subsistence as an integral component of the economic structure, Engels viewed the evolution of labor and family within the capitalistic framework as two sides of the same coin. Engels considered the inequality between the sexes as an effect of the economic oppression of women, based on the patriarchal and monogamous family structure that transformed the management of a household from a public institution into a private service. In his vision, the man assumed the role of the bourgeois, while the woman, whether a wife or a prostitute, occupied the position of the proletariat. According to Engels, the proletarian revolution would destroy capitalism and the traditional patriarchal family would disappear along with the inequality between genders and the commodification of sex. Engels insisted that complete freedom in marriage would only be attainable with the abolition of capitalistic production and the property relations it fostered. He added that mating-search, marriage, and monogamy were other forms of private property and that the predominance of men in the private sphere was a direct consequence of his economic predominance within the public sphere. Both would vanish with the abolition of capitalism.

As it is well-known, Marxists of the time accepted Engels' perspective without further questioning it. They were not much interested in the woman question, with the only exception of Clara Zetkin who followed Engels' critique, and Russian free love activist Alexandra Kollantai who was very popular for advocating free love as a measure for women's emancipation (Kollontai, 1918 [1971]). By aligning themselves with Engels' arguments, they were critical of prioritizing political issues, such as suffrage, as well as legal goals, such as Marriage Acts, which they believed primarily benefitted middle-class women and reinforced the division between capitalists and proletarians (Becchio, 2020).

Among classical liberals and other non-Marxist scholars of the time, the debate on marriage encompassed a range of perspectives, including at least three different viewpoints: supporters of traditional marriage as it was inherent in the logic of the separate spheres; detractors of the doctrine of separate spheres who eventually criticized the institution of marriage per se without calling for its abolition; and libertarians, especially in the United States, who promoted the abolition of marriage as well as free love as a result of rejecting monogamy.

Economists and social reformers of the time, who belonged to the first group, predominantly embraced arguments in favor of the centrality of the family rather than the importance of the individual: they upheld the biological and cultural superiority of men who were always seen as responsible for the well-being of women and children as well as for social prosperity.

Among supporters of the doctrine of the separate spheres, Helen Bosanquet presented the patriarchal family as the main source for the "welfare of the state" (Bosanquet, 1906, 9). The modern family was seen by Bosanquet as "unstable and broken-down" (Bosanquet, 1906, 195) because the traditional household management, which was considered the exclusive domain of women, was threatened by women's entry into the workforce. She justified her argument by adopting an interpretation rooted in the notion of opportunity cost: "both [women] and their husbands know that their service in the home are far more valuable, even from an economic point of view, than if they were themselves earning" (Bosanquet, 1906, 200). She insisted on the notion of family wage and on the necessity for children to be constantly under the supervision and care of their mothers, especially in a frantic period of rapid transformation as it was at that time. She emphasized that the "economic significance of the family" lies in its efficiency as the primary economic agent. She wrote: "in the Family, and in the Family alone, are combined the forces which determine the quantity of the population with the forces which determine its quality; and without this combination the decay of a people is inevitable" (Bosanquet, 1906, 232).

In picturing family in such terms, Bosanquet presented men as the heads of the family, but differently from supporters of the patriarchal family, who presented women as servants or slaves, she depicted women as the "center" of the family, the main care-providers in charge of the education of children "a duty that cannot be delegated" (Bosanquet, 1906, 279). This perspective differed from the views of many activists in the United States, where public debates were focused on creating a new woman who could play an active role in both public and private spheres. In Bosanquet's view, such an option would be detrimental to the welfare of society.[13]

On the opposite side of the spectrum, American libertarians of the nineteenth century claimed that social roles based on gender, as well as privileges related to gender, should be discarded in favor of the concept of individuals as self-owners. By blaming marriage as a major expression of the subjection of individuals to the state, they converged toward the principle of free love that implied the rejection of marriage and traditional family structure. A notable name of the time, almost completely forgotten, was Angela Heywood[14], who wrote: "the ceremony of legal marriage by a third person who represents society, debars us from personal responsibility, invades personal liberty, and exhibits the weakness of accepting conventional force rather than essential right as the arbiter of love relations" (as in McElroy, 2001, 35).

A much better-known libertarian of the time was Moses Harman, the editor of *Lucifer, the Light Bearer*, which was an anarchical publication that promoted birth control and free love and depicted marriage as an institution that systematically enslaved women. He wrote:

> I believe in Freedom, Love, and Wisdom, Knowledge. I put Freedom first (…) I do not believe in marriage. Marriage destroys freedom and compels slavery. Marriage kills love and incarnates hate. Marriage is the inveterate foe of wisdom and incarnated ignorance (…) Marriage is unjust to women depriving them of their right of ownership and control of their person, of their children, their name, their time, and their labor (as in McElroy, 2001, 97–100).[15]

---

13 As pointed out by Morrow (2000), Bosanquet's conservativism was grounded on a moral vision of a social unity that required the maintenance of separate spheres.

14 Along with her husband Ezra, Angela Heywood was the editor and publisher of *The Word: a Monthly Journal of Reform*, an organ of the American Labor Reform League and the New England Labor Reform between 1872 and 1893. It presented a confluence of the radical reform projects of its time, from free love, free expression, and feminism to labor reform. In her pamphlet, *In the Shadow of a Man* she argued in favor of the abolition of speculative income, women's slavery, war government, and pleaded for free use of land, no rents, dividends, and profit, as well as interests.

15 Moses' daughter, Lillian was in a domestic relationship with another libertarian, Edwin Cox Walker. The two considered themselves a feminist couple and declared themselves to be married. Between 1886 and 1887, they went to jail for making their ideas public.

Libertarian feminists of the time, such as Voltairine de Cleyre and Emma Goldman, converged toward Benjamin Tucker's periodical *Liberty*, (1881–1908).[16] They rejected both marriage and the state as well as the critique of socialists who only adopted the class criterion without considering that capitalism and patriarchy are distinct systems, albeit they might co-exist (Kraditor, 1981).[17] They made the same mistake as socialists, albeit being on the opposite side of the political spectrum: just as socialists reduced gender to class, implying that women's emancipation would be a consequence of eliminating classes as shaped within capitalism, libertarians reduced gender to individuality, thus women's emancipation would have been a consequence of getting rid of the state as depicted in some utopian literature.

Between conservativism and anarchism, there were milder positions among economists and social reformers of the time. Although they disagreed on the legal nature of marriage and the limits of state interest in marriage, they realized that marriage was a social institution quickly evolving mainly as an effect of the new role of women in the public sphere. Furthermore, they got acquainted with new data about divorce, which revealed a significant increase in cases, especially in the United States. As Eby (2014) wrote, many progressive scholars insisted on a private transformation of marriage based on the following ideas: spouses should share equal class background, as advocated by Perkins Gilman, to prevent a wife's dependence on her husband's financial approval and earnings; marriage should be validate only by the two spouses, potentially through formal or informal prenuptial agreements, with no specific legislation or religious interference; monogamy should be a free choice between partners, never enforced by legislation and not an issue in case of divorce; divorce should be equally accessible for each partner.

Perkins Gilman was very critical about marriage and she often described it in sarcastic terms. In a pamphlet dated 1885, she wrote:

[16] On *Liberty,* Lysander Spooner condemned suffrage for both women and men, being it a form of recognition of the power of the state over individuals (McElroy, 1992).

[17] Their position was well summed up by Elshtain (1982, 1989): feminist libertarians of the time compared the State to 'Mr. Right' and claimed that to wed themselves to a man as well as to a public identity is a mistake.

"Look at the majority of marriages now existing! If they are made in heaven let us try some earth-made ones!" (Perkins Gilman 1885, 7).[18] She considered marriage mainly influenced by social pressure, a necessity rather than a choice, and she insisted on considering the urgency to teach both sexes how to cultivate the mind and its power of expression rather than the body and its sexual attraction.[19] Perkins Gilman intensively wrote against traditional marriage. In one of her first published short stories, *The Unexpected* (1890), she presented a man happily married to a woman professionally more successful than him.[20] In her first short ghost story, *The Giant Wistaria* (1891a), she pointed out the consequences of stigmatizing illegitimate births.[21] In *An Extinct Angel* (1891b), she attacked the cult of domesticity that depicted women as passive creatures whose lives were totally absorbed by serving their husbands and children.[22] In *Women and Economics* (1898), she defined marriage as a lottery.

In *The Yellow Wall-Paper* (1892) marriage is portrayed as a prison in which the main character, a young wife and mother, was actually segregated inside her house by her husband.[23] Maybe inspired by Wollstonecraft's *Maria,* Perkins Gilman described women as underestimated

---

[18] As retrieved on August 23, 2023 at: http://essays.quotidiana.org/gilman/advertising_for_marriage/.

[19] She married twice and had a daughter. After giving her birth, Perkins Gilman suffered of a severe form of post-partum depression that is described in her short novel *the Yellow Wall-Paper* (1892).

[20] The plot is built up on a case of mistaken identity.

[21] Three young couples spent the night partying in a haunted house that hosted the phantom of a young lady who was forced to live isolated in that house one hundred years earlier in order to avoid the scandal resulting from her out of wedlock pregnancy.

[22] It is a fairy tale about the relationship between angels (women) and humans (men) who forced angels to be submissive until intermarriage between angels and humans made angels found and ate the fruit of knowledge. As a result, they lost their angelic status and transformed into humans.

[23] A young mother suffering post-partum depression is confined by her husband to an upstairs nursery in their mansion. The bedroom where she was confined was covered by 'repellant' yellow wallpaper stripped off in big patches. The young mother thought that a woman was trapped in and she decided to free her by stripping the remaining paper off the wall. One day her husband got back home and found his wife creeping around the room and rubbing against the wallpaper. Scared as hell, the man fainted and his wife continued to circle the room, creeping over his body and believing herself to have become the woman trapped behind the yellow wallpaper.

by their husbands, who often downgraded their wives: "John laughs at me, of course, but one expects that in marriage" (Perkins Gilman, 1892 [2019], 179). She saw marriage as a way to trap women within the private sphere especially in case they experienced any form of distress, as in the case of the main character of *The Yellow Wall-Paper*, who suffered from a severe form of postpartum depression.

In 1892, Perking Gilman's husband filed for divorce which became a scandal when she decided to transfer custody of their daughter to her husband and his new wife, as she was constantly traveling across the country to deliver lectures.[24] She mirrored her own experience in the story *The Unnatural Mother* (1895), which featured a young mother who warned her fellow citizens about a flooding in their village instead of putting her baby's safety in the first place. The mother saved the village, dying in the process while her baby survived. Despite her heroic act, she was posthumously blamed for her 'unnatural behavior': "a man's not fit to bring up children, anyhow. How can they? Mothers have the instinct, that is, all natural mothers have. But dear me! There's some as don't seem to *be* mothers, even when they have a child"[25] (Perkins Gilman, 1892 [2019], 160).

Perkins Gilman delved deeper into the distinction between natural and unnatural motherhood in her book, *Concerning Children* (1903a). She scrutinized how society defined a natural mother as one who embodies primitive or even animalistic characteristics, while an unnatural mother represented a more civilized form of motherhood that relies on intelligence, acquired knowledge, and skills. Natural motherhood, shared by various animal species, especially mammals, was often associated with the basic functions of reproduction, self-preservation, providing nutrition, protection, and defense to the young. In contrast, civilized society expected mothers to seek what is best for their children by involving doctors, teachers, and other experts in the child's education. According to Perkins Gilman, the primary duty of motherhood remained the same—to benefit the child—but progress in motherhood, particularly in

[24] Eventually two years later, in 1894, she relinquished full custody of her daughter.

[25] As retrieved on September 1, 2023 at: https://loahared.s3.amazonaws.com/static/pdf/Gilman_Unnatural_Mother.pdf.

providing a better education for children, was often stigmatized as unnatural. Perkins Gilman challenged these traditional notions of childraising and advocated for a more enlightened and progressive approach to motherhood. She wrote:

> No bottle is as good as the breast. 'You cannot improve on nature!' But you can improve in methods of clothing, feeding in later years, house and school building, teaching, and every other distinctly human process (…) The right education of a child to-day requires more than instinct to produce the best results. Because we have not used the helpful influences of association, study, and experience in this most important labor of life, we keep our progress as a living species far below the level of our progress in material improvements (Perkins Gilman, 1903a, 262).[26]

Perkins Gilman, argued that the civilized or unnatural mother took on two additional responsibilities: promoting racial advancement and contributing to environmental progress. These objectives demanded education of girls and their active participation in the public sphere, either as paid workers or as activists. Their new public roles would mean spending less time with their children in terms of quantity, but it would not compromise the quality of time spent with them. She wrote: "We have urgent need of the unnatural mother,—the mother who has added a trained intellect to a warm heart; and, when we have enough of them, the rarest sound on earth will be that now so pitifully common,—the crying of a little child (ibid, 277)".

In *Women and Economics* (1898), she discarded the notion of family wage, which was founded on a concept of marriage characterized by one partner being subjected to the other, rather than a true partnership. Even monogamy, continued Perkins Gilman, was required only for women while male adultery was tolerated given that prostitution was a form of 'social necessity' or 'social evil'. Marriage was often seen as a 'lottery' (the term was commonly adopted by writers of the time),[27] 'a road to fortune' for women who are "carefully educated and trained to realize

[26] As retrieved on September 1, 2023 at: https://www.gutenberg.org/files/40481/40481-h/40481-h.htm#XIV.

[27] See Taylor Mill (Sect. 2.4 of this book).

in all ways her sex-limitations and her sex-advantages" (Perkins Gilman, 1898, 86). Girls' education was totally devoted to give marriage absolute predominance. She wrote: "Marriage is the woman's proper sphere, her divinely ordered place, her natural end. It is what she is born for, what she is trained for, what she is exhibited for. It is, moreover, her means of honorable livelihood and advancement" (ibid, 87).[28]

As a matter of fact, according to Perkins Gilman, marriage was an 'economic beggary' as well as a 'false attitude from a sex point of view': women, if properly educated like men are, would not have to depend on marriage. While the best marriage should be between equals in all aspects: socially, economically, and politically, in the name of individual freedom against the patriarchal family.

Then, Perkins Gilman made a fundamental distinction between marriage and family, which she saw as "two institutions, not one, as is commonly supposed" (ibid, 213). She argued that people often confused "the natural result of marriage in children, common to all forms of sex-union, with the family, a purely social phenomenon" while marriage was recognized and ruled by social norms and by legislation, the family is a natural-social group, "aside from its connection with marriage" (ibid, 213). Nonetheless, instead of promoting the well-being of families, legislators had increasingly focused on norms aimed to regulate marriage and reinforce men's power by preventing women's role in the public sphere. Perkins Gilman also questioned the traditional gender division of labor within the family: she proposed moving household production to the market to benefit from greater specialization and economies of scale. This shift would enable women to choose their own work without being forced to cover traditional roles within families. Following the model of Hull House, she advocated for professionalizing housework and for creating communal living spaces with public kitchens.

Perkins Gilman's book *The Home* (1903b) targeted the cult of domesticity and the separation of spheres as one of the most pernicious aspects of society subjecting women to biases and prejudices and relegating them in a "sphere [which] is wholly in the home". She wrote:

[28] As retrieved on September 1, 2023 at: https://www.gutenberg.org/cache/epub/57913/pg57913-images.html.

> A larger womanhood, a civilized womanhood, specialized, broad-minded, working and caring for the public good *as well as the private*, will give us not only better homes, but homes more beautiful". And she continued: "Humanity *must* associate, that is the primal law of our being (…) Very woman was confined separately, in her private house, to her most separate and private duties and pleasures; and the duties and pleasures of social progress she was utterly denied" (Perkins Gilman, 1903b, 158).[29]

In her *Man-Mad World* (1911), Perkins Gilman blamed the social concept of marriage which she viewed as a "way of safeguarding motherhood; of ensuring 'support' and 'protection' to the wife and children" while only to men was given the chance "to learn the processes of constructive citizenship" by being committed to the public sphere, which was "for men only". Perkins Gilman viewed the separation between the private and public spheres as the application of biological categories to social constructs. She believed that social well-being did not depend on male and masculine values versus female and feminine values, which were elements of the state of nature, but instead required human values based on education and training aimed at increasing the level of social interconnection and cooperation. She wrote: "We are not merely male and female—all animals are that—our chief distinction is that of race, our humanness (…) human characteristics belong to genus homo alone; and are possessed by both sexes (…) Our trouble is that we have not recognized these human functions as such; but supposed them to be exclusively masculine" (Perkins Gilman, 1911, 97).[30]

Chicago economist Marion Talbot quoted Perkins Gilman in her *The Education of Women* (Talbot, 1910) emphasizing the necessity for husbands and wives to work together and share the same duties at home. She pointed out the essential role of urbanism in increasing women's access to education that, in turn, would enhance the well-being of society as a whole. Talbot fought against those who claimed that home was still a woman's sphere, by pointing out that the home has been dramatically

---

[29] As retrieved on September 1, 2023 at: https://www.gutenberg.org/files/44481/44481-h/44481-h.htm#II.

[30] As retrieved on September 1, 2023 at: https://www.gutenberg.org/cache/epub/3015/pg3015-images.html.

changed. She argued that happier individuals contribute to a happier home. Talbot promoted the role of women in the public sphere especially when they got involved in public school education that should be aimed to develop a sense of citizenship, provide knowledge of our present time, and ensure the welfare of children, rather than adhering rigidly to a fixed curriculum. Public schools should encourage gender equality in the marketplace, as well as subjectivity in learning process by overcoming traditional gender-biased education. Nevertheless, Talbot did not discard entirely the doctrine of the separate spheres: she acknowledged that the traditional household was becoming obsolete, but she also highlighted that the home would remain a place for most educated women to exert their influence on society. Talbot combined the notion of the 'new woman' and the traditional system in her book *The Modern Household* (1912), coauthored with her fellow economist S. Breckinridge. The book was an analysis of the best possible management of the house provided by educated women who are expected to deal with consumption, savings, and family income in an efficient way that minimized resource waste and promoted a suitable standard of living for the family. Talbot's ideal system paved the way to the development of home economics within academia (see Chapter 5).

Although influenced by Perkins Gilman, British economist Clara Collet was more aligned with Talbot in de-emphasizing the cult of femininity. Collet had previously written about marriage by presenting it as a condition where women were still "either slaves or rebels, but never loyal subjects" (Collet, 1892 [1910], 24) . History provided examples of marriages of intelligent women, but women of "brilliant intellect", such as "Hannah More, Jane Austen, Maria Edgeworth, Joanna Baillie, Caroline Herschell, Harriet Martineau", had made their mark on history as fulfilled and content women, despite remaining unmarried in order to pursue their vocations. By following Perkins Gilman, Collet depicted the new mother "inclined to look beyond her home for full scope for her powers when thus set free from maternal cares. And, given intelligence, length of years guarantees experience. They refuse to become decrepit and take to the sofa merely because their daughters are grown up, and fathers only require to be amused occasionally in the evening" (Collet, 1899 [1910], 111).[31]

By commenting Perkins Gilman's *Women and Economics*, Collet (1900 [1910]) summarized her critical assessments as follows: marriage was portrayed as an exchange where women secure their livelihood by attracting husbands with their sexual appeal, while men secure wives by providing for them financially. In this process "men have been developing humanity, women have been developing femininity, to the great moral detriment of both men and women" (Collet, 1900 [1910], 114). According to Collet, the separation of spheres can only be prevented by providing access to the public sphere to women, which means to allow them to be economically independent by performing paid work which remains compatible with the responsibilities of motherhood while domestic duties may be better performed by professionals.

Collet shared Perkins Gilman's critique of the notion of marriage as a business transaction, although she disagreed with the idea that feminine attraction was a detrimental tool. Furthermore, Collet did not share Perkins Gilman's reorganization of domestic arrangements. She wrote:

> [Although] I am far from maintaining that a married woman should not do paid work. (…) I see no reason for believing that either wife, husband, or children will be anything but worse off if the wife goes outside the home to earn a living; nor do I know of any skilled work for educated women, requiring daily assiduous attention for the whole day, in which maternity, or the possibility of maternity, would not be a drawback in the eyes of an experienced employer (ibid, 126).

4.3 The Economic Debate on Prostitution

The first echo of the discussion on prostitution arrived in the United States from Europe in the late eighteenth century, when Mary Ann Radcliffe published *The Female Advocate or an Attempt to Recover the*

[31] As retrieved on September 1, 2023, at: https://www.gutenberg.org/files/68623/68623-h/68623-h.htm#PROSPECTS_OF_MARRIAGE_FOR_WOMEN.

Rights of Women from Male Usurpation (1799) by pointing out that women were often forced into prostitution due to poverty and lack of respectable work. She wrote:

> How far the wife was intended to be the slave to her husband, I Know not, but certain we are … how often do we see her sinking under the burden of a household load, whilst the unfeeling husband is lavishing away the substance which ought to be for the comfort and support of the family? … Let us but look at the many unhappy females, who come to ruin through mercenary marriages. (Radcliff, 1799, 95)

During the nineteenth century, the economic and social elements of prostitution sparked a multifaceted debate among reformers. Prostitutes were in a unique position, acting as both owners of capital but also commodities; they served a public function yet were driven by self-interest. Two different approaches emerged: prostitution was seen either as a moral deficiency that might be erased only by an active moral campaign or as a consequence of economic and social misery that might be erased only when women would earn a living wage. In between, there were other explanation for prostitution, such as women's love for material goods or an 'easy way' to earn money. Libertarian Gertrude Kelly regarded prostitution as a form of labor due to the impossibility for women to get other jobs in the marketplace, oppressed by male stereotypes and hindered by charity, which she labeled as a form of hypocrisy (Kelly 1885). As she wrote: "we find all sorts of schemes for making men moral and women religious, but no scheme which proposes to give woman the fruits of her labor" (in McElroy, 2001, 165).

During the Progressive Era and especially later during interwar, social reformers, including economists, were deeply concerned about the issues of prostitution and alcoholism. These two phenomena were on the rise, particularly due to the rapid urban transformation. In fact, the combination of prostitution, alcoholism, and gambling were considered the three principal vices affecting the society, and their combination was defined the 'social evil'.[32] The debate over individual liberty versus the role of the

[32] Between 1920 and 1933, the Prohibition era occurred in the United States: the Eighteenth Amendment made the production, importation, transportation, and sale of alcohol illegal.

state in regulating prostitution and alcohol was central to the political discussion of the time (Thompson, 2000).

The support for alcohol prohibition, which was enforced in the United States between 1920 and 1933, was justified as a means to preserve the integrity of families. Men who frequently indulged in alcohol were often unable to work effectively and were at risk of losing their jobs. Consequently, families faced severe difficulties and even poverty, especially when husbands were the sole breadwinners.

In 1901, Colorado banned women from entering saloons and prevented them from buying alcohol and working in any place that sold alcohol. In fact, at that time, only entertainers and prostitutes were allowed to enter saloons. This law was not seen as oppressive but rather as a necessary measure to uphold good moral standards (Secrest, 2001). Several laws were intended to fight both prostitution and liquor (Kyvig, 1976). Nonetheless, bootlegging became a common activity for some women who made it a way to supplement their existing businesses like grocery stores or food stands (Murphy, 1994; Sanchez, 1998). Furthermore, many women fought against prohibition: for instance, in 1929, socialite Pauline Sabin founded the Women's Organization for National Prohibition Repeal.[33]

Opinions on the nature, the effects, and the remedies for social evil were discordant, although many reformers converged into viewing them intertwined with class, gender, and race. Especially alcoholism and women's sexuality were commonly connected reflecting a society that held women accountable when they entered the public sphere (Kenneth, 1995; Murdock, 1998). Race was a central element in the analysis of prostitution, which was often referred to as 'white slavery': although girls and women of any ethnicity could be forced into it, the main concern was with white women, mainly Southern Italians, Chinese, and

[33] During its first convention, held in Ohio in 1930, they expressed their opposition to the Eighteenth Amendment by pointing out that "any attempt to impose total abstinence by national government fiat ignores the truth that no law will be respected or can be enforced unless supported by the moral sense and common conscience of the communities affected by it" (Kyvig, 1979, 123).

Russian Jews. Moreover, Eastern European Jews and Chinese immigrants were usually singled out as pimps (Donovan, 2003, 2006).[34] However, the direct relationship between immigration and prostitution was a commonly held belief, albeit difficult to prove, as data of the time revealed.[35]

The debate on prostitution was steered by two assumptions: the necessity of an active legislation and the inseparability of the private and public spheres. Prostitution blurred the lines between private and public spheres by juxtaposing issues such as sex work and the low wages of female workers, venereal disease and sexual double standards, and the challenges faced by immigrants with immigration policies. The increased presence of women in the public sphere created significant tensions because it challenged the traditional notion that a woman's role was confined to childbearing and homemaking (Connelly 1980; Smolak, 2013). Anxieties about the place of women in the public sphere were further reinforced by the establishment of entertainment venues, dance halls, picture shows, and amusement parks, especially in big cities. These venues were often frequented by women who were adapting to new social settings, leading to evolving sexual norms and behaviors. Unlike middle and upper-class women, working-class women were more likely to exchange sexual favors for gifts and entertainment, a practice that was often stigmatized as prostitution (Donovan & Barnes-Brus, 2011).

Three main groups were active in the anti-prostitution movement and lobbied for the suppression of prostitution: Christians, physicians, and feminist social reformers. Christians considered prostitution, along with alcoholism and gambling as threats to the Christian home and family that could be corrected with moral education. Physicians were concerned about hygienic consequences such as venereal diseases and

[34] In 1910 the White-Slave Traffic Act passed: it was a federal law that criminalized not prostitution per se. i.e. voluntary sex-work, rather the transportation of "any woman or girl for the purpose of prostitution or debauchery, or for any other immoral purpose".

[35] Sanger (1895) surveyed 2000 prostitutes in New York: 35 percent were Irish, but at that time Irish immigrants were thirty percent of the population. In 1912, the NYC Bureau of Social Hygiene found that thirty percent of prostitutes were immigrants in a population of forty percent of immigrants. Thus, although immigrants were involved in prostitution, they did not represent the majority (Smolack, 2013).

used to support sex education and to promote a regulation of prostitution. They aimed to disrupt the 'conspiracy of silence' that shrouded public discussions about sexuality (Burnham, 1973). Feminist social reformers considered prostitution as a symbol of masculine political and social power.

Female reformers of the time adopted a double strategy. On one side, they used to approach prostitutes by offering maternal care and religious instruction, by applying the principles of true motherhhod. On the other side, they argued for eradicating drunkenness, which made their fathers and husbands violent and abusive, and provided sex education, as in the new woman's agenda. The concept of true womanhood implied a notion of sex as a tool for motherhood and for the well-being of the family and the nation, while the notion of the new woman was much more devoted to fighting venereal disease and eradicating pornography and prostitution. Reformers of both genders attempted to condemn the social evils of prostitution and alcohol by highlighting their detrimental effects on families and society through various means such as poems, articles, posters and speeches, songs, and films. While women's reform associations certainly censured prostitution, as a matter of fact, prostitutes frequently made a better wage than other working women: female brothel owners could make great sums of money, and many married women sometimes resorted to prostitution to supplement their family's income.

Economists of the time discussed prostitution, especially in relation to wage and minimum-wage legislation (see Sections 3.1 and 3.2). Some economists developed the 'parasites' thesis, based on the idea that employed people who got sub-living wages accepted either public or private charity and considered prostitution as an effect of sub-living wages (Seager, 1913). Against this vision, John Bates Clark emphasized the disemployment effects of minimum wages. He wrote:

> If five dollars a week forces persons into vice, no wages at all would do it more surely and quickly, and here is a further claim on the state which no one can for a moment dispute. And, if Seager were correct—that is, if higher income better protected a woman's virtue— what could one say about the effects upon morals of progressive proposals, such as

> hours' restrictions, that lowered women's income? Analytical inconsistency proved a small price for progressives to pay given the rhetorical power of their argument that labor legislation would protect young working women from temptation and moral turpitude. If the progressive case for sex-specific labor legislation was sometimes internally inconsistent, its different arguments all advanced the same claim: that society is better off when women are excluded from work for wages. (Clark, 1913, 294).

Some reformers targeted the 'white slave' traffic to immigrant women (Feldman, 1967). Campaigns against prostitution often depicted racial, ethnic, and class biases, as observed by Rosen (1982). Connelly (1980) argued that this anti-prostitution crusade, coupled with prejudices against new immigrants, was a reaction to women's increasing presence in the public sphere. D'Emilio and Freedman (1988) identified three key elements in the battle against prostitution during the Progressive Era: the double standard of sexuality, which upheld chastity for women and indulgence for men; the scapegoating of the sexual behavior of new immigrants; and the entrance of women into the public sphere, which led to a new approach to sexuality.

Inspired by her job as an obstetrical nurse on the Lower East Side of New York City, Margaret Sanger witnessed the combined effects of poverty, uncontrolled fertility, infant and maternal mortality, and deaths resulting from illegal abortions. This experience motivated her to dedicate herself to the cause of birth control and sex education. Between 1912 and 1917, she wrote numerous articles for the *New York Call*. In her *What Every Girl Should Know* (1917), she blamed the lack of sexual education as the major driver of prostitution.[36] She fought against the Comstock Act of 1873 that had made it illegal to publish, distribute, or possess obscene information, which encompassed details about medications or other methods of abortion and contraception. Sanger aligned herself with feminist reformers who sought to challenge the double standard of sexuality that produced the demand for prostitution.

---

36 Sanger was not immune of eugenics: she proposed the segregation and sterilization of feeble-minded groups and she linked birth control to reducing people of color (Washington, 2006).

Other social scientists, especially those affiliated with settlement houses were primarily concerned with exploring the causes of prostitution in order to eradicate it. Chicago economists and Hull House activists such as Sophonisba Breckenridge, Edith Abbott, Grace Abbott, and Katharine Davis extensively analyzed prostitution.

Davis conducted a comprehensive study on prostitution in New York City by collecting data to investigate the factors that led women to enter prostitution. Her work contributed significantly to what is now recognized as the field of economics and crime (Davis, 1929). She presented three main reasons for entering prostitution: familiar abuse, including parents and husbands forcing women to enter the sex market; personal moral fallacy; economic reasons including inability to work, low wages, and bad conditions in workplaces. Davis pointed out that prostitutes were often imprisoned for acts which were not as serious as other crimes. As a solution, she proposed implementing training programs in prisons that focused on skills like sewing, knitting, cooking, gardening, and other domestic tasks. These skills would provide inmates with the opportunity to find employment as domestic servants upon their release on parole (Bowler et al., 2013).

Nevertheless, Davis applied a double standard to white and black prostitutes. She directed most of her energy to regulating traditional gender norms and the sexual morality of white women and she excluded Black women. Due to racial stereotypes, black women were often considered as naturally inclined to be sexually promiscuous, therefore they were scapegoated for being corrupted and often precluded by programs in reformatories (Lilley et al., 2019).

Edith Abbott and Breckinridge (1912) presented the figure of 'immoral' girls with a bad reputation in the neighborhood, who used to go with bad companies and stay away at night, as the first step toward prostitution, by reiterating gender-stereotypical concerns regarding girls' sexual behavior and by presenting extramarital sexual behavior as deviant.

Grace Abbott (1917) was primarily concerned with immigrant girls victimized by white slavers. By showing data from the time, she pointed out that prostitutes were victims of poverty. She insisted that immigrants, girls of color, working girls, and girls from the countryside were most vulnerable and blameless as they engaged in prostitution to support their families.

With the only exception of Grace Abbott, Hull House reformers assumed weak moral resiliency as one of the elements leading to prostitution (Abrams, 2000). Nonetheless, they also recognized various social factors as contributing to prostitution, including the lack of work, low wages, poverty, the decline of family and community ties, and police corruption. Jane Addams presented both arguments. She echoed the moral weakness of prostitutes, albeit she explicitly explored economic factors such as low wages and factory working conditions, often downplayed by the moral standpoint (Addams, 1912). She wrote:

> although economic pressure as a reason for entering an illicit life has thus been brought out in court by the evidence in a surprising number of cases, there is no doubt that it is often exaggerated. A girl always prefers to think that economic pressure is the reason for her downfall, even when the immediate causes have been her love of pleasure, her desire for finery, or the influence of evil companions (Addams, 1912, 21).

Moreover, Addams seemed to be trapped by the exaltation of the domestic sphere when she stated: "the honest girl will live as a wife and mother, in contrast to the premature death of the woman in the illicit trade" (Addams, 1912, 29).

Besides moral and economic arguments, Addams introduced the lack of proper formal and sexual education for boys and girls as a contributing factor to the issue of prostitution. She was among the reformers who considered the fight against prostitution connected with the movement against alcoholism, based on the argument that under the influence of alcohol, girls are pushed into the sex market. Likewise, prostitutes usually solicit drinks in saloons. Addams also combined equal suffrage and the anti-prostitution movement, by insisting on maternalism. Thus, according to her, any step toward the public spheres by women, such as suffrage, would necessarily have a moralizing effect. Finally, Addams connected prostitution with an economic system that leads to inequality and exploitation by profit-seeking traffickers. Both Addams and G. Abbott expressed particular concern for the situation of women of color who were victims of a double enslavement. Though only Addams explicitly called for the abolition of prostitution by arguing that the historical continuity between white slavery and the enslavement of Black people compelled society to take action against prostitution.

4.4 Women of Color Between Gender and Race Stereotypes

Economists of the time did not deal specifically with women of color, rather they intensively wrote about people of color and women's entering the market force (see Chapter 3). Some economists of the Progressive era tended to be explicitly racist and implicitly chauvinist; influenced by eugenics they considered the willingness to properly work not equally distributed among 'races' by nature. Hence, they perpetuated some empirical studies in economic demography, aimed to point out the inferior quality of work done by people of color.

John Commons held the view that people of color were inherently inferior, which he used to justify the practice of slavery. He argued that their willingness to accept low wages was a result of their innate laziness (Commons, 1907). Statistician Frederick Hoffman's presented people of color as a limitation to the economic progress of the white race (Hoffman, 1896). Conversely, J. B. Clark (1891) rejected the argument of black inferiority and advocated for the extension of economic and political rights to people of color. Nonetheless, he wrote: "a part of the difficulty lies, probably, in the Ne**o's psychology; but that is not so deeply rooted that it cannot be eradicated. It is not, at any rate, permanently in the blood" (Clark, 1891, 95 as in Leonard, 2006).

In an address delivered before the American Social Science Association at Saratoga, on September 6, 1899, Cornell University economist and statistician Walter Willcox declared that people of color were much more inclined toward criminal behavior. He based this assertion on reports of inmates in American prisons, particularly in the South, where the population of people of color was substantial. He wrote:

> The causes may be grouped as defective family life, defective industrial equipment and ability in comparison with their competitors, increasing race solidarity among the ne***es, and increasing alienation from the whites. Southern whites often exaggerate the agency of Northern whites or Northern ne***es in causing the present condition, and thus minimize their own responsibility (Willcox 1899, 27).[37]

Eventually, Willcox did not take any account of the fact that crime was directly related to poor living conditions and that people of color's standard of living were inferior to white people's. Willcox's methods and claims were famously criticized by W. E. B. Du Bois who sought to demonstrate that people of color received an inferior education in the South, which disadvantaged them economically and reinforced prejudices that led to continued discrimination against them. Du Bois advocated for what is now known as cultural pluralism, i.e. the acknowledgment of peculiarity of different ethnicities. His attitude was reinforced by his empirical studies of people of color: he approached the issue of people of color as individuals rather than from a strictly racial perspective. As he wrote: "Ne**o problems are problems of human beings" (Du Bois, 1899, iv) by emphasizing the importance of the economic context and environment as well as the effect of discrimination as a factor inhibiting upward mobility and ambition. Moreover, he emphasized the role of prior conditions in shaping the economic capacities and performance of all workers, including people of color (Prasch, 2008).

As Pressman and Briggs (2020) pointed out, Du Bois proposed two solutions for the inequalities faced by people of color: enfranchisement and self-awareness, i.e. the request to be treated as equal with whites. In fact, as mentioned in Section 4.1, Du Bois was a fervent suffragist who explicitly linked the question of women's enfranchisement with the request of equal rights for people of (any) color. Thus, his activism was oriented in fighting against the double stereotypes associated with gender and race. Nonetheless, like other economists and reformers of the time, he did not pay any special attention to women of color.

---

[37] As retrieved on September 6. 2023 at: https://tile.loc.gov/storage-services/service/rbc/rbaapc/33600/33600.pdf.

As mentioned several times, the condition of belonging to a double minority made the path toward the public sphere more challenging for women of color compared to white women. Women of color were engaged in associational work more frequently than white women. Maria W. Stewart (1803–1879) was the first American woman who gave a memorable speech against slavery and chauvinism in September 1832, which is recorded as one of the first public speech by an American woman. In 1851, Sojourner Truth (1797–1883) delivered the well-known speech *Ain't I a Woman* to strongly denounce the double discrimination she was facing as a woman and as an African-American. She wrote:

> And ain't I a woman? I could work as much and eat as much as a man—when I could get it—and bear the lash as well! And ain't I a woman? I have borne thirteen children, and seen most all sold off to slavery, and when I cried out with my mother's grief, none but Jesus heard me! And ain't I a woman? Then they talk about this thing in the head; what's this they call it? [member of audience whispers, "intellect"] That's it, honey. What's that got to do with women's rights or Negroes' rights? If my cup won't hold but a pint, and yours holds a quart, wouldn't you be mean not to let me have my little half measure full?[38]

In 1833, the bi-racial Philadelphia Female Anti-Slavery Society (PFAS) was established in Philadelphia and included sisters Sarah and Angelina Grimké. Sarah Grimké published a series of letters to her sister Angelina in the *New England Spectator*, later collected under the title *Letters on the Equality of the Sexes* (1837) by complaining about the restrictions on the "miserably deficient" education imposed by the conservative American society on women "[who] are taught to regard marriage as the one thing needful, the only avenue to distinction and to spend their live investing in *fashionable* world". She specifically intertwined the situation of women of color and white women as a form of social degradation and moral injustice. She wrote:

[38] As retrieved on September 6, 2023, at: https://thehermitage.com/wp-content/uploads/2016/02/Sojourner-Truth_Aint-I-a-Woman_1851.pdf.

> There is another class of women in this country, to whom I cannot refer without feelings of the deepest shame and sorrow. I allude to our female slaves. Our southern cities are whelmed beneath a tide of pollution; the virtue of female slaves is wholly at the mercy of irresponsible tyrants, and women are bought and sold in our slave markets, to gratify the brutal lust of those who bear the name of Christians. In our slave states, if amid all her degradation and ignorance, a woman desires to preserve her virtue unsullied, she is either bribed or whipped into compliance, or if she dares resist her seducer, her life by the laws of some of the slave states may be, and has actually been, sacrificed to the fury of disappointed passion. Where such laws do not exist, the power which is necessarily vested in the master over his property leaves the defenseless slave entirely at his mercy, and the sufferings of some females on this account, both physical and mental, are intense.
>
> (...) Nor does the colored woman suffer alone: the moral purity of the white woman is deeply contaminated. In the daily habit of seeing the virtue of her enslaved sister sacrificed without hesitancy or remorse, she looks upon the crimes of seduction and illicit intercourse without horror, and although not personally involved in the guilt, she loses that value for innocence in her own, as well as the other sex, which is one of the strongest safeguards to virtue. She lives in habitual intercourse with men, whom she knows to be polluted by licentiousness.
>
> Can any American woman look at these scenes of shocking licentiousness and cruelty, and fold her hands in apathy, and say, 'I have nothing to do with slavery?' (Grimké, 1837, 51–54).[39]

In her *Letters,* Grimké's demonstrated the equality of the sexes by adopting a twofold religious argument. First, both males and females were created in the image of God. Second, God gave man and woman dominion over other creatures, but not over each other, being them created in perfect equality as they are companions.[40] Later on, she emphasized the importance of women's involvement in the political

39 As retrieved on September 6. 2023, at: http://www.worldculture.org/articles/12-Grimke%20Letters,%201-3.pdf.

40 Grimké assigned equal guilt to both Adam and Eve: after their expulsion from the Garden, they fell from innocence and happiness but not from equality. Gender equality can also be

arena and pointed out that marriage regarded as necessary and the ultimate fulfillment for women prevented women from being active in the public sphere. On one side, before getting married girls' major commitment was to attract men, while after marriage women used to lose individual responsibility and autonomy especially because the marriage laws destroyed women's independence and self-esteem. On the other side, men's attitude toward their wives led men to consider women as domestic comfort and physical pleasure. Moreover, women are often abused within marriages and forced into motherhood.

Nonetheless, Grimké was still under the influence of some gender biases, especially concerning chastity and morality. She did not approve of contraceptive devices that might encourage male promiscuity, instead she called for self-restraint to preserve 'sexual purity'. She did not support divorce and adhered to the cult of domesticity, based on considering the domestic sphere as a woman's special province by adopting a gynocentric position (Barlett, 1988).

In her dissertation on Grimké sisters, composed in the 1960s, Lerner (1988) presented Angelina as the heroine of antislavery, and Sarah as the heroine of early feminism. According to Lerner, Sarah regarded the exclusion of women from the public sphere as a major cause of women's low self-esteem. Laws, rules, and prejudices that separated married and unmarried women had affected women from a psychological point of view. Sarah also had the merit to introduce the notion of class by pointing out the different conditions of working women versus middle-class women. Nonetheless, Lerner also pointed out that Sarah believed in the superiority of women's culture.

Like their white counterparts, black women organized benevolent societies, often with religious affiliations. The leading African-American spokeswoman was Frances Harper. She served as the Superintendent of Colored Work in the Women's Christian Temperance Union (WCTU), which was the largest women's organization of the time (boasting over 175,000 members by 1900). The primary aim of the WCTU was to restrain men's use of alcohol, by preaching about the evils of alcohol and

---

found in the New Testament where it is stated that all are one in Jesus Christ regardless of their gender.

promoting actions in favor of children of alcoholics. Nonetheless, Harper made a great effort, particularly in the South, to prevent white women from blaming the bulk of alcohol abuse on African-American men. Despite her efforts and leadership, women of color were neither represented among the upper level of WCTU management nor by delegates at regional or national meetings.

The prevalence of racism within women's associations led prominent American women of color to establish their own clubs and organizations. This movement created networking opportunities and resulted in the founding of the Colored Women's League in 1892, as well as the National Federation of Afro-American Women in 1895. In 1896, the two associations merged to form the National Association of Colored Women (NACW), which adopted the motto 'Lifting as We Climb'. They viewed their movement as a means to uplift people of color, regardless of gender. In their fight for suffrage, they advocated not only for women's enfranchisement but also for men of color who were still disfranchised (Gray White, 1998).

Summing up, during the nineteenth century, middle-class women of color combined the doctrine of the separate spheres and the cult of true womanhood, supporting both. Meanwhile, they considered race and gender to be inseparable. In fact, women of color were equally involved in the antislavery movement and in the female suffrage movement. In the Progressive Era, things evolved: they moved beyond the doctrine of separate spheres by embracing the ideal of the 'new woman'. They transitioned from organizing private clubs to getting involved in municipal housekeeping; they organized or managed various homes and institutions, started hospitals and public health clinics, created employment services, and initiated programs to train kindergarten teachers and librarians, as white women did. Through their activism, they provided social services that were denied by some states, particularly in the South, and paved the way for improved treatment by local and state politicians, at least in the North.

Similar to white women of the time, separate female institutions boosted the self-esteem of women of color. These institutions introduced them to the public sphere and provided them with supportive circles of friends and coworkers. Many women of color were accustomed to depending on their own initiative, as they lived in a society that denied them access to politics, an equal legal system, and government support. For them, club work became their career and a means to achieve freedom from racial and gender prejudices.

References

Abbott, G. (1917). *The Immigrant and the Community*. Century Co.

Abbott, E., & Breckinridge, S. (1912). The Wage-Earning Woman and the State. A Reply to Miss Minnie Bronson. In *Committee for Woman Suffrage* (pp. 166–174). Boston Equal Suffrage Association for Good Government.

Abrams, L. S. (2000). Guardians of Virtue: The Social Reformers and the "Girl Problem", 1890–1920. *Social Service Review, 74*(3), 436–452.

Addams, J. (1912). *A New Conscience and an Ancient Evil*. Macmillan Co.

Addams, J. (1914). The Larger Aspects of the Woman's Movement. *Annals of the American Academy of Political and Social Science, 56*, 1–8.

Agger, E. (1911). The Antis Answered. *Woman Voter, 2*(9), 9–12.

Baker, J. (Ed.). (2002). *Votes for Women*. Oxford University Press.

Barlett, E. A. (1988). *Sarah Grimké. Letters on the Equality of the Sexes and Other Essays*. Yale University Press.

Beard, C. (1914). Woman Suffrage and Strategy. *New Republic*, 1(December 12), 22–23.

Becchio, G. (2020). *A History of Feminist and Gender Economics*. Routledge.

Becchio, G., & Fiorito, L. (2023). American Academic Male Economists and Women's Suffrage: Another Look at Progressive-Era (Il)Liberalism. *Review of Political Economy, 35*(4), 1162–1178.

Beecher, C. (1872). An Address on Female Suffrage. Delivered in the Music Hall of Boston, in December 1870. In C. Beecher (Ed.), *Woman's Profession as Mother and Educator with views in opposition to Woman Suffrage* (pp. 3–107). MacLean, Gibson, & Co.

Bordin, R. (1993). *Alice Freeman Palmer: The Evolution of a New Woman*. University of Michigan Press.

Bosanquet, H. (1906). *The Family*. Macmillan.

Bowler, A. E., Leon, C., & Lilley, T. (2013). What Shall We Do with the Young Prostitute? Reform Her or Neglect Her?: Domestication as Reform at the New York State Reformatory for Women at Bedford, 1901–1913. *Journal of Social History, 47*(2), 458–481.

Breckinridge, S. (1914). Political Equality for Women and Women's Wages. *Annals of the American Academy of Political and Social Science, 56*, 122–133.

Bronson, M. (1912). *The Wage-Earning Woman and the State*. Woman Patriot Publishing Co.
Buhle, M. J., & Buhle, P. (Eds.). (2005). *The Concise History of Woman Suffrage: Selections from the History of Woman Suffrage*. University of Illinois Press.
Burnham, J. C. (1973). The Progressive Era Revolution in American Attitudes toward Sex. *Journal of American History.*, *59*(4), 885–908.
Carver, T. N. (1918). *Women Suffrage from a Neutral Point of View*. Address Delivered at the Annual Meeting of the Cambridge Branch of the Women's Anti Suffrage Association of Massachusetts, May 13, 1918. A.T. Bliss.
Chaddock, R. (1911). The Antis Answered. *Woman Voter, 2*(9), 9–12.
Clark, J. B. (1891). The Industrial Future of the Ne**o. In I. C. Barrows (Ed.), *Second Mohonk Conference on the Ne**o Question* (pp. 93–101). George H. Ellis.
Clark, J. B. (1913). The Minimum Wage. *Atlantic Monthly, 112*, 289–297.
Collet, C. (1892 [1910]). Prospects of Marriage for Women. In *Educated Working Women*. P.S. King and Sons.
Collet, C. (1899 [1910]). The Age Limit for Women. In *Educated Working Women*. P.S. King and Sons.
Collet, C. (1900 [1910]). Mrs Stetson's Economic Ideal. In *Educated Working Women*. P.S. King and Sons.
Commons, J. (1907). *Races and Immigrants in America*. Chautauqua Press.
Connelly, M. (1980). *The Response to Prostitution in the Progressive Era*. University of North Carolina Press.
Corbin, C. (1909, April 15). Gentle Sex's Duty Lies in Home and Not in Political Realm. *Chicago Tribune*.
Davenport, H. (1916). *The Economics of Feminism. Herbert J. Davenport Papers*. State Historical Society of Missouri.
Davis, K. (1929). *Factors in the Sex Life of Twenty-Two Hundred Women*. Harper & Brothers.
Deegan, M. J. (2003). Katharine Bement Davis (1860–1935). *Women & Criminal Justice, 14*(2/3), 15–40.
D'Emilio, J., & Freedman, E. (1988). *Intimate Matters: A History of Sexuality in America*. Harper & Row Publishers.
Donovan, B. (2003). The Sexual Basis of Racial Formation: Anti-vice Activism and the Creation of the Twentieth-Century 'Color Line.' *Ethnic and Racial Studies, 26*(4), 707–727.
Donovan, B. (2006). *White Slave Crusades: Race, Gender, and Anti-vice Activism, 1887–1917*. University of Illinois Press.
Donovan, B., & Barnes-Brus, T. (2011). Narratives of Sexual Consent and Coercion: Forced Prostitution Trials in Progressive-Era New York City. *Law & Social Inquiry.*, *36*(3), 597–619.

DuBois, E. (1968). *Suffrage: Women's Long Battle for the Vote*. Simon & Schuster.
DuBois, E. (1975). The Radicalism of the Woman Suffrage Movement: Notes toward the Reconstruction of Nineteenth-Century Feminism. *Feminist Studies, 3*(1/2), 63–71.
DuBois, E. (1987). Outgrowing the Compact of the Fathers: Equal Rights, Woman Suffrage, and the United States Constitution, 1820–1878. *Journal of American History, 74*(3), 836–862.
Dubois, E., & Dumenil, L. (2005). *Through Women's Eyes: An American History with Documents*. Bedford/St. Martin's.
Du Bois, W. E. B. (1899). *The Philadelphia Ne**o: A Social Study*. Kraus-Thomson.
Du Bois, W. E. B. (1912a). Votes for Women. *Crisis, 4*(August), 182.
Du Bois, W. E. B. (1912b). Votes for Women. *Crisis, 4*(September), 234.
Eby, C. V. (2014). *Until Choice Do Us Part: Marriage Reform in the Progressive Era*. University of Chicago Press.
Elshtain, J. B. (1982[1998]). Antigone's Daughters. In A. Phillips (Ed.), *Feminism and Politics* (pp. 363–377). Oxford University Press.
Elshtain, J. B. (1989). Antigone's Daughters Reconsidered: Continuing Reflections on Women, Politics, and Power. In S. K. White (Ed.), *Life-World and Politics: Between Modernity and Postmodernity* (pp. 222–235). University of Notre Dame Press.
Ely, R. T. (1908). Economic Theory and Labor Legislation. *American Economic Association Quarterly*, 3rd Series 9(1), 124–153.
Ely, R. T. (1912, May 25). Ely Opposes Suffrage in Address Today. *Wisconsin State Journal*.
Engels F. (1884[1972]). *The Origin of the Family, Private Property, and the State*. Pathfinder Press.
Faulkner, C. (2019). *Unfaithful: Love, Adultery, and Marriage Reform in Nineteenth-Century America*. University of Pennsylvania Press.
Feldman, E. (1967). Prostitution, the Alien Woman and the Progressive Imagination, 1910–1915. *American Quarterly, 19*, 192–206.
Fisher, I. (1913, May 17). Unfair in Some Points. *The Woman's Journal*.
Fisher, I. (1916, August 27). Ten Reasons Why I Shall Vote for Wilson. *New York Times*.
Fisher, I. (1918, December 3). The Suffrage Amendment. *The Evening Post*.
Fitzpatrick, E. (1990). *Endless Crusade: Women Social Scientists and Progressive Reform*. Oxford University Press.

Gray White, D. (1998). *Too Heavy a Load: Black Women in Defense of Themselves, 1894–1994*. Norton.

Grimké, Sarah M. (1837). *Letters on the Equality of the Sexes and the Condition of Women,* Addressed to Mary S. Parker. Isaac Knapp.

Hansen, K. (1994). *A Very Social Time: Crafting Community in Antebellum New England*. University of California Press.

Hoffman, F. L. (1896). The Race Traits and Tendencies of the American Negro. *Publications of the American Economic Association, 11* (1–3):1–329.

Howard, J. (1982). Our Own Worst Enemies: Women Opposed to Woman Suffrage. *Journal of Sociology & Social Welfare, 9*(3), 463–474.

Howard, G. E. (1914). Changed Ideals and Status of the Family and the Public Activities of Women. *The Annals of the American Academy of Political and Social Science, 56*: 27-37.

Hutchinson, E. (1914). The Socializing Influence of the Ballot upon Women. *Annals of the American Academy of Political and Social Science, 56*, 105–110.

Jenks, J. (1907, October 25). No Suffrage for Women: So Says Professor Jenks in Third Lecture of Blumenthal Lecture. *Columbia Spectator*.

Jones, M. (2020). *Vanguard: How Black Women Broke Barriers, Won the Vote, and Insisted on Equality for All*. Basic Books.

Jordan, J., & Sharp, I. (2003). *Josephine Butler and the Prostitution Campaigns: Diseases of the Body Politic*. Routledge.

Kellor, F. (n.d.). *Cloisters in the American Politics*. Katherine S. Dreier Papers, Yale Collection of American Literature, Beinecke Rare Book and Manuscript Library, Yale University.

Kelly, G. B. (1885). The Root of Prostitution. *Liberty*. Vol. 66 (September 12).

Kenneth, R. (1995). *American Women and the Repeal of Prohibition*. New York University Press.

Kerber, L. (1988). Separate Spheres, Female Worlds, Woman's Place: The Rhetoric of Women's History. *The Journal of American History, 75*(1), 9–39.

Kha, H. (2021). *A History of Divorce Law*. Routledge.

Kirkby, D. (1987). The Wage-Earning Woman and the State. The National Women's Trade Union League and Protective Labor Legislation, 1903–1923. *Labor History*, 28(1), 54–74.

Kollontai, A. (1918 [1971]). The Autobiography of a Sexually Emancipated Communist Woman. *Iring Fetscher*.

Kraditor, A. (1981). *The Radical Persuasion, 1890–1917: Aspects of the Intellectual History and the Historiography of Three American Radical Organizations*. Louisiana State University Press.

Kyvig, D. (1976). Women Against Prohibition. *American Quarterly, 28*, 465–482.
Kyvig, D. (1979). *Repealing National Prohibition.* The University of Chicago Press.
Lamb, C. (1811). A Bachelor's Complaint of the Behaviour of Married People. *Essays of Elia (1823)* (pp. 144–397). Edward Moxon.
Ledger, S. (1997). *The New Woman: Fiction and Feminism at the Fin de Siecle.* Manchester University Press.
Leonard, T. (2006). American Progressivism and the Rise of the Economist as Expert. Available at https://ssrn.com/abstract=926635 or https://doi.org/10.2139/ssrn.926635
Lerner, G. (1969). The Lady and the Mill Girl: Changes in the Status of Women in the Age of Jackson. *Midcontinent American Studies Journal, 10*(1), 5–15.
Lerner, G. (1986). *The Creation of Patriarchy.* Oxford University Press.
Lerner, G. (1988). *The Feminist Thought of Sarah Grimkè.* Oxford University Press.
Lilley, T., Leon, C., & Bowler, A. (2019). The Same Old Arguments: Tropes of Race and Class in the History of Prostitution from the Progressive Era to the Present. *Social Justice*, 46(158), 31–52.
Marshall, S. (1986). In Defense of Separate Spheres: Class and Status Politics in the Antisuffrage Movement. *Social Forces, 65*(2), 327–351.
McElroy, W. (1992). *Freedom, Feminism, and the State.* Homes and Meier.
McElroy, W. (2001). *Individualist Feminism of the Nineteenth Century. Collected Writings and Biographical Profiles.* McFarland & Company.
Menchi, S. S., & Eisenach, E. (2016). *Marriage in Europe, 1400–1800.* University of Toronto Press.
Mitchell, W. C. (1915, February 11). *Why the Country Needs Women Voters. Talk for the Woman Political Union*, 663 Fifth Avenue. Wesley Clair Mitchell Papers. Rare Book and Manuscript Library, Columbia University.
Moehling, C., & Thomasson, M. (2020). Votes for Women: An Economic Perspective on Women's Enfranchisement. *Journal of Economic Perspectives, 34*(2), 3–23.
Morrow, J. (2000). Community, Class, and Bosanquet's New State. *History of Political Thought, 21*(3), 485–499.
Murdock, C. (1998). *Domesticating Drink: Women, Men, and Alcohol in America, 1870–1940.* Johns Hopkins University Press.
Murphy, M. (1994). Bootlegging Mothers and Drinking Daughters: Gender and Prohibition in Butte, Montana. *American Quarterly, 46*(2), 174–194.

Mussey, H. R. (1912). College Women and Suffrage. *The Woman Voter, 2*(1), 6–7.
Pattern, S. (1914). The Evolution of a New Woman. *Annals of the American Academy of Political and Social Science, 56*, 111–121.
Pattern, S. (1919). Making National Debts National Blessings. *Annals of the American Academy of Political and Social Science, 82*, 39–51.
Perkins Gilman, C. (1885, September 1). On Advertising for Marriage. *The Alpha* 11, p. 7.
Perkins Gilman, C. (1890 [1995]). The Unexpected. In R. Shulman (Ed.) *The Yellow Wall-Paper and Other Stories.* Oxford University Press, pp. 25–31.
Perkins Gilman, C. (1891a). An Extinct Angel. In R. Shulman (Ed.) *The Yellow Wall-Paper and Other Stories.* Oxford University Press, pp. 48–50.
Perkins Gilman, C. (1891b). The Giant Wistaria. In R. Shulman (Ed.) *The Yellow Wall-Paper and Other Stories.* Oxford University Press, pp. 39–47.
Perkins Gilman, C. (1892). The Yellow Wall-Paper. The New England Magazine. In C. Golden (Ed.), *The Captive Imagination: A Casebook on The Yellow Wallpaper* (pp. 211–241). Feminist Press, 1992.
Perkins Gilman, C. (1895). An Unnatural Mother. In *The Impress,* February 16, pp. 4–5. In R. Shulman (Ed.), *The Yellow Wall-Paper and Other Stories* (pp. 98–106). Oxford UP, 1995.
Perkins Gilman, C. (1898). *Women and Economics.* Small, Maynard and Co.
Perkins Gilman, C. (1903a). *Concerning Children.* Small, Maynard & Co.
Perkins Gilman, C. (1903b). *The Home*. The Cooperative Press.
Perkins Gilman, C. (1911). *Moving the Mountain. Serialized in The Forerunner*, Vol. 4.
Popenoe, P. B., & Johnson, R. H. (1918). *Applied Eugenics.* Macmillan.
Prasch, R. (2008). W. E. B. Du Bois's Contributions to U.S. Economic (1893–1910). *Du Bois Review: Social Science Research on Race*, 5(2), 309–324.
Pressman, S., & Briggs, T. (2020). W. E. B. Du Bois on Poverty and Racial Inequality. In G. Vallet (Ed.), *Inequalities and the Progressive Era* (pp. 224–237). Edward Elgar Publishing.
Robinson, J. H. (1914). *The Biological Argument Against Woman Suffrage*. The Empire State Campaign Committee.
Radcliffe, M. A. (1799). *The Female Advocate or an Attempt to Recover the Rights of Women from Male Usurpation.* Vernor and Hood.
Rosen, R. (1982). *The Lost Sisterhood: Prostitution in America 1900-1918*. John Hopkins University Press.
Rosenberg, R. (2004). *Changing the Subject: How the Women of Columbia Shaped the Way We Think About Sex and Politics*. Columbia University Press.

Sanchez, T. (1998). *The Feminine Side of Bootlegging: Women, Drink and Prohibition in New Orleans*. University of New Orleans Press.
Sanger, W. (1895). *The history of prostitution: Its extent, causes, and effects throughout the world*. American Medical Press.
Scott, A. (1991). *Natural Allies: Women's Associations in American History*. University of Illinois Press.
Seager, H. R. (1911). Why the Working Girl Should Vote. *Woman Voter, 2*(9), 7–8.
Seager, H. R. (1913). The Minimum Wage as Part of a Program for Social Reform. *Annals of the American Academy of Political and Social Science, 48*(July), 3–12.
Seager, H. R. (1914). The Antis Answered. *The Woman Voter 5*(4): 9–12.
Secrest, C. (2001). *Hell's Belles: Prostitution, Vice, and Crime in Early Denver: With a Biography of Sam Howe, Frontier Lawman*. University Press of Colorado.
Smith, I. (2003). The Law and Economics of Marriage Contracts. *Journal of Economic Surveys., 17*(2), 201–226.
Smolak, A. (2013). White Slavery, Whorehouse Riots, Venereal Disease, and Saving Women: Historical Context of Prostitution Interventions and Harm Reduction in New York City During the Progressive Era. *Social Work in Public Health, 28*(5), 496–508.
Sumner, H. (1909). *Equal Suffrage*. Harper & Brothers Publishers.
Talbot, M. (1910). *The Education of Women*. Chicago University Press.
Talbot, M., & Breckinridge, S. (1912). *The Modern Household*. Whitcomb and Barrows.
Thompson, V. (2000). *The Virtuous Marketplace. Women and Men. Money and Politics in Paris, 1830–1870*. The John Hopkins University Press.
Washington, H. (2006). *Medical Apartheid: The Dark History of Medical Experimentation on Black Americans from Colonial Times to the Present*. Anchor Book.
Willcox, W. (1899, September 6). *Ne**o Criminality*. An Address Delivered Before the American Social Science Association at Saratoga.
Wolfe, Al. B. (1913). Manhood Suffrage in the United States. In Mathews S. (Ed.), *The Woman Citizen's Library, Vol. 7: Woman Suffrage, 1687–1736*. The Civics Society.

Part II

The Doctrine of the Separate Spheres Between Rebirth and Rejection (1920s–early 2000s): Marriage Theory in Economics

5

Reviving the Doctrine of the Separate Spheres: The New Home Economics

In the history of economic thought, the term 'home economics' has been used to denote a specific research field that emerged in the United States around the early twentieth century and reached its apex during interwar especially thanks to the work of Chicago female economists who gathered around Marion Talbot, namely Margaret Reid, Elizabeth Hoyt, Hazel Kyrk. They established a further development of home economics, which has been known as 'household economics', a label which is still adopted by the official classification in academic economics.

Home economics, which was the rational management of the household, emphasized an extensive expertise in economic matters, aiming to shape families into ideal and efficient consumers. Intended in such terms, home economics should have been taught to girls who, according to the doctrine of the separate spheres, were ideally suited to become good wives and excellent mothers.

After decades of struggling for a new woman able to overcome the domestic sphere, the emergence of home economics reinforced the doctrine of the separate spheres bringing back women to the household. It is possible to affirm that the image of women within home economics was much more related to the nineteenth-century idea of

G. Becchio, *The Doctrine of the Separate Spheres in Political Economy and Economics*, Palgrave Studies in Classical Liberalism,
https://doi.org/10.1007/978-3-031-51262-9_5

'true womanhood' than to the idea of 'new woman'. In fact, home economics assumed that the division of roles between men and women in the family was more efficient than gender equality, given that women are much more inclined to take care of households than men. What home economics added to the traditional separation of roles was a more rational way of handling family consumption spending as well as the governance of the household.

In the United States, home economics developed a twofold paradoxical effect: on one side, it allowed women to enter academia as faculty members; on the other side, it separated them from the departments of economics (Becchio, 2020; Forget, 2011).

Household economics, which was the economic analysis of all decision makers within a family concerning consumption, savings, and allocation of time between labor and leisure, using their own capital and their own unpaid labor, stressed the centrality of the household production function as a possible substitute for the market. Household economists were focused on understanding consumer issues and working on consumer education in order to improve the national economy.

Like home economists, household economists reinvigorated the doctrine of the separate spheres for two reasons. First, household economists never questioned the role of women within the domestic sphere; second, their work and research had a huge impact on the emergence of the 'new home economics' which occurred in the 1970s, when Chicago economist Gary Becker applied his human capital theory to household economics by extending it to the economics of the family, albeit Becker never gave credit to Margaret Reid for the enormous impact her work had on him. Becker's 'new home economics', which has recently been referred to as 'new household economics' by some historians of economics (Bankovsky, 2020), epitomized the doctrine of the separate spheres within the discipline.

The term 'new home economics' was introduced by Chicago economist Marc Nerlove in 1974 in order to distinguish old home economists from Becker and his followers, including himself. While home economists considered non-economic factors as structural constraints faced by families and introduced in their analysis elements from psychology and other social sciences, new home economists *à la* Becker refused to embed non-economic elements in their optimization model and excluded any possible contributions provided by other disciplines.

Becker developed the new home economics by relying on the supposed natural and biological differences between men and women, while ignoring the enormous influence of social constructions and gendered stereotypes on individual choice. Hence, he justified the traditional division of labor within households and different educational investments for boys and girls as the natural consequences of gender-based biological distinctions. In doing so, Becker's new home economics represented a powerful endorsement of the doctrine of the separate spheres which, upon its resurgence, encouraged women, particularly married women, to conform to the housewife stereotype of the 1950s and 1960s.

Certainly, in the 1950s–1960s, housewives were no longer constrained by legal, social, and political inequality as their grandmothers were. Nevertheless, married women were invited to step back from the public sphere in order to better perform in their 'natural' private or domestic sphere. During this period, very few women worked after marriage; they usually stayed at home to raise children and manage the household. Men were traditionally considered breadwinners and responsible for handling financial matters such as mortgages, legal documents, and bank accounts. In case of a loveless or violent marriage, married women were trapped, without access to money and job. The rate of female college students dramatically dropped down, especially among lower-class women who went straight into the market place until they married. Secondary schools prepared girls for the role of housewives by providing classes in cookery, household management, sewing, and so forth.

Differently from what happened during the Progressive era in settlement houses, when these educational curricula were aimed to develop women's attitude to take care of themselves, to get them independent from a male figure, and eventually to create a sense of community among immigrants and between them and natives, in the 1950s and onward, they rather were aimed to bring back women into the domestic sphere as the only possible way for them to acquire a social status.

Becker's research on marriage and the economics of the family can be regarded as the best application of the doctrine of the separate spheres in economic theory (Becker, 1973, 1974, 1981 [1991]). From Becker's perspective, the theory of marriage seeks to explain the rationale behind the choice to marry and divorce, all the decisions related to the division of labor between spouses, and any other choice-related aspects of child-raising. Becker and his fellow new home economists explained the rationale behind the traditional institution of marriage, by applying the theory of competitive advantage to partners and by adopting the breadwinner/housewife model. Against Becker's marriage and family theory, feminist economics emerged in the 1970s by pointing out the methodological inadequacy as well as the inequality and unfairness of Becker's intra-house allocation, bargaining, and relationships that perpetuated women's discrimination due to gendered stereotypes and subordinated women into the domestic sphere (see Chapter 6). Simply put, following Becker, the doctrine of the separate spheres was efficient while following feminist economists it was inefficient and unfair.

5.1 The Cult of Domesticity Revised: Home Economics and Household Economics

As seen in Chapter 4, women reformers of the Progressive Era were engaged in social work that was largely considered a woman's profession under the assumption that women's domestic responsibilities could be extended to the realm of public societal management. Being active in social work secured women a professional niche in the public sphere (Becchio, 2020; Deegan, 1988; Fitzpatrick, 1990). Hence, social work became interconnected with the cult of domesticity, intended as a celebration of the home as the only safe harbor for individuals in the face of industrialization's dehumanizing effects. Both social work and the cult of domesticity were reserved to women. A similar process happened within academic economics departments where female professors tended to get a position in home economics departments where undergraduate courses were meant to provide fundamental knowledge about home ownership, child development, and sanitation, while graduate courses were designed to address the problems of the home and the household by integrating several existing disciplines as physics, chemistry, political economy, and sociology.

Pioneers of home economics in the nineteenth century in the United States strongly reinforced the doctrine of the separate spheres by considering motherhood as the focal point of domesticity. Sisters Catharine and Harriet Beecher reinforced the concept of 'true womanhood' by portraying the ideal woman as someone educated in the domestic economy. They emphasized that education in domestic life was primarily the responsibility of mothers and considered teaching an extension of women's domestic role (Beecher, 1841; Beecher & Beecher, 1870).

Home economics courses were focused on domestic science, i.e. a system of formal education about domestic matters intended as a way to educate good housewives. Graduates of home economics programs pursued careers in various fields, including industry or marketing; they also worked as dietitians in hospitals. Furthermore, home economics departments tested new products to get the 'woman's perspective' on their products. Although home economics addressed not only to housewives, but to both male and female institution managers and social workers, the home was described in feminine terms, while the market in masculine terms: "a new emphasis on domestic virtue, rather than domestic work, was rooted in genuine fears about the impact of a new emphasis on profits and personal gain that conflicted with traditional religious value" (Folbre, 1991, 466). Home economics′ program for children education was based on some fixed parameters aimed to develop "pupils′ appreciation for home and family life" (Whitcomb, 1929, 5) which have been targeted for boys and men too. Furthermore, all the curricula of home economics in junior and high schools offered a specific program in social relationship among family members which included questionnaires about affectivity and responsibility, money management, investments, and savings.

In 1899, Ellen Swallow Richards brought home economics to the forefront.[1] She organized the first Lake Placid Conference and founded the

[1] Richards was a chemist and the first woman admitted to the Massachusetts Institute of Technology. The Lake Placid Conferences took place regularly every year. In 1908, the conferees

American Home Economics Association (AHEA) in 1908 and its *Journal of Home Economics*, established in 1909. The label home economics was presented as:

> a general name, simply yet comprehensive enough to cover sanitation, cookery and kindred household arts, and instruction in the art or science of living from the kindergarten to the college was not an easy thing to find; (…) a title preferable for the whole general subject of economics; so that it should find a logical place in the college and university (p. 4).[2]

Differently from Beecher's emphasis on the cult of domesticity, Richards emphasized the application of scientific knowledge to the activities within the domestic sphere, a perspective that would later have a profound impact on Chicago economist Marion Talbot.

During the first two decades of the twentieth century, home economics spread up within universities and colleges in the United States. During interwar, it gained a central place as a prominent research field in some economic departments. Home economics movement created a formidable chance of getting an academic position for many women economists who worked on labor economics and social issues. They seized these new opportunities by working on statistics at a time when the economic profession was itself moving towards applied research. Women economists of the time faced a choice. On one side, they could enter well-established universities, where they could teach economic theory but still encountered significant gender discrimination, such as the gender wage gap and the glass ceiling. On the other side, they could join new home economics departments where they faced less competition from male colleagues or work in high schools and primary schools, where they could more easily secure extra funds for independent research projects. As Forget (2011) claimed, many women preferred the second option.

---

funded the American Home Economics Association (AHEA) to make home economics available in primary, junior, and high school curricula, and to fundraise the expansion of the discipline. Richards was elected as the first president.

[2] Quotations are retrieved by the website of the journal: http://hearth.library.cornell.edu.

The initial emphasis on social work, which had characterized the birthing of home economics, disappeared over the decades: during interwar it was substituted by an education, limited and reduced to receipts and commercials, mainly targeted on women. From the 1950s onwards, home economics curricula definitely deviated from scholarly economics.

During interwar household economics emerged as a new research field that dealt with production of goods and services (accommodation, meals, clean clothes, and child care) provided by household members, for their own consumption, by using their own capital and their own unpaid labor. The headquarters of household economics was the University of Chicago, where a group of women economists, Marion Talbot, Hazel Kyrk, Margaret Reid, and Elizabeth Hoyt, introduced and developed the field.[3]

Marion Talbot played and emblematic role in the transition from home economics to household economics within the discipline. She was involved in both the development of home economics within academia and the promotion of household economics. As mentioned, Talbot got inspired by Richards, who was a family friend, with whom she co-edited *Home Sanitation: A Manual for Housekeepers* (1887). In their work, they applied home economics' methods to the field of housekeeping. In 1892, Talbot accepted a position as assistant professor of sanitary science in the department of social science and anthropology at the University of Chicago where, in 1905, she became full professor in the newly founded department of household administration.[4]

In her publications coauthored with Breckinridge (see Chapter 4), she transitioned from a traditional attitude about the domestic sphere to a more progressive perspective. Talbot considered the home as a highly influential place for women to get their voice on society. She regarded the traditional household, where women played passive roles in economic decisions, as outdated. She promoted research on progressive models of

[3] As described by Folbre, the "Chicago case" was a special result of "unusual circumstances, exceptional faculty, and carefully planned collective action" (Folbre, 1998, 37).

[4] Appointed dean of women, Talbot was responsible for the living conditions of the female students. She developed a system of dormitories organized as residential clubs with a self-organized hospitality program and a clubhouse with exercise facilities (James, 1971).

efficiency and scientific management, along with the application of the new technology of the time, to domestic work. She intended curricula and courses for both men and women "as a means of liberal culture, a general view of the place of the household in society, to train men and women for the rational and scientific administration of the home as a social unit" (Talbot, 1936, 149).

Being concerned that home economics would become a female academic ghetto if scientific standards were not upheld, she promoted a more scientific approach to the field. As she wrote:

> The home was rapidly becoming a consuming, rather than a producing, center. This called for less study of methods of domestic manufacturing and more study of those industrial and governmental institutions through whose agency the householder is enabled to care more effectively for her family and household (Talbot, 1936, 152).

Her concern was correct: after her retirement, home economics department was moved from the School of Economics to the School of Education, a process that happened everywhere in the following years (Gillen, 1990). Furthermore, home economics became a neglected field in the history of economics and only recently it has been included into scholars' attention (Bankovsky, 2020; Becchio, 2020; Forget, 2011; Goldstein, 2012; Hirschfeld, 1997; Le Tollec, 2020; Philippy, 2021; Trezzini, 2016).

The transition from home economics intended as the application of a scientific knowledge to domestic matters to a research on efficient family's consumption, i. e. rational consumption, specifically household economics, was partially anticipated by Talbot and Richards, and finally developed by Hazel Kyrk.[5] Kyrk mentored a generation of women, including Margaret Reid and Elizabeth Hoyt: most of them moved between the disciplines of economics and home economics and between government employment and academic appointments as opportunities arose. Reid and Hoyt mentored, in turn, another generation of women,

[5] As rightly pointed out by Philippy (2021), the concept of consumption was central to home economists believing that economics of the time was not properly addressing the issue.

at the University of Chicago as well as at the Iowa State University (Thorne, 1995, 2000).

Founders of household economics focused their attention on family's consumption and its demand curve, behind which unpaid domestic labor stands as an input. They were, especially Hazel Kyrk, mainly influenced by Simon Patten's analysis of consumption (1889), by Thorsten Veblen's theory of conspicuous consumption (1899), and by John Dewey's idea that domestic education was a means for children to develop social interaction and cooperation (1900).[6]

Against the idea of home economics intended as a specialized knowledge about food, clothing, and the household management, Kyrk redefined the nature of home economics as a research field focused on family well-being. Kyrk's first book (1923) dealt with the notion of economic and ethical waste: economic waste results from the inefficient use of productive resources, while ethical waste consists in a misallocation of resources.[7] According to Kyrk, welfare economics should take account of these two related aspects in order to prevent inefficiency, which results from providing unnecessary goods, and unfairness, which results from giving away benefits to people who do not need them, or vice versa.

Following Veblen's ideas, Kyrk affirmed that wastes are the results of social costs associated with using productive resources for luxury and from an unfair distribution. Although Kyrk did not provide any specific recommendation to avoid wastes, she insisted on the role of education in guiding consumers towards a more balanced approach to consumption, akin to Dewey's educational model. Differently from previous home economists, who were much more focused on developing an educational program tailored to girls and women bounded to be perfect wives, Kyrk stressed the significance of exploring the consumption side of

6 From 1896 to 1903, Dewey ran the University of Chicago Lab. School. Dewey's educational program, based on moral responsibility and personal enrichment intended as the final goals of individual life, inspired the home economic movement as a whole, and especially the moral vision behind Kyrk's theory of welfare system (Trentmann, 2012).

7 Kyrk's book was reviewed in *The Quarterly Journal of Economics* by Clara Dickinson (1927). Dickinson criticized Kyrk's thesis, categorizing it as an institutional economic work that could not advance beyond consumption economics. She considered it an example of "sociological economics" based more on a "psychological theory of value" rather than on an "experimental psychology, applied to inductions on concrete quantitative data" (Dickinson, 1927, 343–344).

economics *per se*. She rejected the stereotype of female consumers as primarily emotional, and the marginal utility theory's emphasis upon individual's preferences, Kyrk pointed out the importance of endogenous preferences and the influence of social factors in decision-making process. Finally, she considered maximizing behavior a good assumption for firms, but not for households.[8]

In her following books (1929; 1933) Kyrk applied her analysis of waste to the standard of living of American families in order to define family consumption and to improve it. The two books merged in Kyrk's last publication (1953). Against the individualistic approach, Kyrk claimed that the family was a self-reliant social unit that was shaped in the system of claims, obligations, and mutual responsibilities among its members. In her view, despite the reduced significance of the family as a productive entity, it remained the principal consumer entity. She also insisted on the different social role of men and women and on the peculiarity of the economic status of women able to create use value. She wrote:

> The division of labor between men and women today takes the form of a concentration of the former upon gainful employment and of the latter upon non-gainful. The result is an economic status for the latter that in many ways is in the market contrast to that of other workers. Here is a group producing for use and not for profit, whose incentive to efficiency and effort is not financially reward, and whose returns are largely the health and happiness of others. In a world engaged in creating exchange values these workers are crating use values (Kyrk, 1953, 275).

And she continued:

> It is conjugal status, not competition, that places workers in this field. Their skills do not affect their outcome. It is the money-making power of the men these workers marry that determines whether they have the place and privileges of the rich or the limitations of the poor, not the competence with which they meet their responsibilities (Kyrk, 1953, 276).

[8] As Hirschfeld (1997) and Velzen (2003) pointed out, Kyrk's work anticipated today's feminist economics' critique of the neoclassical assumption of maximization in a value-free framework.

According to Kyrk, the 'vocational divide' in the working life of women and men was further reinforced by marriage. In fact, women usually worked until marriage while men never get acquainted with the skills and responsibilities of household and childcare.

Differently from the past, women were no longer regarded as 'ornaments of the home', rather as the general managers of the household. Nonetheless, Kyrk pointed out the obsolete negative perception regarding the employment of married women, based on a twofold assumption. First, their employment meant neglect of family responsibilities and could lead to disharmony between husbands and wives. Second, their employment deprived a man of a job or depressed men's wages since they were considered supplementary workers. Hence, she pleaded for a more equitable distribution of household responsibilities between genders.

Elizabeth Hoyt adopted an ethical argument, based on a careful use of resource, in order to describe family consumption: her first publication dealt with exchange based on trust rather than profits (Hoyt, 1926), while in her 1950 book she focused on the ethics of consumption. In Hoyt's theory, consumption included not only goods and services, but also the future use of economic resources in the service of consumption. Differently from Kyrk, she did not directly deal with the environmental consequences of consumption by providing a normative standard of consumption, rather with the 'economic awareness and economic planning' of resources for the future without any normative intent.

In her works, Hoyt often used anthropological examples to explain several factors: the role of consumption within the exchange system; the maximization of satisfaction; exchange and other forms of economic relations, such as integration, which are useful to understand economic systems in different cultures. According to Hoyt, there were six basic human interests differently developed in different cultures. Two primary interests (sensory and social) are universally shared; four secondary interests (intellectual, technological, aesthetic, and empathetic) exist in all cultures albeit in different forms. In fact, each culture is typically dominated by one of these secondary interests. For instance, in the Western society, dominated by technological interests, the division of labor between men and women is driven by technological interests that make women more focused on household management and men on competition in the market place (Hoyt, 1928, 1938).

Although in a different way, both Hoyt and Kyrk were embedded in the doctrine of the separate spheres: they insisted on the role of women as heads of their household and on their agency in making decision about the overall well-being of the family as a whole, particularly in the decision-making process related to family consumption.

The economic approach of Margaret Reid was different from that of Kyrk and Hoyt. Reid, who earned her Ph.D. under Kyrk's supervision, was much more focused on isolating economic theory from any extra-economic factor as well as on applying the concept of opportunity cost to the unpaid activities within household production as alternatives to market employment.[9] Moreover, differently from Kyrk and Hoyt, Reid did not assume any ethical stance about the standard of living within the family.

Reid's investigation of the household as an economic supplier agent in competition with the market as well as her distance from any normative approach paved the way to the 'new home economics' later developed by Becker whose analysis of the household was initially centered on the provision of goods and services able to substitute those produced by market.[10] Differently from Becker's endorsement of the traditional division of labor between men and women, Reid emphasized the neglected role of women in the market force and in the national economy as well as the devaluation of their unpaid labor within households (Reid, 1934, 1938).

After clarifying that household production encompasses all unpaid activities within a household, Reid attempted to quantify the economic

[9] Reid considered four alternative methods of valuing household activities: opportunity cost (a measure of the value of the potential earnings foregone because of time spent on household production); retail price (an attempt to estimate value-added by household production by subtracting the cost of purchased inputs from the prices of market substitutes); working costs of hiring someone for household production; the boarding service cost provided in a boarding house (Reid, 1943).

[10] She also inspired Theodore Schultz, Milton Friedman, and Franco Modigliani. Friedman paid homage to Reid in 1957; while Modigliani cited Reid in his Nobel lecture (1985) (Forget, 2022).

value of women's housework. She emphasized that their role in household production was even more significant when considering that many tasks could have been outsourced to paid workers but were instead carried out by wives and mothers. This situation often compelled them to forego the opportunity of higher-paying jobs outside the household (Reid, 1943). Her critical perspective on unpaid labor has been seen as an early expression of feminist economics' critique of Becker's approach to gender issues (Folbre, 1996; Hara, 2016; Yi, 1996).

Despite different nuances in their perspectives, the founders of household economics never fully departed from the doctrine of the separate spheres and accepted the traditional relegation of women to the domestic sphere. While women were no longer subjected to the arbitrary power of their male counterparts, and could take the lead of the household by orienting family consuming, they remained constrained into their traditional role of wives and mothers (Walker, 2003). The analytical framework of household economics opened the gate to the development of standard economics applied to gender issues and the economics of the family *à la* Becker: a step forward for the discipline, maybe a step backward for women.

5.2 Marriage Theory in Becker's New Home Economics: Combining Human Capital and Labor Economics

New home (or household) economics (NHE) emerged in the 1970s when Chicago economist Gary Becker applied human capital theory, which had been introduced a decade earlier by Jacob Mincer, Theodor Schultz, and Becker himself, to the study of family dynamics.

In the 1960s Jacob Mincer and Gary Becker worked together at Columbia University and at the National Bureau of Economic Research, both located in New York City, on labor economics: their research, mainly focused on empirical work, adopted neoclassical microeconomics by emphasizing human capital as the core of labor economics. Human capital, introduced by Mincer (1958), Schultz (1961), and Becker

(1962), encompasses the various factors that compose the quality of labor including workers' physical health, skill level, education, and so forth.

In standard economics, as earlier formalized by Philip Wicksteed (1894) and J.B. Clark (1899), an incremental increase of an output is the effect of the incremental increase of its own input, whether it is capital or labor. Thus, a capitalist earns more than a worker because an additional unit of capital adds more to output than an additional unit of labor. Mincer, Schultz, and Becker extended this reasoning to understanding personal income distribution that is supposed to depend on productivity, which is directly related to the accumulation of human capital. Consequently, differences in wages among workers were explained by variations in their human capital. Therefore, the human capital approach, which soon became dominant, provided a rationale for men earning more than women since an additional unit of male labor was believed to contribute more to output than an additional unit of female labor. Human capital economists applied the same rationale to explain various other forms of inequality or discrimination, whether based on race (e.g., workers of color) or social status (e.g., immigrants).[11]

Here lies the first critical issue of human capital theory: even assuming a direct relationship between the accumulation of human capital, high productivity, and high income, human capital theorists did not problematize the underlying reasons for disparities in the accumulation of human capital, often taking these differences for granted as if they were entirely natural.

Furthermore, there is no inherent explanation for assuming that men (or white people) are naturally able to accumulate a greater amount of human capital than women (or people of color). Rather, the origin of different human capital accumulation should be likely found in power relations based on forms of oppression, such as patriarchy and slavery.

Becker initially followed Schultz, by emphasizing that human capital accumulation was a result of adult people's self-investment (Becker,

[11] Against Wicksell and Fisher, Pareto (1896) pointed out that income was more unequally distributed than human capital because income does not depend only on productivity, rather it is an effect of having the power of controlling resources, which is related to the notion of elites, a matter of sociology rather than economics.

1964); therefore, by following Mincer′s human capital model, he shifted his attention from individuals to families.

Schultz himself was influenced by Becker's application to human capital theory to family issues: in 1974, Schultz edited a book, *Economics of the Family: Marriage, Children, and Human Capital*, which included Becker's first formulation of marriage theory. Schultz described the family as a decision-making unit regarding household production. He intended the economics of the family as an application of the theory of the firm by assuming that the well-being of each family member is integrated into a "unified family welfare function, that there are overheads, and that shadow (nonmarket) prices play an important role in the family's producer and consumer activities, including the bearing and rearing of children" (Schultz, 1974, 8).

Differently from Becker's attitude, Schultz expressed his concern about the application of human capital to education and fertility without including cultural purposes in the model. Yet, he explained that fertility, from an analytic perspective, depends on the preferences of parents. These preferences are limited by the resources available to the parents and the alternative economic opportunities they face. The model took into account factors such as birth control, infant mortality, the health of the parents, and their income and wages. It operated under the "postulate that parents respond to economic considerations in the children they bear and rear and that parents equate the marginal sacrifices and satisfactions, including the productive services they expect from children, in arriving at the value of children to them" (Schultz, 1974, 5).

Schultz's main concern was to make economic theory advanced by applying the notion of investments in human capital to family behavior, in order to provide a theory able to include consumer choice and decisions related to household production. In this model, children are considered a form of human capital investment, i.e. certain expenditures made "to create productive stocks, embodied in human beings that provide services over future periods" (ibid.). This theory is related with Becker's analysis of human time in allocative decisions within a nonmarket framework (Becker, 1965).

Schultz underlined that predominantly the housewife allocates her time in two activities: the choice of consumer goods to be used in the household production (as in Margaret Reid's household economics) and the responsibility for child care, a highly labor-intensive activity which typically relies on mothers only. Thus, according to Schultz, it must be clarified the relation between mothers' human capital and the value of their time while caring for children. In fact, Schultz continued, the education of mothers affects their productivity in the household, including their ability to rear children. He also presented empirical evidence, highlighting the following key points: the most significant cost of having a child, or additional children, is the price of the mother's time, particularly during the early years of each child when more time is needed from mothers; there is a substitution effect between the quality and the quantity (number) of children; investments in the quality of children are directly related to family income; additional schooling for mothers with lower levels of education has a substantial negative impact on family fertility; the response to a better and cheaper contraception can be scrutinized by economic analysis.

In response to critics who believed that this approach could potentially destroy traditional family structures, Schultz answered that, *au contraire*, they were "enriching the role of the family as it is envisioned in the new home economics" (Schultz, 1974, 11). And he was absolutely right: the family envisioned by the new home economics resembled the image of the family that implied a complete acceptance of the traditional division of roles between men and women, with women being regarded as the primary economic agents within the domestic sphere.

Economist Arleen Leibowitz was a student of Mincer's and contributed to Schultz's volume with a chapter on the allocative effect of education in the household (Leibwitz 1974a), later developed in other papers (Leibowitz, 1974b, 1975, 1976, 1977). She played an important role during the early 1970s in the passage from household economics to the new home economics. She pointed out that education has a non-neutral effect of raising the productivity of labor market time more than that of time spent in home production. Thus education pushes women away from the domestic sphere, albeit married women are less likely to enter the labor-force, especially if their husbands have high incomes. However, Leibowitz claimed that human capital investments of women are worthy because education has a positive correlation with the quantity of time devoted to children. This could be due to the fact that more educated mothers either have fewer children or spend more time with each individual child. She clearly specified that while a husband's time can be a substitute for the wife's in meal preparation, the same cannot be said for providing 'physical care' for children. She wrote:

> The significantly positive coefficient on husband's time inputs indicates that for each ten minutes the husband spends in physical care, the wife puts in an additional four minutes. This is not merely an indication of the family's tastes (since these are controlled for by the 'preference' variable), but may indicate true complementarity - increased inputs of husband's time increasing the marginal productivity of the wife's time inputs (Leibovitz, 1974b, 247).[12]

Hence, neither Schultz nor Leibowitz ever questioned the doctrine of the separate spheres, which was totally embedded in their economic framework.

Jacob Mincer played a crucial role in interconnecting human capital and family issues: while studying consumption behavior, he established a negative relationship between the fertility's rate and parents' wages in terms of the opportunity cost of time and he considered the family as the unit of analysis. Additionally, when studying women's labor supply he considered human capital accumulated at home at a pre-school stage (Mincer, 1962, 1963).

In line with Chicago trained economist Glen Cain's work (1966), Mincer focused his research on determining the supply of married women labor. Both of them considered the relationship between the potential earnings of women and the actual earnings of their husbands: they explained the apparent contradiction that the participation rate of married females increased along with the increased earning power of their husbands. They utilized the standard economics model of an individual's labor supply curve, taking into account the income effect (the push-effect resulting from changes in the husband's earnings) and the substitution

[12] As retrieved on September 12, 2023 at: https://www.nber.org/system/files/working_papers/w0027/w0027.pdf.

effect (the pull-effect resulting from changes in the wife's earnings). They argued that the increased labor-force participation of married women was a reflection of their enhanced earning potential, and this effect overshadowed the negative influence of increasing male incomes on female participation rates.

Differently from economists who adopted the overcrowding model, arguing that women, denied entry into many professions, were crowded into unskilled occupations, Mincer analyzed gender discrimination by assuming perfect competition in the labor market, similar to what Becker later did.

The application of Mincer's human capital theory to women's labor supply implied that their traditional low income was based on their natural low productivity, rooted on their low endowment of human capital. Nonetheless, this explanation failed to consider the reality that individual productivity varies among individuals, regardless of their gender, even when their human capital endowment is similar. This productivity cannot be objectively measured unless we accept the *ceteris paribus* assumption, which can lead to unrealistic conclusions. Furthermore, human capital economists put forth a static conception of human capital, while the process of education and skill development is dynamic. In fact, workers who have historically been less educated, such as women over the years, could significantly enhance their skills through proper training. Moreover, a theory should not disregard the origins of the initial disparities in human capital. Human capital theorists, in this regard, fell short by attributing these differences to biological factors rather than recognizing the impact of legal restrictions, cultural biases, and personal constraints. These factors can have a profound effect on individuals who are inherently considered less valuable in terms of human capital, like women or people of color, compared to individuals traditionally perceived as having greater human capital value, such as men.

Mincer's approach was mainly adopted by Becker, who, in 1968 left Columbia to accept a position at the University of Chicago, where he transformed the long-established tradition of household economics into his new home economics (Grossbard, 1993, 2001, 2006).[13]

At the University of Chicago, Becker introduced the 'price theory of marriage' by combining his previous research on human capital (Becker, 1962) and on the allocation of time (Becker, 1965). In Becker's research on human capital, he had provided "a unified and powerful theory" of human capital by placing new emphasis on intangible resources and the trade-off between the alternative uses of time, in order to understand the inequality of income among people. Becker wrote: "women spend less time in the labor force than men and, therefore, have less incentive to invest in market skill" (Becker, 1962, 38). In his research on the allocation of time, Becker assumed that households produce commodities by combining goods and time according to the traditional theory of the firm, based on the minimization of costs. He reinforced Mincer's concept of the substitution effect for married women between housework and labor-force participation by comparing women's time to the poor, children, the unemployed, etc., who "would be more willing to spend their time in a queue or otherwise ferreting out rationed goods than would high-earning males" (Becker, 1965, 316).

In his first article on marriage theory (1973) Becker used human capital theory to explain how households sort breadwinners from homemakers and to define "marriage market in equilibrium". He presented the trade-off between getting married and remaining single dependent positively on spouses' income, human capital, and differences in wage rates. He claimed that, as marriage is a voluntary act, people get married when the utility function for both M (the male partner) and F (the female partner) of being in wedlock is higher of their utility function as unmarried: "the gain is shown to be related to the' complementarity' of their time, goods, and other inputs used in household production" (Becker, 1973, 815).

Among household-produced commodities, Becker included quality of meals, quantity and quality of children, prestige, companionship, love, and health issues. He assumed that all of them could be aggregated in a

13 As Grossbard wrote: "what Mincer and Becker did was to import the tools of microeconomic and econometric analysis, which had been developed in the context of firms, in order to model home-based decisions" (Grossbard, 2001, 105).

single aggregate utility function, with constant returns to scale, used in the same proportion. According to Becker, both M and F increase their utility function because they are neither perfect substituted nor their household commodities, such as love and children, are perfect substitutes in the market. In Becker's terms "complementarity and substitution [are] the major source of the gain of marriage" (ibid, 819).

He wrote:

> the marriage market acts as if it maximizes not the gain from marriage compared to remaining single for any particular marriage, but the average gain over all marriages. A marriage is a two-person firm with either member being the 'entrepreneur' who 'hires' the other at the 'salary' m_1 or f_1, and receives residual profits [and] optimal sorting enables each 'entrepreneur' to maximize 'profits' to given 'salaries' (Becker, 1973, 825).

Several critical points made Becker's model problematic. From a technical point of view, Becker combined two people's utility function in one function; from a cultural point of view, some may be disturbed to consider children and love as commodities, and marriage as a matter of utilitarian calculus. Both concerns, and many more, had been intensively pointed out by feminist economists who criticized Becker's model (see Chapter 6).

Nonetheless, if we remain focused on whether or not Becker's contribution reinforced the doctrine of the separate spheres, we may admit that in the first part of his 1973 article no gender discrimination appears. Though, in the second part of his article, Becker introduced the concept of human capital to highlight men's superior endowment and to justify women's low wages. In doing so, Becker revitalized the family wage theory and identified family roles in a traditional way: he considered the husband as an entrepreneur who hired his wife whose "education is a proxy for traits affecting her non-market productivity". Furthermore, he added that "women with higher nonmarket productivity merry men with higher earning power" (ibid, 834). This further assumption was precisely a reinforcement of the doctrine of the separate spheres: women's nonmarket productivity refers to women's time spent at home by taking care of the family. In Becker's vision, the perfect complementarity stays in this image of the traditional family with a male breadwinner and a female care-provider, without taking any account of why human capital accumulated by men and women was different in terms of quality.

In his second paper on marriage (1974), Becker applied the theory of comparative advantage to explain the division of labor between partners. He expanded his analysis by including caring between mates, polygamy, mate selection, divorce, and remarriage. According to Becker, love between two persons increases their chances of an optimal sorting "because love raises commodity output and caring raises their total income by making part of their output a 'family' commodity" (Becker, 1974, S15). He noted that polygamy tends to be more common among successful men when it is permitted. He also observed that individuals with similar income levels are more likely to marry each other, resulting in the continuation of family income patterns. Additionally, Becker explained that decisions regarding separation and divorce are influenced by incentives and cost–benefit considerations. The incentive to separate or divorce becomes stronger when a person believes that their marriage was a significant "mistake large enough to outweigh the loss in marriage-specific capital" (ibid, S24).

Expanding Becker's economic analysis of divorce, Becker et al. (1977) connected divorce with the rise in women's labor-force participation rates and the fall in fertility rates. They considered child-raising and working within the domestic sphere (the nonmarket sector, in Becker's terms) as "two marriage-related activities", predominantly for women. Authors specified that divorce occurs when the combined utility of partners once dissolved exceeds their combined utility while married. As the optimal marital decision at any moment maximizes the expected value of full wealth over the remainder of life, the decision of divorcing changes in different moments of life. If one partner expects to have less wealth after a divorce than they currently have in their marriage, they should be compensated. Compensation is described as an application of the Coase theorem, according to which "the allocation of property rights or legal liability does not influence resource allocation when the parties involved can bargain with each other at little cost" (Becker et al., 1977, 1144).

This definition of divorce in Becker's terms was not gender-neutral as it might look: in fact, Becker and his coauthors provided a series of example to corroborate their theory that are entirely biased by gender stereotypes and well-grounded on the doctrine of the separate spheres. They assumed that "a person will tend to specialize in acquiring skills that raise market productivity compared to nonmarket productivity if he spends more time in the market sector after marriage as a result of substitution of spouse's time in the nonmarket sector" and vice versa (ibid, 1977, 1146). Therefore, women have traditionally married earlier because their human capital endowment had been focused on household-oriented specialized investments. For this reason, in the optimal sorting model, men marry women "with relatively low earnings potential, greater physical attractiveness, and superior other nonmarket characteristics (…) since [they] have a comparative advantage in specializing in nonmarket investments" (ibid, 1147).

Possible causes of divorce are a larger than expected deviation between actual and expected earnings in marriage; discrepancies between partners regarding intelligence, social background, religion, or race, which were underestimated at a first stage; marriage at a young age especially if consequences of accidental premarital pregnancies that make women "less valuable to other potential mates" (ibid, 1151). Moreover, as authors wrote, the probability of remarriage depends directly on male earnings and inversely on female earnings and the number of children from previous marriages.[14]

Both labor economists and new home economists who worked between the 1960s and the 1970s endorsed the traditional approach of analyzing why women do what they do (either stay at home or join the labor force) and largely ignored why they do not make different choices. This is particularly relevant for married women, whose choice between home and job depends on the attitude of their husbands towards sharing domestic responsibilities within the household; social pressure on the sacred role of motherhood; perception of discrimination in job market in terms of salaries and mobility; affordability of daycare. Labor economists

[14] Becker addressed the topic of divorce in a later article coauthored with Tomes in 1986. They explained the increasing trend in divorce rates as a result of rising real wages, combined with the increased opportunities to substitute capital for labor in housework. In this context, specializing one member of the household entirely in household production became less efficient (Becker & Tomes, 1986).

and new home economists never questioned the doctrine of the separate spheres and they took for granted that the comparative advantage of a different human capital specialization would have benefitted both agents in equal terms: men, specialized in market-oriented educational investments, who rule the public sphere, as well as women, specialized in household-oriented investments, who rule the private sphere. However, this assumption did not consider that the two spheres are not equal in terms of power and personal empowerment.

5.3 Becker's *Treatise on the Family*: The Doctrine of the Separate Spheres on Steroids

In 1981, Becker published *A Treatise on the Family*, which may be regarded as his general systematization of the new home economics. An enlarged edition was published ten years later, in 1991. In his Nobel Prize Lecture (Becker, 1992), Becker admitted that writing his *Treatise* "was the most difficult sustained intellectual effort" he ever took: it required six years that left him "intellectually and emotionally exhausted".[15] Becker's book embedded some developments of marriage theory that had been meanwhile published by other new home economists, not only colleagues, but also "students who wrote dissertations on the family, or relevant to the family, during their participation in our Workshop on Applications of Economics [at the University of Chicago]" (Becker, 1991, xi).

In his *Treatise*, Becker's endorsement of the doctrine of the separate spheres was completed. He began by defining marriage as a long-term commitment to assure that women were not abandoned and to protect them from life's troubles: "since married women have been specialized to childbearing and other domestic activities, they have demanded long-term 'contracts' from their husbands to protect them against abandonment and other adversities" (Becker, 1991, 30). Even more astonishing

[15] As retrieved on September 13, 2023 at: https://www.nobelprize.org/uploads/2018/06/becker-lecture.pdf.

was his explanation of the sexual division of labor, as a consequence of women's "heavy biological commitment to the production, feeding, and caring of children" (ibid, 38), that led him to the conclusion that the time of men and women were not perfect substitutes, but complementary: "households with only men or only women are less efficient because they are unable to profit from the sexual difference in comparative advantage" (ibid, 39).

Given the biological differences between men and women and the comparative advantage of the traditional division of labor between husbands and wives, Becker analyzed the optimal investment in human capital for men (H^1) and for women (H^2). According to Becker, men and women maximize their own utility function by choosing the optimal path of H^1 and H^2 and the optimal allocation between the market and household sectors. The allocation of time would be optimal when the marginal product of working time equals the marginal product of household time. If all members of an efficient household have different comparative advantages, no more than one member would allocate time to both the market and household sectors.

Analytically, the biological differences between men and women which lead to different investments in human capital (market-oriented for males versus household-oriented for females) assume that an hour spent in working in the household and in the market by women is not a perfect substitute for an hour of the time of men when they make the same investments in human capital. If women have a comparative advantage over men in the household sector, an efficient household run by a married couple would allocate the time of women mainly to the household sector and the time of men mainly to the market sector.

Becker further reinforced his vision by asserting that specialized investments in comparative advantage also serve to perpetuate the traditional division of labor between partners. According to him, this sharp sexual division of labor between the market and household sectors, observable in all societies, can be attributed partly to the benefits derived from specialized investments and partly to inherent differences between the sexes. He pointed out that as the labor-force participation of married women increased in Western countries, the benefits they gained from marriage diminished. Simultaneously, the appeal of divorce grew, as the sexual division of labor within households became less advantageous. This shift in the dynamics of marriage led to a decline in fertility because child care became more challenging after a marriage dissolves.[16]

According to Becker, household members agree to maximize a single utility function, subjected to a budget constraint. This utility function was the sum of all family members' income and he posed a benevolent head of the family (the husband/father) by assuming that his preferences fairly reflect his concern for the welfare of other family members and that he is able to adjust allocations in response to family members' behavior. Becker argued that the presence of an altruistic member of the family who makes positive transfers to others is sufficient to induce rational family members to maximize family income. The resulting distribution was the one that maximizes the altruist's utility function subject to the family's resource constrain. If a family member (a "rotten kid") tries to raise his own consumption by lowering the consumption of others, the head of the household may reduce transfers to him in order to induce him to properly behave.

Becker wrote:

> Investments in children with 'normal' orientations reinforce their biology, and they become specialized to the usual sexual division of labor. Investments in 'deviant' children, on the other hand, conflict with their biology, and the net outcome for them is not certain. For some, their biology might dominate and they would seek a deviant division of labor, with men in the household and women in the market. (Becker, 1981 [1991], 40)

Therefore, Becker insissted, specialized market-oriented investments on boys and specialized household-oriented investments on girls lead to highest returns for society as a whole.

Summing up, in his *Treatise,* Becker considered marriage as a long-term commitment to assure protection to women, and he regarded

---

[16] In Becker's first study on fertility (1960), he provided an explanation for the historical decline in fertility observed in industrialized countries and urban settings. He suggested that parents make a conscious choice to increase their investments in the human capital of their children, focusing on improving the quality of their offspring, while simultaneously reducing the number of children they had, affecting both the quantity and quality of children.

market-oriented education for boys and household-oriented education for girls as optimal strategies, by arguing that highest returns are reached in a society where roles are specialized on the basis of gender differences. Similarly, he explained the decision to divorce by constructing a total utility function of a couple and considering bargaining costs: divorce resulted in efficiency if it provided more utility than staying married.

Becker never hid his preference for the traditional family rooted on the doctrine of the separate spheres. In the "Introduction" of the enlarged version of his *Treatise* (1991), he candidly declared that in the last thirty years the family "has been radically altered, almost destroyed" by several factors: the rapid growth in divorce rates which forced children to grow up in households with only one parent; the increased number of married women workers, including mothers with young children, that "has reduced the contact between children and their mothers and contributed to the conflict between the sexes in employment as well as in marriage"; the decline of fertility which increased "rates of divorce and labor force participation of married women". Furthermore, Becker wrote: "conflict between the generations has become more open, and today's parents are less confident than those of earlier years that they can guide the behavior of their children" (Becker, 1991, 1).

In Becker's words, the "alteration, almost destruction" of the family was women's faults: by ignoring that they are biologically and culturally oriented to providing care in the domestic life rather than to be competitive in the public arena, women left the domestic sphere and entered the labor force, in order to get a position in the public sphere. Their new status led them to have less children and eventually, being finally economically independent, to divorce and to raise their children by themselves. Becker never mentioned the unfairness of women's subjection in the private sphere, mostly the only option they had, and still have in some context. He did not spend a word on the notion of responsibilities within the household that should be shared by men and women. For example, Becker took for granted that after a divorce, children are raised by one parent only, which is often true, but he did not mention that this is mainly due by fathers' negligence.

Even when Becker himself admitted that women in the labor force have suffered from discrimination, he somehow justified discrimination in terms of natural differences between men and women, although in some ambiguous terms.

He wrote:

> I do believe that biological differences are very important in explaining why women traditionally have done most of the child rearing, the main lesson from my analysis of an efficient division of labor is not that biology or discrimination causes the traditional division of activities between men and women. Rather (...) that even small amounts of market discrimination against women or small biological differences between men and women can cause huge differences in the activities of husbands and wives (Becker, 1991, 4).

He continued by admitting:

> a sizable gap is expected when women have specialized in household activities, have invested little in market human capital, and have allocated most of their energy to the household [and that] an efficient division of labor is perfectly consistent with exploitation of women by husbands and parents - a 'patrimony' system- that reduces their well-being and their command of their lives (ibid.).

Finally, Becker concluded:

> the gain to men from exploitation tends to increase when the allocation of resources, including the division of labor between men and women, becomes more efficient and raises output of goods and services (ibid.)

and lamented that his critics "fails to appreciate that exploitation is largely a separate issue from efficiency in the division of labor by gender" (ibid.). Becker did not explain the source of exploitation and did not admit that building a theoretical model to explain the traditional division of labor between men and women in terms of efficiency reinforced the existing system, unless he explicitly acknowledged that the system was efficient, albeit unfair as based on discrimination.

For Becker, the source of discrimination was personal prejudice. If Becker's theory of discrimination of blacks in the labor market (Becker,

1957) is applied to women in the labor market, we obtain that, according to him, discrimination in the market place by any group (either men or white men) reduced their own real incomes as well as those of the discriminated minority (either women or blacks). Thus, an incentive existed for non-discriminating behavior in the labor market, and if enough non-discriminatory employers hired a relatively cheap source of labor (women and blacks) they could eliminate the wage differential between genders and ethnicities. Becker added that discriminated workers would still experience premarket discrimination due to customers who would pay a higher price in equilibrium because they prefer not to conduct business with women and black people. Critics of Becker pointed out that discrimination is rarely a matter of personal preference. It implies a multitude of cultural, social and political factors that require a more sophisticated explanation than a general equilibrium model.

Further developments in standard economics applied to gender issues followed Becker's suggestion, either by implementing his model or by correcting it, in order to reinforce it and to demonstrate the cogency of the interpretation of family behavior in terms of rational choice theory.

5.4 Beyond Becker: Standard Economics on Marriage Theory

Becker was not the only Chicago economist who dealt with the economics of marriage. Before Becker, Paul Samuelson's (1956) consensus model proposed that each member of the family behaves as if there were a family utility function that all attempt to maximize. This assumption allows the family to be analyzed as a single unit, with a family income and a joint budget. Thus, any effect of a property income or government transfer goes to the family as a single unit. Milton Friedman (1976) considered marriage as a nonprofit firm able to organize household production just as a central authority organizes production and distribution in a collective society.

The publication of Becker's *Treatise* had an enormous influence on the spread of the economic modeling of marriage: in the 1980s and

1990s, many standard economists mainly reinforced Becker's approach by providing some modification. According to economist Shoshana Grossbard, a student of Becker's at that time, there were two main types of analysis occurring at the University of Chicago in the 1970s. Marriage markets were explained using either partial equilibrium models based on price theory, drawing from economists like Alfred Marshall and Milton Friedman, or by employing optimal sorting models as in new home economics marriage theory, which relied on rational choice models. Grossman pointed out that Chicago economists of the time (including herself) were more interested in the price model of marriage, and that Becker himself shifted from the former model (Becker, 1973, 1974) to the latter (Becker, 1981) (Grossbard, 2010).

Like Becker, Charlotte Phelps (1972) viewed marriage as a bi-lateral form of contract aimed at maximizing each partner's utility function, and she considered families to be like firms: two people get married in order to reduce negotiation costs between partners. Differently from Becker, she emphasized the role of happiness, linked to mutual love, as the decisive factor in the decision to marry or remain single, and she affirmed that happiness is greater in a marriage than in a single household. Moreover, she deemphasized Becker's biological explanation of the division of roles between husbands and wives by introducing love and caring as fundamental elements of a household's equilibrium: for instance, she stated that some women enjoy to completely devote their time and effort to the family. Although traditional households played an important role in Phelps' model, she never used her theory to offer a foundation for housewives' specialization in household production, and differently from Becker, in some of her later papers, Phelps admitted that marital sorting depends mainly on gender role norms, which can be either traditionally related to patriarchy or based on a more egalitarian approach (Phelps, 1988, 1991).

Chicago economist Mark Nerlove (1974) summarized earlier criticism of Becker's marriage price theory. First and foremost, the fact that the model was too simple to rightly cope with the complexity of marriage theory and identified the following four main problems within the new home economics (Becchio, 2020).

First, as in Samuelson's model (1956), the mechanism of maximization applied to a household's expected utility function shaped on the utility function of a single decision maker, i.e. the husband/father figure, failed to consider the well-being of children and other family members.

Second, an oversimplified economic theory of fertility assuming two inputs (husband's time and wife's time) used to produce three household's goods (number of children, quality of children, and 'other satisfactions'). Both Willis (1973) and DeTray (1973) assumed that children numbers and children quality are time-intensive for mothers, neglecting some essential dynamics of investments in children quality: for instance, they ignored that in many societies and families, the eldest son was often the beneficiary of the bulk of the investment in the human capital decided by the parents.

Third, the set of assumptions about the allocation of time of women was static and it actually did not explain educational investments, female labor-force participation, and, consequently, fertility.

Fourth and last, an insufficient attention had been paid to the quality of the time resources passed down through generations by assuming that husbands devoted themselves full time to the market and wives devoted themselves full time to the household.

Major critiques of the new home economic stated that it predicted the obvious: the composition of a family was strongly associated with women's labor-force participation; highly educated married women participated to a greater extent in the labor force and they worked more hours than less educated married women; married women tended to withdraw from the labor force when they had children, being children more female time-intensive than other commodities produced within the home.

In 1977, Margaret Reid, who was still a faculty member in the economics department at Becker's time, pointed out that new home economic was a development of household economics, rather than of home economics, as the label might suggested. According to Reid, what was really new in Becker's approach was the formal technique adopted to scrutinize phenomena such as the allocation of family time for activities in nonmarket production, as well as the factors influencing joint decisions by spouses regarding market and nonmarket production and the balance between production and consumption.

According to Reid, Becker's model was unrealistic: the assumption of perfect rationality was at least problematic; path dependence effects on household demand and on labor-force participation were not acknowledged; the status quo of social gender dynamics as well as the role of traditions and conventions were never questioned. Furthermore, by considering the family as a maximizing unit able capable of providing an optimal outcome, the model offered a definition of rational behavior which "deals with *ex ante* behavior not the *ex post* appraisal of its outcome" (Reid, 1977, 182).

As Grossbard pointed out, most intra-house decision-making models developed after Becker's articles oscillated between the individual level and the aggregate level. On the individual level, partners engage in games, whether cooperative or non-cooperative. On the aggregate level, they share a joint welfare function or a joint production function, as in Becker's price theory of marriage, which was based on the individual allocation of time by two married individuals who contribute to a household function.

In early 1980s, standard economists tried to replace Becker's unitary models of the household with models of household's decisions makers with their own preferences and their own constraints. By following Samuelson (1956), other economists assumed that households have a social welfare function (Apps & Rees, 1988; Chiappori, 1988), albeit they did not differentiate their model from Becker's interpretations of allocation of time.

Bargaining models of marriage assumed that households play either cooperative games (Manser & Brown, 1980; McElroy & Horney, 1981) or non-cooperative games (Konrad & Lommerud, 1995). Manser and Brown (1980) and McElroy and Horney (1981) applied Nash's bargaining model to households: spouses cooperate in the process of bargaining to get a Pareto-efficient (optimal) solution, but if they do not cooperate a threat point can be reached and separation and divorce may occur.[17]

Konrad and Lommerud (1995) provided a marriage model where two family members can choose whether to be free-riders, allocating their time in ways that primarily benefit themselves, rather than contributing to the production of a family public good, such as childcare or caring for elderly parents. In this model, they assumed an absence of love or altruism, and family members are only interdependent in their mutual concern for the public good. The game played between the two is a one-shot game fully non-cooperative. According to the authors, "even in such a setting there will be a tendency towards specialization between spouses in market work and the provision of child care according to comparative advantage in market work and household production" (Konrad & Lommerud, 1995, 585). Paradoxically, as authors suggested, in efficiency models, the comparative advantage reinforces traditional roles in the family, while in non-cooperative family models, where family members act strategically, there is an expectation of less drastic specialization between the spouses. This is because the spouse specializing in household production is not adequately compensated by the other.

Grossbard (1984) presented marriage as an exchange of household labor between spouses in order to show that the labor-force participation of married women depends on the sex ratio of those eligible for marriage, and that income variations have a greater influence on wives' labor supply than on husbands'. In a later paper she presented the idea that the share of household income which benefits a particular spouse depends on the specific cultural framework of the marriage market (Grossbard & Neuman, 1988).[18]

---

17 Threat points refer to the outside options available to individuals, indicating the resources each person could access if they were not a part of the household. Therefore, within the household, each individual must secure at least this amount of resources, or they may choose to leave the household. The analysis of these threat points contributed to develop cooperative bargaining models.

18 The paper examines the labor-force participation of married Jewish women in Israel, considering marital sorting based on age and ethnicity. The central hypothesis is that the value of time and, consequently, labor force participation, may vary depending on the specific circumstances within a marriage market. The study anticipates that certain characteristics of wives, which are highly regarded in the marriage market, will be linked to lower labor-force participation. Conversely, attributes of husbands that are valued in the marriage market are expected to be

The model proposed by Lundberg and Pollak (1993) is the most interesting in terms of the doctrine of the separate spheres. They conceptualized household members as joint decision makers regarding some matters while maintaining separate spheres regarding other issues, and assumed 'exogenous separate spheres', where each person specializes in a particular sphere. Their 'separate spheres bargaining model' was intended as a new model of distribution of resources within marriage. It differed from divorce threat bargaining in several ways. First, the threat point was not divorce but a non-cooperative equilibrium that was defined in terms of traditional gender roles and gender role expectations. Second, the non-cooperative equilibrium may actually be the final equilibrium, which means that spouses may not fully cooperate or reach a Pareto-efficient outcome.[19] Their separate spheres model was thus consistent with the view that distribution between women and men in two-parent families depends on which parent receives the child allowance payment.

Authors considered specialization by gender a pervasive aspect of family life, with men being responsible for earning income in two-parent families, and women being responsible for supplying household services. They suggested a 'separate spheres equilibrium' in the family that required a minimal coordination among spouses: each spouse is considered a decision maker within their own sphere, able to optimize their decisions under the constraint of their individual resources. While in non-cooperative marriages, the division of labor based on traditional gender roles emerges without explicit bargaining, in cooperative bargaining marriages spouses negotiate, monitor, and enforce agreements, which can lead to transaction costs. These transaction costs can include the time and effort required for communication, negotiation, and monitoring of household tasks and responsibilities. Hence, a non-cooperative solution is optimal for couples with high transaction costs or low expected gains from cooperation.

associated with higher participation rates among wives. The inclusion of such characteristics, like a husband being older than his wife, enhances the explanatory capacity of labor-force participation regressions.

19 They conducted a comparison between two child allowance schemes: one involves a cash transfer paid to the mother, while the other entails a cash transfer paid to the father. In cases of divorce, their assumption is that the mother assumes the role of the custodial parent and receives the child allowance.

Akerlof and Kranton (2000) proposed a refined version of Becker's model by pointing out that any deviation from standard behavior based on gender identity is highly costly. Elul et al. (2002) pointed out that albeit a cooperative marriage, which implied equity at home as well as in the marketplace, would be optimal, it will be risky and costly because family and market may behave unfairly, unless institutions, such as prenuptial agreements are introduced in order to improve fairness (Waldfogel, 1998).

Grossbard (1993, 2015, 2018) proposed a 'work in household' (WiHo) model which questioned the doctrine of the separate spheres at least by rejecting the traditional gender stereotypes and by presenting the differences between partners in gender-neutral terms. Her WiHo model distinguished between couples' economic decisions within household activities that may benefit a spouse and couples' economic decisions that do not benefit a spouse. WiHo model applied price theory to households by considering households as firms, husbands as employers, and wives as workers, by following Becker. It assumed that there are markets for different types of men and women and that an 'equilibrium price of WiHo' may be reachable in each submarket. Moreover, in WiHo model, optimization is not rejected, albeit it is pursued by individuals rather than by households as in the new home economics approach. Nonetheless, Grossbard's model rejected Becker's notion of benevolent husband able to optimize on behalf of the family. In Grossbars's model family members are independent decision makers and they do not necessarily cooperate. Furthermore, the institutional framework may provide exchanges of WiHo for WiHo, or WiHo for money as well as in-kind gifts.[20]

Basu (2006) tried to combine theoretical models, empirical investigations, and anthropological insights, albeit his model did not eliminate the traditional dichotomy of the separate spheres. He rightly pointed out that the time spent by women in the household can vary across geographical and social areas. This implies different policies, although policy

[20] WiHo model has been later expanded by including public goods along with private goods (Grossbard, 2003). According to Grossbard, a major advantage of WiHo is the inclusion of the old distinction between home production and leisure previously introduced by Margaret Reid (Becchio, 2020).

models usually imply a male breadwinner. Conversely, as Basu claimed, it is fundamental to understand the relation between household balance of power and household behavior. As he pointed out, the standard unitary model of the household is based either on two adults who have the same preference or on one of them who takes all the decisions, as if it were a single household's utility function. Cooperation emerges when a collective approach to modeling the household is adopted by considering that each agent has his/her distinct utility function and that the household maximizes a weighted average of these two functions, with the weights capturing the balance of power in the household. Hence, Basu introduced a Nash bargaining model of the household, which accommodates asymmetric power dynamics and acknowledges that the extent of asymmetry and the threat point can significantly influence household decisions. He also pointed out the limitations of standard economic models that often reinforce the traditional division of labor between men and women, in line with the doctrine of the separate spheres, confining women's decision-making power to the domestic sphere.[21]

Some new developments of assortative matching consider the role of preferences and research costs, age, education, race, ethnicity, and income inequality (Lee & McKinnish, 2018; Mansour & McKinnish, 2014). For instance, the tendency to get married to a partner with the same level of education, especially among higher-skill professionals, has been explained as an effect of a lower cost in researching and meeting potential partners (which usually occurs while people are attending college, at least for the first marriage) rather than as an effect of shared preferences, which are expected among partners with the same education (Mansour & McKinnish, 2018a, 2018b). More recently, the idea that marital sorting depends on the benefit of marriage as an alternative to remaining single has been reinforced by data sets provided by dating websites (Hirsh et al., 2010).

[21] As Duflo and Udry (2003) observed, Nash bargaining models of households can look very different depending on what we take to be the threat point in a non-cooperative equilibrium. Basu insisted on the idea of domains of control that may be more germane to household decision making and not merely a feature of a breakdown in cooperation. In this approach a woman's power would be reflected in part by the size of the domain of her decision.

Summing up, from a historical standpoint, the doctrine of separate spheres reached its peak in Becker's new home economics. By incorporating the traditional division of labor between men and women into a standard economics model, the system of women's confinement to the private sphere was justified in the name of efficiency.

Home economists and household economists before Becker analyzed the formation of family's consumption and eventually whether it was possible to influence them, in order to raise family's standards of living. Becker applied standard/neoclassical economics model to the economics of the family 'as if'—in Milton Friedman's terms—preferences among family members were given. Until mid-1970s, he described the economics of the family in Marshallian terms, by adopting a model of partial equilibrium, by following human capital economists such as Mincer, Schultz, and Cain. Later, in his *Treatise* Becker described the economics of the family as a process of optimization within a general economic equilibrium theoretical framework based on a division of labor between partners whose roles are biologically and culturally determined (Becker, 1981).

Hence, while old home economists and household economists, with the only exception of M. Reid, were much more oriented towards a *normative* approach in analyzing the economY of the family, Becker adopted a *positive* approach by describing the economicS of the family. Capital letters, Y and S, as well as italics, are intentional: by applying standard economics, Becker provided a 'scientific' description of family's behavior, which will be deeply criticized later, especially by feminist economists (see Chapter 6) and by other non-standard/heterodox economists (Averett et al., 2018; Becchio, 2020; Berik & Kongar, 2021; Jacobsen, 2020; Nelson, 1995; Orozco Espinel & Betancourt, 2022).[22]

However, Becker's approach was praised and highly recognized: in 1992, the Sveriges Riksbank conferred him the Prize in Economic Sciences in Memory of Alfred Nobel with the following motivation: "for having extended the domain of microeconomic analysis to a wide

[22] A more extensive bibliography on the subject is in Chapter 6.

range of human behavior and interaction, including nonmarket behavior"[23] which included discrimination, crime and punishment, besides household and family issues.

While some new home economists, in Chicago and elsewhere, have made certain contributions to enhance Becker's initial approach, they have, in many cases, implicitly adhered to the doctrine of separate spheres. They have not critically examined the origin of the traditional gender division of labor, based on women's dual role in the job market and within the household. Furthermore, while women were somehow encouraged to participate in the public sphere, there has been a lack of emphasis on husbands sharing equal responsibility within the private sphere.

The revival of the doctrine of the separate spheres by new home economics occurred in a historical moment (the 1970s) during which the sexual and cultural revolution was spreading in the Western society. Traditional women's roles within the domestic sphere were being strongly criticized as products of patriarchy. Women's studies were examining norms related to gender, class, and race to understand the cultural origins of social inequalities. Various initiatives aimed at addressing gender discrimination were emerging across academic disciplines. Nonetheless, standard economics—via Becker—explained the underlying rationale of these gender-related norms, by portraying the role of women as caregivers in the private domestic sphere and the role of men as breadwinners in the powerful public sphere as efficient and natural outcomes of the preferences of married men and women.

References

Akerlof, G., & Kranton, R. (2000). Economics and Identity. *The Quarterly Journal of Economics, 115*(3), 715–753.

Apps, P. F., & Rees, R. (1988). Taxation and the Household. *Journal of Public Economics, 35*(3), 355–369.

[23] As retrieved on September 10, 2023 at: https://www.nobelprize.org/prizes/economic-sciences/1992/press-release/.

Averett, S., Argys, L., & Hoffman, S. (Eds.). (2018). *The Oxford Handbook of Women and the Economy*. Oxford University Press.
Bankovsky, M. (2020). A History of Early Household Economics: Improving the Family's Contribution to Industrial Production and Rationalizing Family Consumption. *Oxford Economic Papers, 72*(4), 1–21.
Basu, K. (2006). Gender and Say: A Model of Household Behavior with Endogenously Determined Balance of Power. *The Economic Journal, 116*(511), 558–580.
Becchio, G. (2020). *A History of Feminist and Gender Economics*. Routledge.
Becker, G. (1957). *The Economics of Discrimination*. University of Chicago Press.
Becker, G. (1960). An Economic Analysis of Fertility. *NBER* (pp. 209–240). Columbia University Press.
Becker, G. (1962). Investment in Human Capital: A Theoretical Analysis. *Journal of Political Economy, 70*(5, Part 2), 9–49.
Becker, G. (1964). *Human Capital: A Theoretical and Empirical Analysis, with Special Reference to Education*. National Bureau of Economic Research.
Becker, G. (1965). A Theory of the Allocation of Time. *The Economic Journal, 75*(299), 493–517.
Becker, G. (1973). A Theory of Marriage: Part I. *Journal of Political Economy, 81*(4), 813–846.
Becker, G. (1974). A Theory of Marriage: Part II. *Journal of Political Economy, 82*(2), 11–26.
Becker, G. (1981 [1991]). *A Treatise on the Family*. Harvard University Press.
Becker, G. (1992). *The Economic Way of Looking at Life*. Nobel Prize in Economics Documents 1992–1991, Nobel Prize Committee.
Becker, G., Landes, E., & Michael, R. (1977). An Economic Analysis of Marital Instability. *Journal of Political Economy, 85*(6), 1147–1187.
Becker, G., & Tomes, N. (1986). Human Capital and the Rise and Fall of Families. *Journal of Labor Economics, 4*(3), 1–39.
Beecher, C. (1841). *A Treatise on Domestic Economy, for the Use of Young Ladies at home, and at School*. Wm. A. & Co.
Beecher, C., & Beecher, H. (1870). *Principles of Domestic Science as Applied to the Duties and Pleasures of Home: A Text-Book for the Use of Young Ladies in Schools, Seminaries and Colleges*. J.B. Ford.
Berik, G., & Kongar, E. (Eds.). (2021). *The Routledge Handbook of Feminist Economics*. Routledge.
Cain, G. (1966). *Married Women in the Labor Force: An Economic Analysis*. University of Chicago Press.

Clark, J. B. (1899). *The Distribution of Wealth*. Macmillan.
Chiappori, P. (1988). Rational Household Labor Supply. *Econometrica, 56*(1), 63–90.
Deegan, M. J. (1988). *Jane Addams and the Women of the Chicago School, 1892–1918*. Transaction.
DeTray, D. (1973). Child Quality and the Demand for Children. *Journal of Political Economy, 81*(2), 570–595.
Dewey, J. (1900). *The School and Society*. University of Chicago Press.
Dickinson, C. (1927). A Theory of Consumption by Hazel Kyrk. *The Quarterly Journal of Economics, 38*(2), 343–346.
Duflo, E., & Udry, C. (2003). *Intrahousehold Resource Allocation in Cote D'Ivoire: Social Norms, Separate Accounts and Consumption Choices* (NBER Working Paper No. w10498).
Elul, R., Silva-Reus, J., & Volij, O. (2002). Will You Marry Me? A Perspective on the Gender Gap. *Journal of Economic Behavior and Organization, 49*(4), 549–572.
Fitzpatrick, E. (1990). *Endless Crusade: Women Social Scientists and Progressive Reform*. Oxford University Press.
Folbre, N. (1991). The Unproductive Housewife: Her Evolution in Nineteenth-Century Economic Thought. *Signs: Journal of Women in Culture and Society, 16*(3), 463–484.
Folbre, N. (1996). For Margaret, with Thanks. *Feminist Economics, 2*(3), xi–xii.
Folbre, N. (1998). The Sphere of Women in Early Twentieth Century Economics. In H. Silverberg (Ed.), *Gender and American Social Science: The Formative Years* (pp. 35–60). Princeton University Press.
Forget, E. (2011). American Women and the Economics Profession in the Twentieth Century. *Oeconomica, 1*(1), 19–30.
Forget, E. (2022). Margaret Gilpin Reid (1896–1991). In R. Cord (Ed.), *The Palgrave Companion to Chicago Economics* (pp. 343–356). Palgrave Macmillan.
Friedman, M. ([1962] 1976). *Price Theory*. Aldine Publishing Company.
Gillen, A. (1990). Talbot, Marion. In R. Lunin Schulz & A. Hast (Eds.), *Women Building Chicago, 1790–1990* (pp. 865–868). Indiana University Press.
Goldstein, C. M. (2012). *Creating Consumers: Home Economists in Twentieth-Century America*. University of North Carolina Press.
Grossbard, S. (1984). A Theory of Allocation of Time in Markets for Labor and Marriage. *The Economic Journal, 94*(376), 863–882.
Grossbard, S. (1993). *On Economics of Marriage*. Westview Press.

Grossbard, S. (2001). The New Home Economics at Columbia and Chicago. *Feminist Economics, 7*(3), 103–130.
Grossbard, S. (2003). A Consumer Theory with Competitive Markets for Work in Marriage. *Journal of Socio-Economics, 31*(6), 609–645.
Grossbard, S. (2006). The New Home Economics at Columbia and Chicago. In S. Grossbard (Ed.), *Jacob Mincer: A Pioneer of Modern Labor Economics* (pp. 37–49). Springer.
Grossbard, S. (2010). How "Chicagoan" Are Gary Becker's Economic Models of Marriage? *Journal of the History of Economic Thought, 32*(3), 377–395.
Grossbard, S. (2015). *The Marriage Motive: A Price Theory of Marriage. How Marriage Markets Affect, Employment, Consumption, and Savings*. Springer.
Grossbard, S., et al. (2018). Marriage and Marriage Markets. In S. Averett (Ed.), *The Oxford Handbook of Women and the Economy* (pp. 55–73). Oxford University Press.
Grossbard, S., & Neuman, S. (1988). Labor Supply and Marital Choice. *Journal of Political Economy, 96*, 1294–1302.
Hara, N. (2016). Unpaid Labor and the Critique of Political Economy in Home Economics and the New Household Economics: From the Feminist Economics Perspective. *The History of Economic Though, 58*(1), 1–20.
Hirsh, G., Hortasçsu, A., & Ariely, D. (2010). Matching and Sorting in Online Dating. *American Economic Review, 100*(1), 130–163.
Hirschfeld, M. L. (1997). Methodological Stance and Consumption Theory: A Lesson in Feminist Methodology. *History of Political Economy, 29*(Suppl. 1), 189–211.
Hoyt, E. (1926). *Primitive Trade: Its Psychology and Economics*. Kegan Paul, Trench, Trubner and Co., Ltd.
Hoyt, E. (1928). *The Consumption of Wealth*. Macmillan.
Hoyt, E. (1938). *Consumption in Our Society*. McGraw-Hill.
Jacobsen, J. (2020). *Advanced Introduction to Feminist Economics*. Edward Elgar.
James, E. T. (Ed.). (1971). *Notable American Women, 1607–1950*. The Belknap Press of Harvard University.
Konrad, K. A., & Lommerud, K. E. (1995). Family Policy with Non-cooperative Families. *Scandinavian Journal of Economics, 97*(4), 581–601.
Kyrk, H. (1923). *A Theory of Consumption*. Houghton Mifflin Company.
Kyrk, H. (1929). The Place of the Economic and Social Studies in the Home Economics Curriculum. *Journal of Home Economics, 21*(6), 488–494.
Kyrk, H. (1933). *Economic Problems of the Family*. Harper & Brothers Publishers.

Kyrk, H. (1939). The Development of the Field of Consumption. *Journal of Marketing, 4*(1), 16–19.

Kyrk, H. (1953). *The Family in the American Economy*. Chicago University Press.

Le Tollec, A. (2020). *Finding a New Home (Economics): Towards a Science of the Rational Family, 1924–1981*. Université Paris-Saclay.

Lee, W., & McKinnish, T. (2018). The Marital Satisfaction of Differently-Aged Couples. *Journal of Population Economics, 31*(2), 337–362.

Leibowitz, A. (1974a). Home Investments in Children. In T. Schultz (Ed.), *Economics of the Family, Marriage, Children, and Human Capital* (pp. 432–452). The University of Chicago Press.

Leibowitz, A. (1974b). Education and Home Production. *American Economic Review, 64*(2), 243–250.

Leibowitz, A. (1975). Education and the Allocation of Women's Time. In F. Juster (Ed.), *Education, Income, and Human Behavior* (pp. 171–197). National Bureau of Economic Research and Carnegie Commission.

Leibowitz, A. (1976). Years and Intensity of Schooling Investment. *American Economic Review., 55*(3), 321–334.

Leibowitz, A. (1977). Parental Inputs and Children's Achievements. *Journal of Human Resources., 12*(2), 242–249.

Lundberg, S., and Pollak, R. A. (1993). Separate Sphere Bargaining and the Marriage Market. *Journal of Political Economy, 101*(6), 988–1010.

Manser, M., & Brown, M. (1980). Marriage and Household Decision Making: A Bargaining Analysis. *International Economic Review, 21*(1), 31–44.

Mansour, H., & McKinnish, T. (2014). Couples' Time Together: Complementarities in Production versus Complementarities in Consumption. *Journal of Population Economics, 27*(4), 1127–1144.

Mansour, H., & McKinnish, T. (2018a). Marriage Market Search and Sorting. In S. Averett, L. Argys, & S. Hoffman (Eds.), *The Oxford Handbook of Women and the Economy* (pp. 35–53). Oxford University Press.

Mansour, H., & McKinnish, T. (2018b). Same-Occupation Spouses: Preferences or Research Costs. *Journal of Population Economics, 31*(4), 1005–1033.

McElroy, M. B., & Horney, M. J. (1981). Nash Bargained Household Decisions: Toward a Generalization of the Theory of Demand. *International Economic Review, 22*(2), 333–349.

Mincer, J. (1958). Investment in Human Capital and Personal Income Distribution. *Journal of Political Economy., 66*(4), 281–302.

Mincer, J. (1962). Labor Force Participation of Married Women: A Study of Labor Supply. In H. G. Lewis (Ed.), *Aspects of Labor Economics* (pp. 63–105). Princeton University Press.
Mincer, J. (1963). Market Prices, Opportunity Costs, and Income Effects. In C. Carl (Ed.), *Measurement in Economics* (pp. 66–82). Stanford University Press.
Nelson, J. (1995). Feminism and Economics. *Journal of Economic Perspectives, 9*(2), 131–148.
Nerlove, M. (1974). Household and Economy: Toward a New Theory of Population and Economic Growth. *Journal of Political Economy, 82*(2), S200–S218.
Orozco Espinel, C., & Gomez, B. R. (2022). A History of the Institutionalization of Feminist Economics through Its Tensions and Founders. *History of Political Economy, 54*(S1), 159–192.
Pareto, V. (1896). *Cours d'Économie politique professé a l'Université de Lausanne.* F. Rouge.
Patten, S. (1889). *The Consumption of Wealth*. Publications of the University of Pennsylvania.
Phelps, C. (1972). Is the Household Obsolete? *The American Economic Review Papers and Proceedings, 62*(1/2), 167–174.
Phelps, C. (1988). Caring and Family income. *Journal of Behavioral Economics, 10*, 57–76.
Phelps, C. (1991). The Disappearance of Polarized Altruism. *Journal of Economic Behavior and Organization, 15*, 91–113.
Philippy, D. (2021). Ellen Richards's Home Economics Movement and the Birth of the Economics of Consumption. *Journal of the History of Economic Thought, 43*(3), 378–400.
Reid, M. (1934). *The Economics of Household Production.* Wiley.
Reid, M. (1938). *Consumers and the Market*. F. S. Crofts.
Reid, M. (1943). Trends in the Work of Married Women. *Marriage and Family Living, 5*(1), 80–83.
Reid, M. (1977). How New Is the 'New Home Economics'? *Journal of Consumer Research, 4*(3), 181–183.
Richards, E., & Talbot, M. (1887). *Home Sanitation: A Manual for Housekeepers*. Whitcomb & Barrow.
Samuelson, P. (1956). Social Indifference Curve. *Quarterly Journal of Economics, 70*(1), 1–22.
Schultz, T. W. (1961). Investment in Human Apital. *American Economic Review, 51*(1), 1–17.

Schultz, T. (1974). Fertility and Economic Values. In T. Schultz (Ed.), *Economics of the Family: Marriage, Children, and Human Capital* (pp. 3–22). University of Chicago Press.
Talbot, M. (1936). *More Than Lore: Reminiscences of Marion Talbot, Dean of Women, The University of Chicago, 1892–1925*. University of Chicago Press.
Thorne, A. (1995). Women Mentoring Women in Economics in the 1930s. In M. A. Dimand, R. Dimand, & E. Forget (Eds.), *Women of Value. Feminist Essays on the History of Women in Economics* (pp. 60–70). Edward Elgar.
Thorne, A. (2000). Elizabeth Ellis Hoyt (18–1900). In M. A. Dimand, R. Dimand, & E. Forget (Eds.), *A Biographical Dictionary of Women Economists* (pp. 215–219). Edward Elgar.
Trentmann, F. (2012). Consumer Society Revised: Affluence, Choice, and Diversity. In R. Jessen & L. Lange (Eds.), *Transformations of Retailing in Europe after 1945* (pp. 19–33). Routledge.
Trezzini, A. (2016). Early Contributions to the Economics of Consumption as a Social Phenomenon. *European Journal of the History of Economic Thought, 23*(2), 272–296.
Veblen, T. (1899). *The Theory of the Leisure Class*. Macmillan.
Velzen, S. (2003). Hazel Kyrk and the Ethics of Consumption. In D. Barker & E. Kuiper (Eds.), *Toward a Feminist Philosophy of Economics* (pp. 38–55). Routledge.
Waldfogel, J. (1998). The Family Gap for Young Women in the United States and Britain: Can Maternity Leave Make a Difference? *Journal of Labor Economics, 16*(3), 505–545.
Walker, S. (2003). Professionalisation or Incarceration? Household Engineering, Accounting and the Domestic Ideal. *Accounting, Organizations and Society, 28*(7–8), 743–772.
Whitcomb, E. (1929). *Trends in Home Economics Education, 1926–1928*. Bulletin n. 25. Department of Interior Bureau of Education.
Wicksteed, P. H. (1894). *An Essay on the Co-ordination of the Laws of Distribution*. London School of Economics.
Willis, R. (1973). A New Approach to the Economic Theory of Fertility Behavior. *Journal of Political Economy, 81*(2), S14–S64.
Yi, Y. (1996). Margaret G. Reid: Life and Achievements. *Feminist Economics, 2*(3), 17–36.

6

Feminist Economics and the Doctrine of the Separate Spheres

Feminist economics officially emerged in 1992, when feminist economists founded the International Association for Feminist Economics (IAFFE). Three years later they founded the academic journal *Feminist Economics*. Nonetheless, feminist economics has a long story that began at least two decades earlier (Becchio, 2020). During the 1970s and the 1980s, many women economists, such as Randy Albelda, Drucilla Barker, Barbara Bergmann, Susan Feiner, Marianne Ferber, Nancy Folbre, Ulla Grapard, Julie Nelson, Jean Shackleford, and Myra Strober, have been engaged in a twofold battle. First, they struggled against the underrepresentation of women economists in academia.[1] Second, they converged in an articulated critique to Becker's new home economics which led them to deeply criticize and often reject standard economics as a whole.

[1] In 1971, during the Annual Meeting of the AEA, in a session titled 'What economic equality for women required' the *Women's Caucus* was established. The Caucus formally invited the Executive Committee of the AEA to recognize the need for greater openness to women in economics departments (Chassonnery-Zaïgouche et al., 2019; Cohen, 2019).

G. Becchio, *The Doctrine of the Separate Spheres in Political Economy and Economics*, Palgrave Studies in Classical Liberalism,
https://doi.org/10.1007/978-3-031-51262-9_6

Influenced by feminist philosophy of the time, which led to the sexual revolution and the emergence of the second wave of feminism, feminist economists combined a feminist agenda with economic research, in order to achieve the emancipation and empowerment of women in the economy. Their research project started with a profound critique of the economics of the family and the traditional division of labor between partners as presented in standard economics. In doing so, feminist economists aligned themselves to the general critique to the doctrine of the separate spheres provided by feminists.

From a philosophical point of view, feminist philosophers contrasted the doctrine of the separate spheres by providing three possible reactions against it.

First, by following the classical liberal tradition, some feminist philosophers denied any essential differences between men and women, which had led to the doctrine of the separate spheres, by underlining that gender stereotypes, which assign women to the domestic sphere and men to the public sphere, have been shaped by culture and social norms and are not the results of natural differences, being individuals all equal regardless of gender (Haslanger, 2000; Scott, 1988).

Second, some feminists admitted that women are naturally more inclined to provide care work than men and, therefore, a sex-based division of labor is welcome, provided it is voluntary and not imposed by social pressure. Nonetheless, they emphasized that care work has never been properly valued and its importance has always been underestimated (Gilligan, 1982; Noddings, 1986).

Third, some feminists believed that even if there is a biological and cultural rationale behind the doctrine of the separate spheres, social structures have traditionally been shaped in a masculine way that has damaged women by making them victims of poverty, injustice, domestic violence, and any sort of inequality (MacKinnon, 1989; Rhode, 1997).

As a matter of facts, the doctrine of the separate spheres was often used as an explanatory and a normative framework for justifying gender inequality and men's power over women. Although it has been intensively criticized by feminist scholars as a means to perpetuate gender inequalities, some feminists, including feminist economists, more orientated to the second and third approaches, which tend to endorse the argument of the superiority of the feminine over the masculine, might have perpetuated what they had initially hoped to displace: gender-biased social roles. In fact, when some feminists, including some feminist economists, propose to overcome gender inequality by suggesting policies which help women to better perform their traditional role within the private sphere, they paradoxically reinforce the doctrine of the separate spheres that becomes a friend of some feminist agenda rather than a foe. Instead, it is possible to move beyond the doctrine of the separate spheres when the responsibilities of the private sphere are equally shared between men and women and when women actually become as powerful as men within the public sphere.

Regardless of which of the three approaches they were oriented towards, feminist scholars and feminist economists converged on some general points. They recognized men's dominance in every cultural, economic, and political realm (the public sphere). They pointed out that women's subjection within the family (the private sphere) was primarily the effect of the institution of marriage, structured in a way that favored men over women. They highlighted that the emergence of strict gender social roles within both private and public spheres reinforced the patriarchal system and the discrimination against women and other minorities.

Between the 1970s and the 1980s, feminist economists were especially focused on rejecting Becker's theory of marriage, which they considered grounded on assumptions biased by traditional gendered stereotypes that simultaneously ignored the separate identities of family members and underestimated non-economic factors. Furthermore, they criticized the gender specialization in education that traditionally made women, the lower-income partner, much more vulnerable in case of divorce or breakups.

Hence, feminist economists provided a model that included care work, love, power, and obligation as well as the role of cultural and social norms, all of which are wrongly explained or simply ignored by marriage theory *à la* Becker. Some feminist economists explicitly pointed out that Becker's theory of marriage, grounded in a general cultural devaluation of women and social roles associated with women that led to gender discrimination of any kind, reinforced the doctrine of the separate spheres. They pointed out some evident applications of the doctrine of the separate spheres in many new home economics' assumptions such as: optimal decisions depending on the different skills of different members; the division of labor within households depending on biological and cultural differences between men and women; the allocation of women's time to the household and of men's time to the market as rational; marriage seen as a long-term commitment to assure the protection of women; specialized market-oriented investments in boys and household-oriented investments in girls as optimal strategies (Barker & Feiner, 2004; Bergmann, 1995; Lamanna et al., 2014; Paterson & Lewis, 1999; Schultz, 1974).

Nonetheless, by rejecting Becker's standard approach applied to gender issues, many feminist economists advocated the transformation of the male world into a female world—intended as more emotional and less competitive. This approach was quite common among many feminist philosophers of the time who have especially influenced some feminist economists (Carter & Williams, 2003; Fricker & Hornsby, 2000). As mentioned earlier, this attitude may somehow reinforce the doctrine of the separate spheres. Other feminist economists, more politically oriented toward classical liberalism, such as Bergmann, Nelson, McCloskey, tend to prefer a long-run project aimed at promoting an educational system focused on equal opportunities in the job market. In Bergmann's words: "[a system where] women [are] incorporated into the 'male world' of money exchange, with a distribution of jobs similar to that of men" (Bergmann, 1998, 76), and an equal share of responsibilities between spouses when it comes to housework. These measures and commitments would actually render the doctrine of the separate spheres obsolete.

As the final section will show, the road toward gender equality in both spheres remains long even today. Recent data revealed that there are still structures and obstacles that hinder women's full participation in various fields, and the situation got worse especially after the COVID-19 pandemic, as shown by the Global Gender Gap Report 2023 (World Economic Forum, 2023). Gender equality in both spheres requires either overcoming the idea of the separation of the spheres, by considering the public role of the private sphere, i.e. the public role of family, or sharing responsibilities between men and women in both the private and the public sphere. These solutions are not mutually exclusive. Moreover, today's notion of family and marriage requires a more articulated and complex analysis that takes account of new cultural stances, including same-sex marriage and the role of other gender identities, in both Global North and South, and eventually highlights whether the intra-house dynamics of non-traditional families differs from traditional families or not.

6.1 Feminism, Gender Equality, Care, and the Doctrine of the Separate Spheres: Friends or Foes?

Gender equality is the result of the application of a set of cultural values that implement the idea that men and women are equals in both the private and the public sphere. Consequently, working on gender equality implies the adoption of a political agenda able to provide a voice for the minority group (women) and ultimately promote any possible way to reduce and eliminate inequality and discrimination. There are at least three main different visions of gender equality that lead to different political strategies: achieving equal opportunities (inclusion principle); supporting differences between the feminine and the masculine (reversal principle); transforming establishing gender-biased norms (displacement principle) (Squires, 2005; Verloo & Lombardo, 2007; Walby, 2005).

The combination of these three visions belongs to the history of feminism which had been developed in three waves (-nineteenth century; 1960s–1970s; 1990s–). Though feminism is not, and has never been, a monolithic cultural movement: the feminist spectrum goes from conservative to radical. Nor does feminism features a single political stance: feminism includes classical liberalism and socialism, along with their subgroups. Given the historical, cultural, and political differences within feminism, feminist groups may differ in many aspects according to their cultural and political orientation.

Classical liberal feminists rely on the inclusion principle: they insist on the equality between men and women and emphasize the urgent need to remove educational and legal barriers that prevent women from earning and thriving as much as men in the labor market. They may support some progressive measures in order to accelerate gender equality in the name of personal freedom. Conversely, conservative feminists, albeit accepting the inclusion principle, refuse affirmative action to improve women's conditions and are much more inclined to let the market, embedded in the Rule of Law framework, address and solve gender inequality (Posner, 1989).

Radical feminists are more focused on the reversal approach and refuse the idea that women must either play the male game or be compensated for not having been admitted to the game. They advocate for affirmative action, such as establishing criteria for promoting women over men.

Socialist feminists and post-modernist feminists are focused on the displacement principle. The former are oriented towards emancipating subordinate minorities through a revision/rejection of the capitalistic structure (McAfee & Howard, 2018). The latter reject the dilemma of equality versus difference as well as the binary heteronormativity as a norm and they consider the doctrine of the separate spheres as a way adopted by men to get power over women.

The broad cultural and political spectrum of feminism was a major concern for the founders of feminist economics. In the first editorial of the journal *Feminist Economics*, Strassmann wrote: "In recognition of the diversity of feminist thought, the journal will claim no one definition of feminism, and will welcome the multiplicity of feminism currently present in economics as well as those that may emerge when new voices are drawn into this forum" (Strassmann, 1995, 2).

Yet, feminist economists agreed with other feminist scholars in considering feminism as a general movement for the emancipation and empowerment of women. Furthermore, the majority of them agreed on considering that men's dominance historically prevailed in society in any cultural, economic, and political sphere and on maintaining that sexual differences have generated strict gender social roles within both private and public life that have reinforced the subjection of women in various fields.

Besides political and cultural differences, feminist scholars broadly agree on the idea that, regardless of differences in the feminist political and cultural spectrum, intersectionality is the only way to construct a feminist agenda that takes account of gender, class, age, sexual orientation, ethnic origins, ability, and other inequalities (Banks, 2021; Collins & Bilge, 2020; Crenshaw, 1991; Folbre, 2021; Nussbaum, 2000).[2] They also agree on criticizing the gendered dichotomy between private and public spheres by assuming a broader definition of 'political' that includes private issues traditionally excluded from the public sphere, such as education, care work, domestic violence, and so forth and by considering the private sphere politically oriented (Kantola, 2006; Lombardo & Meier, 2006; Moller Okin, 1998; Olsen, 1985; Pateman, 1983; Stratigaki, 2004).

Feminists argue that the doctrine of the separate spheres must be reconsidered by regarding the domestic realm of the family as part of the political sphere. In fact, they consider families not as natural orders, rather as social institutions upon which the state cannot help but interfere. Feminist criticism against the view of the family as a non-political agent is mainly based on the rejection of the idea that family is a place where harmony reigns; rather, as often happens, conflicts, power relations, and a scarcity of resources determine conflicting dynamics within the family. These conflicts require the intervention of the state and some regulation. Furthermore, coercion and convention have played a fundamental role in shaping families, which are ruled by laws that may or may not allow and regulate divorce, polygamy, same-sex marriages, out of wedlock children's rights, adoptions, property inheritance, and so forth. Finally, families are political entities as they are the place where children, who are future citizens, learn to handle moral issues.

As seen in Part I, traditionally codified rules as well as social norms reinforced men's power and women's subjection. In dysfunctional families, women usually have been and still are subjected to oppression, including domestic violence and abuses; in functioning families, women have been and still are subjected to the double burden, i.e. to an unequal division of labor which combines their active role in the workplace and almost completely relies on them in providing intra-household care

[2] For instance, as Goldin (1977) pointed out, Black American women have had the highest labor participation rate among women since the late nineteenth century.

(Hochschild, 1989). Moller Okin (1989) introduced the concept of 'cycle of vulnerability' in order to describe the vicious circle in the interaction between women's unequal position at workplace and their unequal position at home.

Feminists' plead for overlooking the doctrine of the separate spheres is also an effect of the situation faced by women in parenting which often constrains them and hinders their performance at work. The asymmetry between men and women in the job market due to the double burden faced by women, leads many women to remain economically dependent on their male partners and much more vulnerable to poverty in case of split-ups or divorce. This situation perpetually reinforces men's power within the marriage (Bergmann, 1986; Folbre, 1994; Sen, 1990).

The doctrine of the separate spheres also affected the different educational paths for girls and boys, which tend to reproduce the role played within the family by their parents (Chodorow, 1978). Supporters of the doctrine justify the domestic division of labor as a free choice made by women. Feminist responses argue that a free choice made within an unfair framework does not justify the unjust system.

In feminist perspectives, the doctrine of the separate spheres reproduced gender inequality in every sector. For instance, when the doctrine of the separate spheres is applied to labor, it leads to the dichotomy of labor and care, as well as paid and unpaid work, which are based on the subordination of women. Care is not viewed as a shared responsibility of men and women, rather as an individual responsibility of women who bear the double burden and face obstacles in their participation in the public sphere (Budlender & Hewitt, 2002; Lovenduski, 2005). Moreover, Phipps and Burton (1998) and Phipps et al. (2001) showed that time for oneself is much more stressful for women than for men. This situation exacerbates inequality within double-earner marriages. In fact, as they pointed out, the household utility framework suggests that only the total time for either the husband or wife matters, regardless of the way in which time is structured. This framework fails to consider that few husbands take on their wives' unpaid work responsibilities when their spouses joined the market labor force.

The role of care is especially controversial when feminists deal with the doctrine of the separate spheres. Some feminists, namely cultural feminists, consider caring as a peculiar feminine trait against the masculine tendency to be careless. They celebrate traditionally feminine qualities by claiming that women are innately superior to men. In doing so, feminists reinforced the doctrine instead of making women free from it, as they encourage women to play their traditional roles, designed by men and for their convenience, which appear inconsistent with any form of equality (Gilligan, 1982). For instance, MacKinnon (1987) pointed out that women value care because men value women for providing it.

The category of care is also adopted by some feminists who argue that the dichotomy between the public and the private spheres has been used, and continue to be used, to perpetuate women's oppression within liberal discourses (Armstrong & Squires, 2002). The authors suggest that liberalism cannot actually overcome the doctrine of the separate spheres because liberalism is compromised by the incorporation of traditional patriarchal norms, albeit it proposes a gender-neutral system based on equality among individuals regardless of their gender. According to them, the liberal discourse of individual autonomy is grounded in a theory of the self that is not a neutral description of human nature. Rather it derives from an exaltation of masculine norms that prioritize a notion of rationality which does not fit with women's nature, based on love and compassion rather than strength and competition. Hence, not only have women been denied the rights and privileges granted to the 'rational individuals' (men) in liberal societies, but also the care work performed by women has been devaluated. Hence, Armstrong and Squires identified classical liberals with standard economics *à la* Becker's based on a theory of the self as a rational maximizer agent. They do not consider two major arguments though. First, the classical liberal tradition and standard economics are not the faces of the same coin. Second, classical liberal tradition and a progressive agenda aimed at reducing inequalities are entirely compatible, as in the case of feminist economist Barbara Bergman (see Sect. 6.3 in this chapter).

Feminist scholar Carole Pateman (1988) claimed that the political freedom of individuals simultaneously entails the sexual subordination of women in marriage: patriarchy was relocated into the private domain and reformulated as complementary to civil society. Moller Okin (1989, 1998) claimed that the principle of non-intervention in the private sphere has been used by the state to justify inaction, formally denying its responsibility to intervene in familial disputes on the grounds that it is essential to limit state intervention in civil society and personal relations.

Against an abstract commitment to equality, West (1999) emphasized the role of women as primary caretakers mainly because they are naturally emphatic with the weakest, being them traditionally subjected to men's power. The significance of caring, both as a practice and as a moral stand, has generated a large feminist literature on the 'ethic of care' (Bubeck, 1995; Tronto, 1993).

Consistently with the ethic of care, many feminist economists, such as England and Folbre (1999), plead the state to implement specific support for caregivers and their dependents (Kittay, 2020). The capability approach by Nussbaum and Sen (1993) followed that direction too. Although women are responsible for raising children and developing children's capabilities, which are an asset for the society as a whole, women's work as caregivers is undercompensated and they are disproportionally in poverty. Hence, England and Folbre (1999) second Sen's argument and advocate for adequate support for children, who are considered 'public goods', and their caregivers, mainly women.

Against the care movement, which has, in some ways, reinforced the dichotomy between the public and private spheres, Franke (2001) pointed out that focusing on women as mothers and on the necessity to improve public support for mothers reinforces the 'maternalization' of women and the commodification of women's reproduction. While Case (2001) argues that those who are likely to benefit the most from a better support for care are male breadwinners while women without children are likely to bear the most burden. Hence, Case proposed equal parenting by partners and a monitored state provision directly to children.

The discussion around motherhood is crucial. If a woman decides not to be a mother, some people will stigmatize her, especially in some cultural context. If a woman decides to become a mother, she is likely to be primarily seen as a mother and likely be stigmatized if she prioritizes other tasks in her life. In fact, a series of disincentives become apparent: mothers earn less money than other workers, as they often work fewer hours while carrying the double burden; mothers' low wages do not end when their children grow up; working mothers of infants are often sleep-deprived as well as leisure-deprived; working mothers are affected by workplaces that are usually not designed in terms of space and time for caregiving responsibilities; pregnancy or absences associated with pregnancy or caregiving may lead working mothers to get fired or to quit their job, especially in countries without welfare measures *ad hoc*.

Nonetheless, M. Becker pointed out (2002) that in spite of the amount of disincentives to being a mother, eighty percent of working women are mothers, maybe because they "must experience something of value in mothering relative to their other options for meaningful work and relationships" (Becker, 2002, 70). For this reason, M. Becker presented a feminist approach that offers benefits to all members of society, not just women: an approach that rejects hyper-masculinity and praises traditionally feminine qualities, such as care, caretaking, and valuing relationships, without pressuring women to adopt traditionally feminine attributes and to repress masculine ones (Becker, 1999). She wrote:

> Patriarchy is a social structure, not a conspiracy among men. It is not always intentional; men need not intend to oppress women. (...) Men as well as women are damaged by patriarchy. For example, masculine men are hurt when they learn to repress emotions and to deny their needs for connection and intimacy. Although a man cannot be oppressed as a member of the group culture, because men as a group are not oppressed, subgroups of men can be oppressed (Becker, 1999, 30).

Motherhood is inevitably linked with the notion of marriage and family. Understanding the role of marriage in women's lives as well as the nature of family as an institution are fundamental aspects within any feminist agenda. The feminist analysis and critique of marriage, which can be dated back to the eighteenth and nineteenth centuries (see Chapter 2 and 4), has traditionally been rooted in the idea that marriage reinforces the traditional subjection of women. In societies where traditional patriarchy is still dominant, unmarried women are subjected to their fathers' will, and once they get married their subjection is simply transferred to their husbands' will. In soft-paternalistic societies, the legal protection eventually provided by marriage perpetuates women's economic and social dependence on their husbands. Either way, harms to women resulting from marriage are a direct effect of the doctrine of the separate spheres. As scrutinized in Chapter 5, standard economics played a crucial role in providing a marriage theory that reinforced the doctrine and consequently the status quo. Against the standard economics' perspective on the economics of the family, feminist economics provided an alternative marriage theory and a different economics of the family.

6.2 Challenging Becker's Economic Approach: Marriage Theory in Feminist Economics

Deeply influenced by feminist philosophy, feminist economics combines economic theory and a feminist stance by criticizing the neoclassical/standard approach to gender issues, which was seen as *malestream*, i.e. an approach based on an economic agent behavior who makes choices by adopting a very masculine attitude rooted in strength and competition, without including the 'feminine sphere', which is more oriented toward care and compassion (Nelson, 1993).

Against the traditional analysis of marriage provided by standard economics, feminist economists considered marriage as a social institution whose complex dynamics have too often been grounded in gender inequality, which persists in the intra-house dynamics of caring as well as in the dynamics of divorce and breakups. Differently from standard economics, which assumed gender inequality in the distribution of resources (including material provisions, leisure time, and investments in education in favor of boys) as *ceteris paribus* conditions, feminist economists scrutinized marriage by explicitly including social pressures as well as tacit and explicit rules and traditions related with age, classes, race, religion, sexual orientation, and gender identities. Moreover, feminist economists pointed out the relevant role of the legal framework which enormously affects the dynamics of marriage and divorce as well as other formal legal partnerships. Finally, feminist economists promoted economic policy aimed at improving the condition of women and children, especially considering that the marriage rate has been dropping in the last three decades, divorces have increased as well as lone parenthood and same-sex parenting.

From the perspective of the history of economic ideas and analysis, the first target of feminist economists was to challenge Becker's contribution on marriage theory and the economics of the family (summarized in Becker, 1981), which was mainly based on the analysis of intra-household allocation, as if there were a marriage market aimed at achieving a Pareto-optimal equilibrium (Blau & Winkler, 2018). Hence, feminist economists rejected Becker's approach by pointing out that it was grounded in a general cultural devaluation of women and social roles associated with women that led to gender discrimination of any kind (Barker & Feiner, 2004; Bergmann, 1995; Paterson & Lewis, 1999). According to feminist economists, although new home economists, following Becker, had partially enriched his original approach by introducing endogenous preferences that finally considered the role of social structures, they did not provide any model able to include the economics of care, as feminist economics does (England, 1993 [2003]; Folbre, 2001; Folbre & Nelson, 2000; Jacobsen, 2020; Woolley, 1999, 2003).

In her book, *Woman's Role in Economic Development*, Ester Boserup (1970) emphasized gender as a basic factor in the division of labor within family, both in developing and in developed countries. Despite the rhetoric of the doctrine of the separate spheres insisted on women's labor entirely devoted to the domestic sphere, Boserup pointed out several factors against this vision that were connected with an alternative analysis of marriage. First, women are breadwinners too, especially in some cultures and countries. Second, in some communities, there is a correlation between women's work and land holding that may explain polygamy, giving men control on more land assigned to their different wives. Third, the idea that land ownership belonged to men only is not commonly shared, rather it was introduced by European colonialism.

Boserup (1987) noticed that Becker relied only on biological differences, based on the idea that women are intrinsically more productive at child bearing than men, to explain the division of labor between household and other activities; and that the application of the rational choice theory to the supposed-lower marginal productivity of women's labor justified the idea of the inferiority of women. Moreover, according to Boserup, Becker overemphasized competition in market marriage by neglecting power relations and social pressure and by assuming harmony of interests between partners as well as an equal distribution of consumption and leisure between them.

Robert Ferber and Francesco Nicosia (1972) accused new home economics of being grounded in traditional gendered stereotypes that systematically ignored the separate and autonomous identities of the family members. Robinson and Converse (1972) considered the new home economics' model of household as oversimplified and biased in considering the failure of husbands to share burdens of household activities with their partners rational, rather than unfair. Another problem related to the new home economics model was the fact that it failed to take into account of differences across social classes and income groups. Berk and Berk ([1976] 1978) pointed out that the new home economics was irrelevant in terms of policy as it did not capture the presence of conflicts among family members as well as the effects of power control within the families. John P. Robinson (1977) claimed that the new home economics' methodological assumptions included the role of wives as the only partner to perform household tasks, the failure to contemplate lifetime in earning potentials, and "the unrealism and fuzziness of joint preference functions" (Robinson, 1977, 178).

Marianne Ferber and Bonnie Birnbaum (1977a, 1977b) criticized the new home economics because it failed to consider the discrepancies between the real world and their model, which adopted families as maximizing agents and ignored empirical evidence in time series that had shown that when husbands' wage increases, his wife dose not spend less time in the labor market and more time at home. Moreover, differently from what is supposed by the new home economics, data present extensive evidence that, on average, husbands of women working outside the home spend very little more time working at home.

As Nancy Folbre (1986, 1998c) originally pointed out, Becker's unitary model of the household was awkward because it assumed either that all household members have the same preferences, pool all resources, and agree on all decisions, or that one household member makes the decisions for everyone. That model implied social norms based on gender roles, determined by the doctrine of the separate spheres, as exogenous and it assumed that altruism prevails within families, which is problematic in terms of realism and inconsistent with the notion of *homo oeconomicus*. In fact, the selfish economic agent in standard economics does not match with a cooperative and devoted *pater familias*. She stated:

> [Becker's theory] relies heavily on perfect self-interest in the market and perfect altruism in the family. It resembles a caricature of a nineteenth-century separatist idea. It is not exclusively that men are self-interested and women are altruistic, but that the male world in the market is totally self-interested and the female world of the family is total benevolence, total altruism, and lacking in opportunism (Folbre, 1998c, 46).

Folbre rejected Becker's standard economics, idea that inequality is voluntary, and women choose to devote more time and energy to family than to work, which led them to acquire fewer specific market skills, being their intrinsic utility function maximized by marriage and motherhood. She also rejected the standard economics idea that women are not as willing as men to commit themselves to a career, which is used to explain why women are paid less. Regarding Becker's contribution on endogenous preferences, Folbre claimed that Becker failed to explain the evolution of norms, which is not always a matter of neutral distributional efficiency, such as driving on the right or left-hand side; rather it was, and it is often, a matter of political struggle between differently powerful groups, such as men and women.

Finally, according to Folbre, Becker totally neglected an actual analysis of caregiving (both paid and unpaid), which is almost totally provided by women who are also highly concentrated in caring occupations such as teaching, nursing, child care, and elder care. She pointed out that an analysis of what unpaid care contributes to living standards and the development of human capabilities is necessary. Becker ignored that the benefits of his model were the effects of men exploiting women's care work at home (Bowles & Gintis, 1977; Delphy, 1984;

Ferguson & Folbre, 1981; Folbre, 1982) or of men getting jobs and incomes from sectors where women have deliberately been excluded (Hartmann, 1981).

Myra Strober (1987) outlined that the examination of the motivations behind some choices, such as marriage and divorce, had been wrongly explained by Becker's model. She proposed to overcome "reasoned judgement economics to make critical evaluations of personal, familial, occupational, and societal economic alternatives" (Strober, 1987, 145).[3] In the same year, Elaine McCrate (1987) pointed out that Becker's model did not adequately consider the role of conflicts among family members by acknowledging that the solution to the Rotten Kid Theorem is "a static Cournot-Nash non-cooperative equilibrium position" (Becker, 1977, 506). She provided an analysis of the Rotten Kid Theorem by directing her critique at Becker's lack of clarity about the significantly distinct conditions under which men and women bargain and by pointing out that Becker assumed only one family member as the *effective* altruistic one.

Paula England (1993 [2003]) seconded Folbre by presenting Becker's marriage theory affected by the 'soluble conception of self', i.e. an overly simplistic vision of family that overemphasized empathy and connectivity among family members while ignoring the possibility that men might not be altruistic toward their partners and children. According to England, the efforts made by new home economists to amend Becker's model did not succeed in creating a model capable of accounting for both altruism and selfishness in both markets and families. She stated that only the economics of care in feminist economics had taken steps towards "modeling behavior when selfishness and empathy are variables and when preferences can change in response to the environment" (England, 1993 [2003], 53). Julie Nelson underlined that Becker's approach to the economics of marriage, which analyzed marriage in terms of utilities, "has more to do with the comforts of orthodoxy than with the requirements of productive investigation" (Nelson, 1994, 126).

[3] Strober (1995) also criticized Grossbard's thesis, which viewed marriage and employment as substitutes for women, creating a trade-off between the two.

Some other feminist economists criticized Becker's approach, particularly in relation to the doctrine of the separate spheres: way before the publication of Coontz's book (1992), which pointed out that the supposed 'golden age' of family values in the 1950s, based on the male breadwinner, was a very recent and short-lived invention grounded in a form of nostalgia for a mythical and harmonious society, feminist economists had already criticized Becker's attitude to reinforce that nostalgic image that, by the way, positively affects only men.

As Ferber and Birnbaum (1977a) pointed out, the new home economics' notion of family resembled a 'bastion of tradition' rather than a rational maximizing unit. They wrote:

> Clearly tradition is the dominant factor in determining the division of tasks within the family (..) When women are trained for and devote much of their time to household responsibilities, while men are trained for and encouraged to enter the labor market, comparative advantage becomes little more than a self-fulfilling prophecy (Ferber & Birnbaum, 1977a, 21).

As Ferber suggested, tradition played the main role not just in Becker's application of comparative advantage to the division of labor between men and women but also in the work of other standard economists: Willis (1973) assumed that the husband's time spent at home is entirely unproductive. Additionally, Mincer and Polachek (1974) linked the different allocation of time and investments in human capital to gender, offering a tautological argument suggesting that women specialize in housework because they earn less in the labor market, and they earn less in the labor market because they specialize in housework.

Feminist economist Barbara Bergmann viewed marriage as an institution that responded to social norms which had traditionally segregated women to the domestic sphere, thus discriminating them in the public sphere (as discussed in more detail in Sect. 6.3 of this chapter). According to her, traditional gender stereotypes assigned men and women different roles in the economy and society, resulting in significant disparities in power, professional development, social interactions, and the pursuit of individual talents and desires. She argued that three significant developments since the 1970s have challenged the doctrine of the separate spheres and prompted scholars, including economists, to work on addressing these societal changes: the increased participation of women in the paid workforce, the rise of single mothers, and the emergence of feminist economics advocating for policies that promote a more equitable world. In contrast, standard economists defended and justified 'the old regime'. As she wrote: "Becker explained, justified, and even glorified role differentiation by sex" (Bergmann, 1987, 132).

According to Bergmann, standard economists, influenced by Becker, opposed women's calls for affirmative action, as they held "a stereotype attitude about women", and carried a "sexist baggage". They applied the theory of comparative advantage to explain the division of labor between the sexes and the specialization of women in the domestic sphere without acknowledging the discrimination and segregation of women in the private sphere. Bergmann argued that women's traditional roles in the domestic sphere, which resulted in their accumulation of less human capital, should be seen as a form of discrimination rather than a free and rational choice. On the opposite side of the ideological spectrum, according to Bergmann, Marxist economists, focused on building up a system able to destroy inequalities of all kind, do not spend energies by "fighting inequalities here and now" (ibid.). Bergmann claimed that standard economists tend to overemphasize the effect of competition and adopt economic models that ignore or deny the importance of social and psychological factors that lead to discrimination against women. This, in turn, leads to a market that produces unfair and distorted outcomes (Bergmann, 1989).

Drucilla Barker (1995) pointed out that Becker's model of the family was a rationalization and reinforcement for the existing distribution of power and wealth, grounded in discrimination on the basis of race, class, and gender, ultimately favoring men's public roles (Barker, 1995, 35–36). Phipps and Burton (1995) considered Becker's model of household behavior as a formal development of the Victorian ideal of the family, where women were constrained in their role as mothers and wives in the private sphere while being excluded from the public arena. Barker and Feiner (2004) claimed that feminist economics did not romanticize the role of women in the private sphere by assuming their subordinate social status as natural, rather by considering it a form of inequality. They presented a feminist perspective based on five criteria: fairness, participation, economic security, acknowledgment of the potential wastefulness of economic potentiality, and provision of opportunity for all individuals. They encouraged the development of economic models that could challenge and ultimately dismantle the doctrine of the separate spheres.

Frances Woolley (1996) considered some Becker's claim, such as the idea that girls more inclined towards market-oriented activities display antisocial behavior, that divorcees are likely to have troublesome personalities, and that women who marry wealthy men are more attractive than others, as gender stereotypes rooted in the doctrine of the separate spheres.

Gillian Hadfield (1999) explained the doctrine of the separate spheres as a traditional gender divisions of labor aimed at mitigating a coordination problem in the marriage market. In contrast to Becker's assertion that the gender division of labor is driven by biological differences between men and women, Hadfield noted that the basic coordination problem in skill acquisition does not imply that specific tasks must be performed by either men or women. Instead, it suggests that some gender division of labor needs to be specified.

Matthew Baker and Joyce Jacobsen (2007) developed a model that examines how a customary gender division of labor can alleviate coordination issues in the marriage market. Unlike Hadfield (1999), they presented a model in which, given the task segregation specified by a gender division of labor, agents may still choose to learn their specified tasks inefficiently. Their findings revealed that the doctrine of the separate spheres, while potentially beneficial in certain contexts, disadvantaged the gender that had less power and limited individuals' ability to function independently of marriage. They also pointed out that the gender with a distributional advantage tends to possess more marketable labor, making them resistant to changes in labor markets that would enhance the marketability of the other gender's labor. Similarly, they would resist changes in marriage patterns that could increase the likelihood of separation and divorce.

Other feminist economists, such as Katz (1997), Agarwal (1997), and Colander and Woos (1997), raised concerns about Becker's failure to recognize gender-based power relations. They emphasized the importance of incorporating ideology and culture into economic analysis. Specifically, Katz suggested moving away from the standard cooperative bargain model and adopting an interdisciplinary feminist-institutional approach in order to better understand the dynamics behind marriage and divorce. Agarwal criticized the descriptions of intra-household dynamics by new home economists, who characterized them as a mix of cooperation and conflict without considering qualitative factors and external elements. She stressed the significance of gender-based discrimination beyond the household, such as in the labor market, communities, and the state. Colander and Woos criticized the application of human capital theory to the analysis of gender inequality in the labor market, including gender pay gap: they argued that attributing such disparities solely to free choice neglected the role of discrimination against women.

Some feminist economists, like Iversen (2003), followed Sen's marriage model (1990) that portrays marriage as a 'cooperative conflict'. Spouses benefit from cooperation in providing household goods and services, including cohabitation, caring of the children, and so forth. Yet, they are in conflict over household distribution, which includes any allocation of surplus produced by household division of labor, and largely varies accordingly to different social and cultural framework. Sen had also pointed out that, particularly in developed countries, there are fewer and fewer households with women staying at home, as the majority of women work outside of the home; this shift requires women to balance their role in both private and public spheres. Iversen's applied Sen's capability approach to intra-household inequality when evaluating people's well-being: in a domestic relationship, an individual well-being will depend not only on her own capabilities but also on those of her significant other. The analysis of capability approach from a feminist perspective had drawn a special attention to domestic power imbalances, which had been ignored by both new home economists and by welfare economists who did never take account of intra-house inequality.

Woolley (1993) listed six specific feminist challenges to standard economics: developing models capable of explaining endogenous preferences; acknowledging that people make systematic mistakes; insisting on the tremendous importance of gender stereotypes; finding out factors that shape the institutions that privilege or disadvantage women; developing a better economic model of caring and reproductive activity.

She emphasized that ignoring effects of unequal outcomes in specific demographic group in the name of efficient markets can diminish economists' relevance in policy discussions. She also underlined that while feminist economists may not always share the same views, they recognize the importance of accurately modeling factors like power dynamics within households, gender bias in resource allocation favoring sons over daughters, and unequal access to land and capital markets. Accounting for these factors, especially through considering intra-household allocation rather than relying on a unitary household model, can lead to significantly different policy recommendations.

Finally, Woolley pointed out that the challenging form of gender bias was the invisibility of women in standard economics' male-oriented modeling: standard economists tended to regard the private sphere as a black box by treating the household as a single individual. This model was possible only by assuming that the interests of women and children were subsumed interests of the male breadwinner. Yet, as she wrote: "building models of the family according to the standard economic rules, that people maximize their own well-being (which may depend upon the well-being of all people) subject to some set of constraints, fails to yield explanations or predictions about family behavior" (Woolley, 1993, 495).

Recently Averett et al. (2018) wrote that today's differences between standard economics of gender and feminist economics are more evident in their policy focus rather than in their theoretical foundations. However, Jacobsen (2018) has highlighted that there are still significant differences between the two approaches. The economics of gender is primarily concerned with understanding how gender differences lead to diverse economic outcomes using the framework of standard economics, based on individual preferences. In contrast, feminist economics takes a more comprehensive approach by exploring how conventional methods of measuring economic outcomes have been shaped, and how applying a feminist economic perspective to various areas, including marriage theory, labor supply, earnings determination, endogenous preferences, and their interaction with care work, can lead to different predictions and results. Furthermore, standard economics of gender heavily relies on econometrics and mathematical models by reducing storytelling to zero (McCloskey, 1990).

When family structure matters, as it does in feminist economics, one must consider human capital investments related to the type of family and society. Feminist economics, as seen in Bergmann's crowding model (Bergmann, 1974a), accounts for these aspects. In her model, women may either choose or be compelled to work in sectors traditionally labeled as 'pink-collar' due to discrimination in other sectors. This discrimination results in lower wages even in sectors that are not inherently discriminatory. A similar effect can be observed among self-employed women, especially in microcredit situations. Women may find themselves constrained to operate in sectors with lower capital requirements due to their lack of access to capital markets for larger loans.

In labor economics, feminist economists considered how social and cultural institutions within societies can reinforce the gender division of labor and create obstacles for individuals seeking to deviate from traditional roles, even when such deviations might be economically efficient for individual households. In fact, in standard labor economics model, the wage of the optimizing agent is assumed exogenous; human capital investments are made in advance, so they are exogenous to the current labor supply decision; gender pay gap is also due to market power as women tend to be in monopsonized labor markets and being tied movers due to their family ties. Standard economics considered these factors effects of individual preferences. Feminist economics pointed out that expecting discrimination played a fundamental role in women's decisions that cannot be reduced to simple preferences: expecting discrimination might lead women to enter specific sectors and to refrain from investing in market skills, including the reluctance to make career-enhancing moves.

Furthermore, feminist economists emphasized that the intersectionality of gender disparities with other forms of disparities related to race and ethnicity may have a multiplicative effect and result in additional costs, whether physical or real.

Finally, feminist economists took seriously the nature of caring labor and the decreasing bargaining power of care workers in the labor market. As Folbre pointed out, care work is a form of being held hostage for caregivers, mostly women: it is hard for them to go on strike, and caretakers have high needs and generally low assets especially when it comes to children and the disabled (Table 6.1).

Table 6.1 The economics of marriage and the division of labor between partners: Becker's standard approach versus feminist economics' approach

Becker's standard approach	Feminist economics' approach
The division of labor within households depends on biological and cultural differences between men and women which led men to perform better in the public sphere and women to perform better in the private sphere	The division of labor within households depends on gendered stereotypes that assigned men to the public sphere and women to the domestic sphere by determining the subjection of the latter to the former
The allocation of women's time to the private sphere and of men's time to the public sphere is a matter of individual preferences and it is rational and efficient	The allocation of women's time to the private sphere and of men's time to the public sphere is an effect of power relations within a patriarchal system, which is unfair
Labor segregation and gender wage gap are natural consequences of the specific division of labor between partners, with women who freely choose to devote themselves much more to the private sphere rather than to their commitment in the public sphere (their career)	Labor segregation and gender wage gap are consequences of the specific division of labor between men and women which is socially constructed, and usually not freely chosen by women
A single household's utility function depends on the male breadwinner family who is supposed to be benevolent	A single household's utility function is a nonsense and the male breadwinner might be not benevolent at all
Given the condition listed above, marriage is seen as a long-term commitment to assure women to be protected within the private sphere	Given the condition listed above, marriage is seen as a form of coercion for women who often carry the double burden of being in the workforce and the only care-providers in the household
Specialized market-oriented investments on boys and household-oriented ones on girls are optimal strategies to strengthen the status quo	Specialized market-oriented investments on boys and household-oriented ones on girls are gendered stereotyped strategies which are in favor of boys/men

6.3 Going Beyond the Doctrine of the Separate Spheres: Barbara Bergmann's Combination of Feminist Economics and Classical Liberalism Against Becker's Approach

Barbara Bergmann's work on the theory of marriage represents one of the most important critiques of Becker's approach to the economics of the family. Her contributions on this specific topic, which were published between 1974 and 1986, often in response to Becker's work of the same period, played a pivotal role in the emergence and the development of feminist economics as an autonomous research field.

As mentioned earlier, Bergmann identified the doctrine of the separate spheres as the primary obstacle to women's emancipation. She rejected the justification for it offered by standard economics, which failed to acknowledge discrimination and segregation and insisted that women's traditional role in the domestic sphere was an efficient allocation of their labor and a free choice. She specifically argued that Becker's new home economics was inadequate in understanding the dynamics of families. Finally, she outlined her own policy proposals to enhance family condition.

Almost unique in her position among feminist economists, she integrated a feminist perspective, which called for affirmative action to diminish market discrimination and eliminate gender stereotypes concerning women's domestic roles, with a classical liberal vision, focused on the role of market and political institutions in providing the means necessary to facilitate women's emancipation as active participants in the public sphere.

When asked in an interview what type of feminism she advocates, Bergmann replied that she supported "the total commodification of family work where we dismantle the female sphere, the unpaid family work" against the maintenance of the traditional female spheres by adopting some form of rewards for care work (Saunders & King, 2010, 311). She firmly believed that the only possible way to reach gender equality was a "totally androgynous model" that does away with gender stereotypes and barriers (Bergmann, 1998). She explained that this transition towards gender equality will be completed through a significant program of government supporting "high commodification" of care work, making possible for women to be embedded "into the 'male world' of money exchange, with a distribution of jobs similar to that of men" by concluding that some women "must play the male game" (Bergmann, 1998, 79–82).[4]

Bergmann specifically worked on the economic theory of marriage in the 1980s, after having devoted most of her efforts in analyzing the economics of discrimination during the 1970s. Bergmann's first economic analysis of marriage was an unpublished study (Bergmann, 1974b) on the effects of divorce on women and children in the United States. She criticized the common opinion according to which American middle-class women who devoted themselves to full-time unpaid household management should be happy with their status because their standard of living was higher than ever. Bergmann tried to show that this opinion perpetuated a stereotype that did not correspond to the real situation of many American housewives, who were mainly bored by their lives, as pointed out by Betty Friedan's *The Feminine Mystique* (1963).

According to Bergmann, the analysis of the data provided by the Bureau of Labor Statistics revealed that women's occupational segregation and overcrowding was more severe than any occupational segregation and overcrowding due to race: the traditional division of labor in households, the gender labor gap in high-skilled jobs, and the gender wage gap had reinforced and perpetuated discrimination against women who were not allowed to enter more remunerative jobs.

She strongly attacked the doctrine of the separate spheres by rejecting the common opinion that women's discrimination in the market was compensated by their husbands taking care of them and providing a good standard of living. As the dramatic rise in divorce rates showed, women wanted to leave their marriages although their economic situation was likely to worsen without their soon-to-be ex-husbands' income.

---

[4] On this specific aspect of Bergmann's feminist agenda, see Folbre (1998b).

Bergman insisted that, between 1960 and 1972, data also revealed a fifty-six percent increase in households headed solely by women who were often forced to rely on welfare due to the employment segregation they faced.[5] Hence, Bergmann promoted affirmative action to combat women's employment segregation, such as quotas as well as legal procedure to force separated or divorced fathers to consistently provide paid child care, that would help prevent any form of self-segregation of women at home.[6]

Her paper "The Economic Risk of Being a Housewife", published in 1981, in the *American Economic Review* (Bergmann, 1981c), represented a direct response to Becker's approach to marriage theory. Contrary to Becker, who rationalized the traditional gendered-biased division of roles in the separate spheres, Bergmann emphasized that the massive presence of women entering the labor force had transformed the traditional division of labor between men and women within the family. She targeted "Becker's encomium to the advantages of the division of labor among spouses" by defining it biased by "its perspective of a male member of a traditional family" (Bergmann, 1981c, 81).

According to Bergmann, being a housewife was much riskier than working in many occupations. The risks of being a housewife included unpaid duties like housekeeping and childcare, exposure to physical hazards in domestic accidents, a higher likelihood of domestic violence compared to physical assaults in the workplace, and non-cash, untaxed benefits instead of a regular salary. Furthermore, variability in payoff resulting from the possibility of marriage ending in divorce was high and the financial and emotional trauma of getting divorce far surpassed the distress of losing a job. Moreover, while the relationship between former employers and employees ends after the contract termination,

---

[5] Bergmann's archival material reveals that she was working on a research proposal for an adequate and equitable economic support system for children whose divorced fathers did not provide them any regular financial support (Bergmann, 1981a). Her research proposal was intended to be a book, composed of eleven chapters, but it instead appeared only in partial form in an article published in 1981 (Bergmann, 1981b) and later revised and included (again in partial form) in her book *The Economic Emergence of Women* (Bergmann, 1986).

[6] Bergmann worked on proposing an adequate and equitable economic support system for children whose divorced fathers did not provide them any regular financial support (Bergmann, 1981a).

the role of ex-husbands in women's lives remains central in case of children. In fact, ex-husbands usually are responsible for alimony and child support that are often unpaid or irregularly provided.

Hence, Bergmann concluded by considering that being a housewife, i.e. devoting women's time and skills to the domestic sphere, was not properly a choice, otherwise it should have been chosen equally by men; rather it can be regarded as a 'caste'. Like in any other caste system, traditional roles are reinforced by social pressure and by specific education, in this case, the traditional education for girls (which included the 'Prince Charming legend') played a fundamental role. While Becker justified this situation as the effect of a rational choice based on human capital theory, Bergmann pointed out that women who leave the caste usually are forced to confront "employment discrimination", "social stigma" on divorced women, and the "social pressure on wives not to seek paid employment" (Bergmann, 1981c, 84).[7]

Another crucial publication by Bergmann appeared in 1983 (later reprinted in Bergmann, 1990). Bergmann specifically targeted new home economists based in Chicago as the group of "mainline economists", who analyzed the economics of marriage by invoking the theory of comparative advantage to reinforce the traditional division of labor between the sexes. Bergmann shared other feminist economists' concerns and critiques about the new home economics' marriage theory, such as the benevolence of the male breadwinner and the natural propensity of women to take care of children due to the nature of biological motherhood which makes women more responsible for child-rearing than fatherhood. Bergmann considered these assumptions unrealistic and heavily gender stereotyped, thus unable to seriously analyze the motivations to marry, the evolution of the contribution of partners at home and in the market, and the distribution of family resources among spouses and children (Bergmann, 1983 [1990]).

Three years later, in 1986, Bergmann systematized her contribution to marriage theory by publishing *The Economic Emergence of Women*

---

[7] In another article dated 1981, mainly focused on the decrease in the flow of financial support from separated fathers to children, she portrayed marriage as an obsolete institution intended "to limit the number of 'fatherless' children" (Bergmann, 1981c, 106).

(second and enlarged edition dated 2005). As she has done previously, she defined the traditional division of roles between men and women within families and society as a 'sex-role caste system' based on what has traditionally been denoted as the doctrine of the separate spheres that never took into account women's employment discrimination and was reinforced by Becker's human capital theory, which deliberately ignored that men and women compete in segregating markets (Bergmann, 1986).

Bergmann clearly pointed out that since women had gradually entered the job market a social transformation occurred and radically challenged the rationale of the doctrine of the separate spheres, based on employment discrimination against women and men's evasion of housework. Bergmann explicitly accused Becker to ignore that employment discrimination made the theory of comparative advantage appropriate rather than the other way around. Furthermore, Becker reduced both sex and racial discrimination in the job market to personal preferences by ignoring the role of social pressure that may heavily influence individuals' choice, such as men neglecting housework and child care.

After Becker received the Nobel Prize, Bergmann felt the urgency of pointing out that his way of dealing with marriage theory and the division of labor was a huge step backward toward the doctrine of the separate spheres. According to Bergmann, although Becker's work earned recognition from the Nobel Prize committee, it "failed badly" in providing "a realistic appreciation of actual problems that are being encountered and the policies that might be applied to them". Bergmann criticized "the paucity of factors" that Becker considered as "proofs of his diagrammatic and algebraic modes of characterization and persuasion" as well as his "tendency to idealize the phenomenon under examination as optimal", subjected to be ruined by any specific policy. In her view, Becker's work on the family "concentrates most of his attention on the Victorian ideal of the family, although it appears he would judge the harem, a still more retrograde version of the family, to be even more praiseworthy" (Bergmann, 1995 [1996], 10).

According to Bergmann, Becker's analysis of the family was misleading and unable to understand especially three topics: polygamy versus monogamy, altruism, and fertility. First, in Becker's work, women do better under polygamy than under monogamy, as their price for selling themselves into marriage under polygamy is higher. Second, Becker thought that an altruistic individual derives positive utility from the increase in another's consumption and, given the state of the labor market, in which men have access to better jobs than women do, the benevolent member is the male breadwinner. Finally, Becker explained fertility by pointing out that people have children accordingly to their standard of living, which are influenced by the inheritance of capital they get and the rate of return on that capital.

In Bergmann's view, Becker's argumentation on these three topics was biased by "a naive, not to say boyish, faith in the ability of pared-down models with as few as two variables to produce truth, even where the situation being analyzed has many variables, most of which cannot be represented handily on a supply-and-demand curve diagram" (Bergmann, 1995 [1996], 11). Against Becker's three arguments, Bergmann pointed out that the advantages of polygamy for women are false as "in societies that allow polygamy, the status of women is abysmal"; Becker's implicit assumption that all males are altruists is false and ridiculous; finally, speaking of fertility, Becker considered irrelevant some factors of prime importance, such as availability of contraception and abortion as well as the role of religion and social norms in determining relations between partners and children, and the position of women in the society.

As some feminist economists underlined, Bergmann's emphasis on equal access to the labor market allowed her to explore public policies aimed at ensuring equal opportunity for men and women in the labor market (Folbre, 1998a, 1998b; Olson, 2007; Olson & Emami, 2002). During the last decade of her life and intellectual production, she worked on two more research projects, specifically related to the economic theory of marriage and the family. They were: *The Challenge of Single Motherhood* (Bergmann, 2003), a book proposal focused on policy measures for single mothers,[8] and *The Decline of Marriage and What To Do About It*, a book proposal on the decline of the institution of marriage, which was partially embedded in a working paper she presented at the University of

[8] It remained unpublished mainly because Bergmann was unable to find a publisher, as letters in her archive indicate.

Linz (Bergmann, 2008). Bergmann noted that the long-term decline in marriage rates raised several economic and emotional challenges, particularly regarding the upbringing of children. While conservatives expressed concern about the decline of marriage, viewing it as a potential threat to society, liberals accepted this trend and suggested that the decrease in married couples had been compensated for by the rise in couples cohabiting without marriage. Bergmann pointed out that while conservatives accurately diagnosed the issue, their proposed solutions were neither necessarily effective nor appropriate.

Again, in her last publication on marriage theory, Bergmann directly attacked Becker's *Treatise* and his followers, who attributed the decline of marriage to the introduction of new technologies that facilitated women's work at home and pushed them into the labor force, by reducing the efficient specialization within marriages.

Bergmann insisted on a feminist agenda that encompasses a two-part approach: equal job market opportunities for both genders and an equal distribution of household responsibilities between spouses in order to transform marriage into "a loving alliance between two economically and socially equal people" (Bergmann, 2005, 9).

Hence, her feminist agenda involved implementing affirmative action measures to balance the division of labor in both work and family between men and women as the only path to achieving gender equality.

Bergmann's position aligned with contemporary classical liberal feminists who endorse specific policies aimed at diminishing gender inequality and emphasizing the importance of promoting an educational system that ensures equal opportunities in the job market, along with promoting equitable sharing of responsibilities between spouses in household. This combination of short-term policy measures and long-term educational commitments represents the only way to make the doctrine of the separate spheres obsolete (Bergmann, 2005).

Differently from classical liberal feminists of the eighteenth, nineteenth, and early twentieth centuries, who confined feminism's political role to opposing laws that treated women differently from men,

Bergmann belonged to a more contemporary classical liberal feminist tradition, often referred to as egalitarian-liberalism, which includes figures like Rawls, Moller Okin, Nussbaum, and Sen, who actively advocated for policies aimed at bolstering women's personal and political autonomy. These policies encompassed areas like anti-discrimination laws, affirmative action, and welfare state programs.

Some authors, such as Horwitz (2015), pointed out that classical liberalism may offer a non-conservative defense of the family as well as it may provide a meaningful theory of the family that does not rely on the concept of the traditional family, rooted in heterosexual marriages, and can encompass various family structures, including domestic relationships, same-sex marriages and queer families. Drawing from Hayek's concept of spontaneous order and emphasizing the interplay among culture, society, and individuals, as well as Mises' emphasis on the idea of social cooperation, Horwitz defined the family as a continuously evolving and privately organized social institution that fulfills functions that cannot be substituted by either the State or the community.

As Horwitz rightly suggested, since the nineteenth century, the doctrine of the separate spheres "became a social myth that performed the function of reconciling the promise of equality inherent in marriages based on consent and love with the objective differences in each gender's access to resources and power" (Horwitz, 2015, 90). The effect was that women became more dependent on marriage than ever before. Economists, from Victorian England to new home economics, exacerbated the situation by depicting women's choice to dedicate themselves entirely to household production as a rational choice. Conversely, Horwitz continued:

> from a Hayekian perspective, the spheres themselves did not disappear; what changed in the twentieth century was that both spheres were open to both genders. However, without gender to demarcate those spheres in a socially visible way, it was easy to forget that they still existed and that there were meaningful differences between them (Horwitz, 2015, 100).

Classical liberal feminists consider marriage (or domestic relationship) as an equal partnership, and plead for men's involvement in child care. They also support abortion and planned parenthood, which are linked to individual autonomy. Their primary goal is gender equality in the public sphere, including equal access to education, equal pay, and the elimination of job sex segregation. They champion legal changes and policies to make this possible. They also address private sphere issues that hinder equality in the public sphere and encourage a shared responsibility between partners in managing households. Some feminist critics have accused their position of evaluating women's success using male standards, as in the case of Bergmann, who explicitly invited women to play the game by following the male rules.

The crucial point for classical liberals like Bergmann is that they do not consider these values to be inherently masculine; instead, they view them as human values applicable to any individual, regardless of their gender, ethnicity, sexual orientation, or class. The publications of Friedan's works (1963, 1981) contributed to this perspective. She rejected the notion of female superiority and advocated for social androgyny, particularly in her earlier writings. Although in her later works, she replaced competition with cooperation, androgyny, which involves a blend of stereotypically male and female qualities, remained the primary means to achieve gender equality.

One possible solution in terms of policy, according to Bergmann, could be to implement a model similar to Sweden's approach to balancing responsibilities between parents in child rearing and homemaking. This model includes parental leave in case of the birth or adoption of a child, paid medical leave, and other welfare measures. The goal is to enable women to combine motherhood and a career while also encouraging men to share the traditionally female-dominated responsibilities of parenthood. Nonetheless, data reveal that the double burden on women persists, as only a small percentage of men take advantage of the possibilities provided by this type of policy (Figart et al., 2002). This outcome further supports Bergmann's idea that family policy alone does not solve the problem of the double burden for women that requires the elimination of gender inequality in the labor force, by including measures like a temporary system of quotas, equal pay legislation, incentives for female employment, and more. These measures should be accompanied by a general cultural shift that, in the long run, will lead to a different attitude toward care work, making it a central part of men's values and attitudes.

6.4 Are the Separate Spheres Still Separate Today?

There is no unique answer to this question. The answer depends on geographical areas, political frameworks, and social rules that vary across different cultures. The answer also depends on two major phenomena: the entrance of women into the labor force, which is related to their agency in the public sphere, and the status of women within marriages and families, which is related to the dynamics involving women in the private sphere.

There is no doubt that for millennia, the phenomenon of women's underrepresentation in the public sphere had originated gender inequality in education, in politics, in the economy, in leadership role, and so forth. As we have seen, starting from the eighteenth century the battle for women's empowerment within the public sphere has continually gained momentum. Legal rights, access to all levels of education, women's suffrage, and women's participation in the labor force have all contributed to reducing gender inequality in the public sphere.

We have also observed changes in the status of women in the private sphere. The emergence of the cult of domesticity, combined with the notion of 'true womanhood', which began in the nineteenth century and was paradoxically reaffirmed and strengthened by new home economics, effectively confined women to the domestic sphere. Though the sexual revolution and the introduction of contraception, abortion, and divorce have significantly expanded women's self-determination and control over their lives in the private sphere. Additionally, more recently, the recognition of domestic relationships and same-sex marriage has broadened the traditional concept of the family. The interplay of these two major developments has been scrutinized by gender studies in order to comprehend the origins of gender inequalities and to assess the existing gender disparities in both spheres.

Gender studies, which have evolved over the past decades, were designed to elucidate the mechanisms of women's subordination and to offer potential solutions to achieve gender equality by proposing strategies to redress the historical disadvantages women have faced in terms of autonomy, resource access, and leadership.[9] As we have seen, political economists and economists endeavored to comprehend power dynamics within the labor force and households. They adopted micro-analyses of decision-making, proposed economic policy measures, and developed economic theories related to marriage and the family. Gender studies help economics to analyze gender stereotypes in order to explain the economic and social status of women and men, as well as the gender disparities that traditionally favor men, leading to discrimination against women.

The integration of gender studies into economics has resulted in a more consistent and robust framework for explaining gender-based economic inequality and discrimination. It helped in understanding the distinction between inequality and discrimination while also emphasizing their inherent interconnections. Since all social interactions are influenced by gender, and these interactions are driven by social status, discrimination emerges when women's and men's statuses are subjected to stereotyping while inequality may or may not be the effect of a form of discrimination. Moreover, the collection of empirical data in specific datasets helps to explain economic phenomena related with gender stereotypes and discrimination.

Although gender issues have been studied through different and sometimes opposite analytical tools by standard economists and by feminist economists, the two approaches have gradually converged, especially lately. This convergence has become increasingly evident, particularly in recognizing that closing gender disparities can significantly enhance a nation's overall prosperity. While they may differ in terms of theory and methodology, both standard economics and feminist economics have

[9] Since the 1990s, the word 'gender' has been introduced into academic language.

contributed to the understanding of the enduring division between the 'separate spheres' and have laid the groundwork for an economic policy agenda designed to address and reduce gender inequality.

The aim of any economic policy, which takes gender issues seriously, is to scrutinize several factors such as: the cost of gender inequality in macro-sectors, including business; the role of gender assumptions in global policy; the way to increase economic empowerment for women; the cost of gender inequality in labor market; the possibility to introduce quotas; the role of gender in sustainability, health and innovation, women empowerment, and the correlation between women empowerment and economic development (Bohnet, 2016; Cassar & Katz, 2016; Duflo, 2012). An economic policy agenda usually incorporates empirical research that demonstrates how cultural differences related to gender roles, such as those influenced by religion, family structure, and language, have emerged as a consequence of specific historical situations. These gender roles tend to persist even when the circumstances that initially gave rise to them change. This is particularly evident in very stable environments where cultural norms and expectations may endure over time.

Gender equality was one of the fundamental principles of the European Union's treaties (Rome 1957, Amsterdam 1997, Lisbon 2007/2009). In 1995, the United Nations introduced the United Nations Development Program (UNDP), the Gender-Related Development Index (GDI), and the Gender Empowerment Measure (GEM) to monitor and assess data related to gender inequalities and disparities in various sectors around the world.

As Myra Strober pointed out in her powerful autobiography (2016), written for students who are—in her words—neither aware of the present situation nor of the history of women's emancipation, various forms of gender inequality persist globally. Today gender inequality includes the gender pay gap, occupational segregation in lower-paying sectors, the glass ceiling, which refers to the fact that men are more likely to be promoted than women, and career penalties for mothers. As we can observe, traditional gender issues persist.

Global datasets eventually help to understand the present situation. Since 2006, the World Economic Forum has been annually publishing the Global Gender Gap Report.[10] International organizations, such as OECD and ILO, as well as national institutes of statistics, regularly report data on gender inequalities. Their common aim is to ensure that both women and men can fully participate as equal partners in private and public life, equally sharing responsibilities in decision-making process and gaining access to opportunities to improve their lives.

Overall, data indicates that women's position in the public sphere is still subordinate to men's in nearly every field, with the exception of education, around the world. However, the extent of this inequality varies, and its causes range from legal subordination to cultural norms, from social pressures to a lack of institutional support. Global datasets confirm that the higher gender gap the lower the economic performance of a society. Nonetheless, the systemic inequality between men and women persists.

In the public sphere, women's underrepresentation may be regarded as a dramatic limit to the economic well-being of the society as a whole and a drastic obstacle to the increase of GDPs. In the private sphere side, data reveal that the phenomenon of the double burden is still mainly carried by women.

The Global Gender Gap Report (2023) reveals that "not only was women's participation slipping globally, but other markers of economic opportunity were showing substantive disparities between women and men" (World Economic Forum, 2023, 33).[11]

In the economy, gender labor gap, gender wage gap, and gender entrepreneurship gap represent the three most significant forms of gender inequality.

[10] The World Economic Forum's last report (2023) benchmarks 146 countries. It ranks countries according to gender equality rather than women's empowerment in order to better measure inequality and how it performs. It assesses gender disparity on a scale from 0 (indicating high disparity) to 1 (indicating gender parity). This scale allows for the measurement of progress made by any country toward achieving gender parity. Gender gaps are evaluated across four thematic dimensions including 'Economic Participation and Opportunity', i.e. female over male ratio in labor force participation, gender wage gap at the same level for similar work, female over men ratio at the top positions (World Economic Forum, 2023). As retrieved on February 3, 2023 at: https://www3.weforum.org/docs/WEF_GGGR_2022.pdf.

[11] As retrieved on September 30, 2023, at: https://www3.weforum.org/docs/WEF_GGGR_2023.pdf.

The gender labor gap includes the access to labor market as well as the opportunities for career advancement. It is influenced by the fact that societal expectations continue to push boys and girls toward gender-stereotyped career paths, regardless of their actual proficiency in subjects at school. Women often choose part-time jobs in sectors like education and healthcare to balance work and family responsibilities, leading to lower pay. In contrast, men often prefer full-time positions in fields like finance, banking, and insurance when they do not have the same caregiving responsibilities.

Many OECD governments consider the best way to reduce barriers to women's employment by proposing a more accessible childcare and increasing flexible work arrangements for a better-quality job. Women's lower labor force participation might be explained by the higher probability of interrupting their careers to take care of their family, and the higher likelihood of working part-time. This aspect significantly reduces the number of women who get a promotion to advance in their career or who reach top positions in workplaces. The phenomenon is known as the 'leaky pipeline', or 'glass ceiling', and it involves top positions in both private and public sectors, including academia.

The gender wage gap includes wage discrimination in same level jobs and refers to the median annual pay of all women who work in a year, compared to the pay of a similar cohort of men.[12] It directly depends on gender labor gap, women's preference for part-time jobs, pink ghettoes that usually includes lower-paid jobs, and glass ceiling that makes upgrading more difficult for employed women.

Across OECD countries, the gender wage gap is higher in sectors such as information and communication, technology, finance, and in personal services. Possible causes for gender wage gap include discrimination and underestimation of women's skills.[13]

---

12 The gender wage gap should not be understood as a situation where men and women working the same job at the same place are paid differently, as such discrimination is illegal in many countries.

13 As retrieved on September 30, 2023 at: https://www.oecd-ilibrary.org/sites/ea13aa68-en/1/3/1/index.html?itemId=/content/publication/ea13aa68-en&_csp_=cb036b49c30b2b5e419ca33b85864294&itemIGO=oecd&itemContentType=book.

The OECD Report (2023) reveals that gender pay gap persists in every OECD country:

> Across OECD countries, on average, the unadjusted gender pay gap stands at 11.9% – meaning that the median full-time working woman earns about 88 cents to every dollar or euro earned by the median full-time working man. This gap varies widely across countries, ranging from 1.2% in Belgium to 31.1% in Korea. The gap gets even larger when looking at the income *all* working women and men – not only full-time workers – take home at the end of the year, as women tend to spend fewer hours in paid work than men. Women are overrepresented in part-time jobs, and men are overrepresented in jobs with long work hours, throughout the OECD. This mechanically reduces pay tied to work hours, and it contributes to gender inequalities in complementary and variable components of pay as well (OECD Report, 2023).[14]

According to the OECD Report, the gender pay gap is due to horizontal occupational segregation (with women overrepresented in fields that pay relatively lower wages) and vertical occupational segregation (with men and women concentrated in different job levels, and women underrepresented in management roles and on Boards).

Decades of public policies and legal efforts in education, labor markets, and social protection systems have contributed to narrowing the gender pay gap. However, governments and employers need to make even greater efforts to overcome the negative income effects of horizontal and vertical occupational segregation, inequalities in unpaid work, and discrimination against women. To address this longstanding gender inequality, OECD governments are increasingly implementing practical policy measures, including pay gap calculators and anti-discrimination laws. Nobel laureate Claudia Goldin has promoted a solution that does not necessarily require government intervention or increased responsibility on the part of men. Instead, it involves changes in the labor market by reducing the disproportionately high rewards for individuals who work long hours (Goldin, 2014).

[14] As retrieved on September 28, 2023 at: https://www.oecd-ilibrary.org/sites/ea13aa68-en/index.html?itemId=/content/publication/ea13aa68-en.

The gender entrepreneurship gap measures the differences between the number of female and male entrepreneurs, in both traditional entrepreneurship and social entrepreneurship, as well as the challenges women face in accessing credit. It may depend on macro elements, such as the overall institutional framework, gender stereotypes, and government policies (Doe, 2017; Welter, 2010) as well as on micro elements, such as individual expectations and motivations (Jamali, 2009; Klyver et al., 2013).[15]

The Global Entrepreneurship Monitor (2022/2023) reveals that globally women are more likely than men to work as entrepreneurs in sectors that are less competitive and less profitable.[16] This process reinforces occupational segregation in entrepreneurship. Women entrepreneurs prefer to run small business, better if lone-firms. The gender entrepreneurship gap is narrower among young and unmarried people while it is higher among elders. Most recent data reveal that:

> the relative gender gap for ownership of established businesses tends to be smaller than the relative gender gap for new entrepreneurs (34 out of 49 economies) suggesting that either greater equality between genders starting new businesses is a recent phenomenon that has yet to work its way into established businesses, or businesses started by women may have a lower rate of transition into established businesses than those started by men (GEM, 2022/2023, 89).[17]

---

15 Self-employment has traditionally been associated with a full-time labor market activity, but lately it has evolved to take on various forms, known as hybrid or informal entrepreneurship (i.e. forms of self-employment combined with employment, education and/or volunteer work), group entrepreneurship (i.e. self-employment in a team), and freelancers (i.e. self-employed people who undertake project-based work, often in creative industries). Informal entrepreneurship is growing especially in developing countries where women's access to capital is heavily limited.

16 Since 1999, Gender Entrepreneurship Monitor (GEM) has been collecting data about entrepreneurship in over 100 economies by adopting a multi-phase measure of entrepreneurship that includes potential entrepreneurs, intentional entrepreneurs, nascent entrepreneurs, established business owner, discontinued entrepreneurs, and new entrepreneurs.

17 As retrieved on September 30, 2023 at: https://www.gemconsortium.org/reports/latest-global-report.

There are significant differences among geographical areas and countries. In low GDP countries, women are more likely to choose self-employment as it may be the best way for them to support their families, with women often serving as the primary breadwinners. Women's entrepreneurship tends to be concentrated in sectors such as manufacturing, farming, and tourism. Additionally, entrepreneurship often attracts women with lower levels of education.

Women entrepreneurs often encounter challenges related to financial education and the lack of adequate policies designed to promote access to credit.[18] Cultural factors, including migration and the communal support system for childcare in rural communities, can make portfolio entrepreneurship more accessible for women.[19] However, the gender gap in social entrepreneurship presents different dynamics.[20] Unlike the situation in traditional entrepreneurship, the number of women social entrepreneurs is lower in developing countries compared to those in developed countries, where, apparently, women entrepreneurs tend to prioritize social goals more than their male counterpart.[21]

Regarding the institution of marriage and its role in the gendered division of labor, which still plays a crucial role in reinforcing or eventually debunking the doctrine of the separate spheres, things have evolved significantly over the course of the twentieth and early twenty-first centuries. In the Western society equality between partners, either married or in domestic relationships, in terms of formal legal status, has

---

[18] Since 1995, the World Bank has started a special program of regular credit and microcredit to promote entrepreneurship among women. As reported by the *World Bank Gender Action Plan 2016–2021* microcredit is especially dedicated to the "poorest individuals, and women make up 85.2% of this group".

[19] In low-income countries, women tend to be portfolio entrepreneurs rather than serial entrepreneurs, i.e. they invest their skills and efforts across multiple micro-firms, aiming to increase their chances of earning a sufficient income to support their families, instead of concentrating their entrepreneurial activities within a single firm.

[20] The notion of social entrepreneurship has been introduced in the 1950s (Bowen, 1953). Social entrepreneurship has been defined as "entrepreneurial activity with an embedded social purpose" (Austin et al., 2006, 2) or "the pursuit of sustainable solutions to neglected problems with positive externalities" (Santos, 2012, 335). In the past decades, researches on social entrepreneurship are dramatically increased, especially in low-income countries (Bloom, 2009; Ghauri et al., 2014), targeting possible way towards women empowerment (Datta & Gailey, 2012). For a review of the literature on social entrepreneurship, see Saebi et al. (2018).

[21] See for example (Hechavarria et al., 2012; Huysentruyt, 2014; Nicolás & Rubio, 2016).

been completed. However, the formal legal equality has not necessarily translated into a corresponding substantive equality between partners. There is still a disparity in the division of time and labor when it comes to child-rearing and household activities. This situation continues to place a disproportionate burden on women, or on the partner who has less power in same-sex couples. Eventually prenuptial agreements might help[22]: if intended not merely as a set of conditions in case of separation and divorce, but as agreements between spouses on how to properly handle the conditions within the new household. These agreements could address the division of labor and child-rearing responsibilities, offering a potential solution to the issue of the double burden.[23]

Summing up, the doctrine of the separate spheres is no longer a myth, but gender inequality in the workforce and within household still persists. Women have dramatically increased their position in the public sphere. Yet women's unpaid work in the private sphere is still predominant. The COVID-19 pandemic has further exacerbated this situation, and the current cost of living disproportionately affects women, who continue to earn and accumulate less wealth than men. To address these issues, economic policies aimed at closing gender gaps in labor, access to finance, resources, and opportunities, as well as broader educational efforts, should focus on eliminating the gender stereotypes that still play a fundamental role in perpetuating gender inequalities.

Datasets on marriage also provide valuable insights. The most recent OECD dataset from 2022 shows that marriage rates have declined in nearly all OECD countries over the past few decades, accompanied by

---

22 Prenuptial agreements may enable partners to organize their rights upon marrying, and eventually facilitating the procedure of divorce. While in some countries, such as the United States, Belgium and the Netherlands, prenuptial agreements are a well-known institution regularly adopted by couples, in other countries they have not achieved legal recognition or status.

23 Several studies have shown that prenuptial agreements have notable effects on individuals' behavior. For instance, couples who opt for joint ownership of property in their prenups tend to maintain a more balanced division of labor within the household (Hamilton, 1999). Moreover, empirical investigations suggest that prenuptial agreements can contribute to a significant reduction in divorce rates, particularly because they are typically designed to safeguard the financial interests of economically well-off spouses in the event of a divorce (Leeson & Pierson, 2016). Additionally, spouses' perceptions of the fairness in the division of labor in marriage are considered a fundamental element for maintaining a healthy household (Brinig & Nock, 1999; Rainer, 2007).

increases in the average age at which people get married and higher divorce rates. While common historical trends are observed, there are significant differences across countries in the ages at which individuals first marry. Cohabitation has become a significant form of long-term partnership, and as of 2022, same-sex marriages are formally recognized in 24 OECD countries.[24]

OECD dataset also scrutinizes unpaid work, a critical aspect of family dynamics that disproportionately affects women. Unpaid work encompasses various categories: domestic activities that include all tasks related to maintaining a household, except for time exclusively spent caring for a child or another person; the combination of home activities, such as cleaning, washing, repair work, or caring for pets etc., and non-home activities such as volunteer work, shopping, etc.; care work that covers the time spent caring for a child or another adult, including the supervision and the education of a child, as well as any activity related to childcare. The data clearly indicate that women disproportionately shoulder the burden of care work as a primary activity when compared to men. In many cases, this means women spend around twice as much time, if not more, on care work within the household.[25] These findings underscore the urgent need for a more equitable distribution of household responsibilities within marriages and relationships to achieve greater gender equality. Addressing this division of labor is essential for promoting more balanced and fair partnerships within families.

Marriage, or the equivalent long-term domestic relationship between two people regardless of their gender, is neither an exclusive romantic union of two people, nor a private bargaining of two rational agents. Rather, it is a form of cooperation and coordination that involves individuals and families. When we view it through this perspective, the doctrine of the separate spheres may be finally overcome. Indeed, reducing gender inequality in the public sphere is contingent upon transforming the dynamics of the private sphere. This necessitates a new paradigm for marriage or partnership in which both individuals

---

[24] As retrieved on October 1, 2023 at: https://www.oecd.org/els/family/SF_3_1_Marriage_and_divorce_rates.pdf.

[25] As retrieved on October 1, 2023 at: https://www.oecd.org/els/family/LMF2_5_Time_use_of_work_and_care.pdf.

equally share the responsibilities of caring for their family and advancing their careers. Despite women having entered the public sphere, men have yet to fully embrace equal responsibilities in activities traditionally associated with the private sphere. Getting rid of the doctrine of the separate spheres and promoting gender equality as well as women's empowerment and responsible parenting are some of the most powerful instruments for enhancing human and social capital, thereby effecting positive change in our global society. Political economy and economic theory played a significant role in analyzing, either reinforcing or criticizing, the dynamics of the doctrine of the separate spheres and its influence on the well-being of women, men, and children. This book has tried to describe this influence by tracing the history of economic ideas on gender issues, dating it back to the multifaceted discussions on these matters that emerged in early modern period among scholars of the time up to the split between standard economics and feminist economics.

References

Agarwal, B. (1997). Bargaining and Gender Relations: Within and Beyond the Household. *Feminist Economics, 3*(1), 1–51.

Armstrong, C., & Squires, J. (2002). Beyond the Public/Private Dichotomy: Relational Space and Sexual Inequalities. *Contemporary Political Theory, 1*(3), 261–283.

Austin, J. E., Stevenson, H., & Wei-Skillern, J. (2006). Social and Commercial Entrepreneurship: Same, Different, or Both?'. *Entrepreneurship Theory and Practice, 30*(1), 1–22.

Averett, S., Argys, L., & Hoffman, S. (Eds.). (2018). *The Oxford Handbook of Women and the Economy*. Oxford University Press.

Baker, M., & Jacobsen, J. (2007). Marriage, Specialization and the Gender Division of Labor. *Journal of Labor Economics, 108*(4), 663–679.

Banks, N. (2021). Intersectional Identities and Analysis. In G. Berik & E. Kongar (Eds.), *The Routledge Handbook of Feminist Economics* (pp. 118–126). Routledge.

Barker, D. (1995). Economists, Social Reformers, and Prophets: A Feminist Critique of Economic Efficiency. *Feminist Economics., 1*(3), 26–39.

Barker, D., & Feiner, S. (2004). *Liberating Economics: Feminist Perspectives on Families, Work and Globalization*. The University of Michigan Press.
Becchio, G. (2020). *A History of Feminist and Gender Economics*. Routledge.
Becker, G. (1977). Reply to Hirshleifer and Tullock. *Journal of Economic Literature, 15*(2), 506–507.
Becker, G. (1981 [1991]). *A Treatise on the Family*. Harvard University Press.
Becker, M. (1999). Patriarchy and Inequality: Towards a Substantive Feminism. *University of Chicago Legal Forum, 1*(3), 21–88.
Becker, M. (2002). Care and Feminists. *Wisconsin Women's Law Journal, 17*(1), 57–110.
Bergmann, B. (1974a). Occupational Segregation, Wages and Profits When Employers Discriminate by Race and Sex. *Eastern Economic Journal, 2*(3), 103–110.
Bergmann, B. (1974b). *The Struggle of Women in the United States* (Unpublished. Barbara Bergmann's Archive). Duke University.
Bergmann, B. (1981a). *Proposal for a Study: The Provision of Adequate, Equitable and Assured Economic Support for Children* (Unpublished. Barbara Bergmann Archive). Duke University.
Bergmann, B. (1981b). The Share of Women and Men in the Economic Support of Children. *Human Rights Quarterly, 3*(2), 103–112.
Bergmann, B. (1981c). The Economic Risks of being a Housewife. *The American Economic Review, 71*(2), 81–86.
Bergmann, B. (1983 [1990]). Feminism and Economics. *Women's Studies Quarterly, 18*(3/4), 68–74. Reprinted from *Academe: Bulletin of the American Association of University Professors, 69*(5), 22–25.
Bergmann, B. (1986). *The Economic Emergence of Women*. Basic Books.
Bergmann, B. (1987). The Task of a Feminist Economics. In C. Farnham (Ed.), *The Impact of Feminist Research in the Academy* (pp. 131–147). Indiana University Press.
Bergmann, B. (1989). What the Common Economic Arguments Against Comparable Worth Are Worth. *Journal of Social Issues, 45*(4), 67–80.
Bergmann, B. (1990). Women's Role in the Economy: Teaching the Issue. *Women's Studies Quarterly, 18*(3/4), 6–22.
Bergmann, B. (1995). Becker's Theory of the Family: Preposterous Conclusions. *Feminist Economics, 1*(1), 141–150. Reprinted in *Challenge* (1996), 39(1), 9–12.
Bergmann, B. (1998). The Only Ticket to Equality: Total Androgyny, Male Style. *Journal of Contemporary Legal Issues, 9*, 75–86.

Bergmann, B. (2003). *The Challenge of Single Motherhood* (Unpublished. Proposed Chapter Outline. Barbara Bergmann's archive). Duke University.

Bergmann, B. (2005). *The Economic Emergence of Women* (2nd enlarged edition). Palgrave Macmillan.

Bergmann, B. (2008). *The Economic Consequences of the Decline of Marriage* (Working paper n. 0818). Department of Economics. Johannes Kepler University of Linz.

Bergmann, B. (undated, presumably between 2005 and 2008). *The Decline of Marriage and What To Do About It* (Unpublished Chapter Outline. Barbara Bergmann's archive). Duke University.

Berk, R., & Berk, S. ([1976] 1978). A Simultaneous Equation Model for the Division of Household Labor. *Sociological Methods & Research, 6*(4), 431–468.

Blau, F., & Winkler, A. (2018). *The Economics of Women, Men, and Work* (8th ed.). Oxford University Press.

Bloom, P. (2009). Overcoming Consumption Constraints through Social Entrepreneurship. *Journal of Public Policy & Marketing, 28*(1), 128–134.

Bohnet, I. (2016). *What Works: Gender Equality by Design.* Harvard University Press.

Boserup, E. (1970). *Woman's Role in Economic Development*. George Allen & Unwin.

Boserup, E. (1987). Inequality between the Sexes. In J. Eatwell, M. Millgate, & P. Newmann (Eds.), *Social Economics* (pp. 165–170). Palgrave Macmillan.

Bowen, H. (1953). *The Social Responsibilities of the Businessman.* Harper & Brothers.

Bowles, S., & Gintis, H. (1977). The Marxian Theory of Value and Heterogeneous Labor: A Critique and Reformulation. *Cambridge Journal of Economics, 1*(2), 173–192.

Brinig, M., & Nock, S. L. (1999). *The Division of Labor, the New Marriage, and Marital Instability*. Available at SSRN: https://ssrn.com/abstract=162730

Bubeck, D. (1995). *Care, Gender and Justice*. Clarendon Press.

Budlender, D., & Hewitt, G. (2002). *Gender Budgets Make Cents. Understanding Gender Responsive Budgets.* Commonwealth Secretariat.

Carter, N., & Williams, M. (2003). Comparing Social Feminism and Liberal Feminism. In J. E. Butler (Ed.), *New Perspectives on Women Entrepreneurs* (pp. 25–50). Information Age.

Cassar, A., & Katz, E. (2016). *Gender, Behavior, and Women's Economic Empowerment* (CDG Background Paper, pp. 1–27). Washington DC: Center for Global Development.

Case, M. (2001). How High the Apple Pie? A Few Troubling Questions about Where, Why, and How the Burden of Care for Children Should Be Shifted. *Chicago-Kent Law Review, 76*, 1753, 1758.

Chassonnery-Zaïgouche, C., Cherrier, B., & Singleton, J. (2019). *"Economics Is Not a Man's Field": CSWEP and the First Gender Reckoning in Economics (1971–1991)* (SSRN Working paper). Available at https://papers.ssrn.com/sol3/papers.cfm?abstract_id=3510857

Chodorow, N. (1978). *The Reproduction of Mothering*. University of California Press.

Cohen, J. (2019). The Radical Roots of Feminism in Economics. *Research in the History of Economic Thought and Methodology, 37A*, 85–100.

Colander, D., & Woos, J. (1997). Institutional Demand-Side Discrimination Against Woman and the Human Capital Model. *Feminist Economics, 3*(1), 53–64.

Collins, P., & Bilge, S. (2020). *Intersectionality*. Polity Press.

Coontz, S. (1992). *The Way We Were. American Families and the Nostalgia Trap.* Basic Book.

Crenshaw, K. (1991). Mapping the Margins: Intersectionality, Identity Politics, and Violence Against Women of Color. *Stanford Law Review, 43*(6), 1241–1299.

Datta, P., & Gailey, R. (2012). Empowering Women through Social Entrepreneurship: Case Study of a Women's Cooperative in India. *Entrepreneurship: Theory & Practice, 36*(3), 569–587.

Delphy, C. (1984). *Close to Home: A Materialist Analysis of Women's Oppression.* University of Massachusetts Press.

Doe, H. (2017). Gender and Business. Women in Business or Businesswomen? An Assessment of the History of Entrepreneurial Women. In J. F. Wilson, S. Toms, A. de Jong, & E. Buchnea (Eds.), *The Routledge Companion to Business History*. Routledge.

Duflo, E. (2012). Women Empowerment and Economic Development. *Journal of Economic Literature., 50*(4), 1051–1079.

England, P. (1993 [2003]). Separative and Soluble Selves: Dichotomous Thinking in Economics. In M. Ferber & J. Nelson (Eds.), *Feminist Economics Today. Beyond Economic Man* (pp. 33–57). The University of Chicago Press.

England, P., & Folbre, N. (1999). The Silent Crisis in U.S. Child Care: Who Should Pay for the Kids? *Annals of American Academy of Political and Social Science, 561*, 39–51.

Ferber, M., & Birnbaum, B. (1977a). The 'New Home Economics': Retrospects and Prospects. *Journal of Consumer Research, 4*(1), 19–28.
Ferber, M., & Birnbaum, B. (1977b). How New Is the 'New Home Economics'? Rejoinder. *Journal of Consumer Research, 4*(3), 183–184.
Ferber, R., & Nicosia, F. M. (1972). Newly Married Couples and their Asset Accumulation Decisions. In B. Strumple, J. N. Morgan, & E. Zahn (Eds.), *Human Behavior in Economic Affairs* (pp. 161–185). Jossey-Bass.
Ferguson, A., & Folbre, N. (1981). The Unhappy Marriage of Patriarchy and Capitalism. In L. Sargent (Ed.), *Women and Revolution: A Discussion of the Unhappy Marriage of Marxism and Feminism* (pp. 313–338). South End Press.
Figart, D., Mutari, E., & Power, M. (2002). *Living Wages, Equal Wages: Gender and Labor Market Policies in the United States*. Routledge.
Folbre, N. (1982). Exploitation Comes Home: A Critique of the Marxian Theory of Labor Power. *Cambridge Journal of Economics, 6*(4), 317–329.
Folbre, N. (1986). Hearts and Spades. Paradigms of Household Economics. *World Development, 14*(2), 245–255.
Folbre, N. (1994). *Who Pays for the Kids?* Routledge.
Folbre, N. (1998a). The Sphere of Women in Early Twentieth Century Economics. In H. Silverberg (Ed.), *Gender and American Social Science: The Formative Years* (pp. 35–60). Princeton University Press.
Folbre, N. (1998b). Barbara, the Market, and the State. *Feminist Economics, 4*(3), 159–168.
Folbre, N. (1998c). The Neglect of Care-Giving. *Challenge, 41*(5), 45–58.
Folbre, N. (2001). *The Invisible Heart: Economics and Family Values*. New Press.
Folbre, N., & Nelson, J. (2000). For Love or Money—Or Both? *The Journal of Economic Perspectives, 14*(4), 123–140.
Folbre, N. (2021). *The Rise and Decline of Patriarchal Systems*. Verso.
Franke, K. M. (2001). Theorizing Yes: An Essay on Feminism, Law, and Desire. *Columbia Law Review, 101*(1), 181–191.
Fricker, M., & Hornsby, J. (Eds.). (2000). *The Cambridge Companion to Feminism in Philosophy*. Cambridge University Press.
Friedan, B. (1963). *The Feminine Mystique*. W.W. Norton and Co.
Friedan B. (1981). *The Second Stage*. Summit Book.
Ghauri, P., Tasavori, M., & Zaefarian, R. (2014). Internationalisation of Service Firms Through Corporate Social Entrepreneurship and Networking. *International Marketing Review, 31*(6), 576–600.
Gilligan, C. (1982). *In a Different Voice: Psychological Theory and Women's Development*. Harvard University Press.

Global Entrepreneurship Monitor. (2022/2023). https://www.gemconsortium.org/reports/latest-global-report
Goldin, C. (1977). Female Labor Force Participation: The Origin of Black and White Differences, 1870 and 1880. *Journal of Economic History, 37*(1), 87–108.
Goldin, C. (2014). A Grand Gender Convergence: Its Last Chapter. *American Economic Review, 104*(4), 1091–1119.
Hadfield, G. K. (1999). A Coordination Model of the Sexual Division of Labor. *Journal of Economic Behavior and Organization, 40*(2), 125–153.
Hamilton, G. (1999). Property Rights and Transaction Costs in Marriage: Evidence from Prenuptial Contracts. *Journal of Economic History, 59*(1), 68–103.
Hartmann, H. (1981). The Unhappy Marriage of Marxism and Feminism: Toward a More Progressive Union. In L. Sargent (Ed.), *Women and Revolution* (pp. 1–41). South End Press.
Haslanger, S. (2000). Gender and Race: [What] Are They? [What] Do We Want Them to Be? *Noûs, 34*(1), 31–55.
Hechavarria, D., Ingram, A., Justo, R., & Terjesen, S. (2012). Are Women More Likely to Pursue Social and Environmental Entrepreneurship. In K. Hughes & J. Jennings (Eds.), *Global Women's Entrepreneurship Research: Diverse Settings, Questions and Approaches* (pp. 135–151). Edward Elgar.
Hochschild, A. (1989). *The Second Shift: Working Parents and the Revolution at Home*. Viking Press.
Horwitz, S. (2015). *Hayek's Modern Family. Classical Liberalism and the Evolution of Social Institutions*. Palgrave Macmillan.
Huysentruyt, M. (2014). Women's Social Entrepreneurship and Innovation. *OECD Local Economic and Employment Development.* OECD Publishing. As retrieved on December 28, 2018 at https://doi.org/10.1787/5jxzkq2sr7d4-en
ILO. (2023). *New Data Shine Light on Gender Gaps in the Labour Market*. https://ilo.org/wcmsp5/groups/public/---dgreports/---stat/documents/publication/wcms_870519.pdf
Iversen, V. (2003). Intra-Household Inequality: A Challenge for the Capability Approach? *Feminist Economics, 6*(2–3), 93–115.
Jacobsen, J. (2018). Women and the Labor Market: A Feminist Perspective. In S. L. Averett, L. M. Argys, & S. D. Hoffman (Eds.), *The Oxford Handbook of Women and the Economy* (pp. 623–641). Oxford University Press.
Jacobsen, J. (2020). *Advanced Introduction to Feminist Economics*. Edward Elgar.

Jamali, D. (2009). Constraint and Opportunities Facing Women Entrepreneurs in Developing Countries: A Relational Perspective. *Gender in Management: An International Journal, 24*(4), 232–251.

Kantola, J. (2006). *Feminists Theorize the State*. Palgrave Macmillan.

Katz. E. (1997). The Intra-Household Economics of Voice and Exit. *Feminist Economics, 3*(3), 25–46.

Kittay, E. (2020). *Love's Labor. Essays on Women, Equality and Dependency*. Routledge.

Klyver, K., Nielsen, S. L., & Evald, M. R. (2013). Women's Self-Employment: An Act of Institutional (Dis)Integration? A Multilevel, Cross-Country Study. *Journal of Business Venturing, 28*(4), 474–488.

Lamanna, M. A., Riedmann, A., & Stewart, S. (2014). *Marriages, Families, and Relationships: Making Choices in a Diverse Society* (12th ed.). Cengage Learning.

Leeson, P., & Pierson, J. (2016). Prenups. *Journal of Legal Studies, 45*, 367–400.

Lombardo, E., & Meier, P. (2006). Gender Mainstreaming in the EU: Incorporating a Feminist Reading? *The European Journal of Women's Studies, 13*(2), 151–166.

Lovenduski, J. (2005). *Feminizing Politics*. Polity Press.

MacKinnon, C. (1987). *Feminism Unmodified*. Harvard University Press.

MacKinnon, C. (1989). *Toward a Feminist Theory of the State*. Harvard University Press.

McAfee, N., & Howard, K. B. (2018). Feminist Political Philosophy. In E. N. Zalta (Ed.), *The Stanford Encyclopedia of Philosophy* (Winter 2018 ed.). https://plato.stanford.edu/archives/win2018/entries/feminism-political.

McCloskey, D. (1990). Storytelling in Economics. In C. Nash (Ed.), *Narrative in Culture: The Use of Storytelling in the Science, Philosophy, and Literature* (pp. 5–22). Routledge.

McCrate, E. (1987). Trade, Merger and Employment: Economic Theory on Marriage. *Review of Radical Political Economics, 19*(1), 73–89.

Mincer, J., & Polacheck, S. (1974). Family Investments in Human Capital: Earnings of Women. *Journal of Political Economy, 82*(Part II), S76–S108.

Moller Okin, S. (1989). *Justice, Gender, and the Family*. Basic Books.

Moller Okin, S. (1998). Gender, the Public and the Private. In A. Phillips (Ed.), *Feminism and Politics* (pp. 116–141). Oxford University Press.

Nelson, J. (1993). Gender and Economic Ideologies. *Review of Social Economy, 51*(3), 287–301.

Nelson, J. (1994). I, Thou, and Them: Capabilities, Altruism, and Norms in the Economics of Marriage. *American Economics Review, 84*(2), 126–131.

Nicolás, C., & Rubio, A. (2016). Social Enterprise: Gender Gap and Economic Development. *European Journal of Management and Business Economics, 25*(2), 56–62.

Noddings, N. (1986). *Caring: A Feminine Approach to Ethics and Moral Education.* University of California Press.

Nussbaum, M. (2000). *Women and Human Development: The Capabilities Approach.* Cambridge University Press.

Nussbaum, M., & Sen, A. (1993). *The Quality of Life.* Clarendon Press.

OECD. (2022). *Family Database.* https://www.oecd.org/els/family/database.htm

OECD. (2023). *Gender Report 2023.* https://www.oecd.org/gender/

Olsen, F. E. (1985). The Myth of State Intervention in the Family. *Journal of Law Reform, 18*(1), 835–864.

Olson, P. (2007). On the Contributions of Barbara Bergmann to Economics. *Review of Political Economy, 19*(4), 475–496.

Olson, P., & Emami, Z. (2002). Barbara Bergmann. In P. Olson & Z. Emami (Eds.), *Engendering Economics. Conversations with Women Economists in the United States* (pp. 53–72). Routledge.

Pateman, C. (1983). Feminist Critiques of the Public/Private Dichotomy. In S. Benn & G. Gaus (Eds.), *Public and Private in Social Life* (pp. 281–303). Croom Helm.

Pateman, C. (1988). *The Sexual Contract*. Stanford University Press.

Paterson, J., & Lewis, M. (Eds.). (1999). *The Elgar Companion to Feminist Economics.* Edward Elgar.

Phipps, S., & Burton, P. (1995). Social/Institutional Variables and Behavior within Households: An Empirical Test Using the Luxembourg Income Study. *Feminist Economics, 1*(1), 151–174.

Phipps, S., & Burton, P. (1998). What's Mine is Yours? The Influence of Male and Female Incomes on Patterns of Household Expenditures. *Economica, 65*(260), 599–613.

Phipps, S., Burton, P., & Osberg, L. (2001). Time as a Source of Inequality within Marriage: Are Husbands More Satisfied with Time for Themselves than Wives? *Feminist Economics, 7*(2), 1–21.

Posner, R. (1989). Conservative Feminism. *The University of Chicago Legal Forum, 1*, 191–217.

Rainer, H. (2007). Should We Write Prenuptial Contracts? *European Economic Review, 51*(2), 337–363.

Robinson, J. (1977). The 'New Home Economics': Sexist, Unrealistic, or Simply Irrelevant? *Journal of Consumer Research, 4*(3), 178–181.

Robinson, J., & Converse, P. (1972). Social Changes as Reflected in the Use of Time. In A. Campbell & P. Converse (Eds.), *The Human Meaning of Social Change* (pp. 17–86). Russell Sage.

Rhode, D. (1997). *Speaking of Sex: The Denial of Gender Inequality*. Harvard University Press.

Saebi, T., Foss, N., & Linder, S. (2018). Social Entrepreneurship Research: Past Achievement and Future Promises. *Journal of Management, 45*(1), 70–95.

Santos, F. (2012). A Positive Theory of Social Entrepreneurship. *Journal of Business Ethics, 111*(3), 335–351.

Saunders, L., & King, M. (2010). An Interview with Barbara Bergmann: Leading Feminist Economics. *Feminist Economics, 12*(3), 305–316.

Schultz, T. (Ed.). (1974). *Economics of the Family, Marriage, Children, and Human Capital*. The University of Chicago Press.

Scott, J. W. (1988). *Gender and the Politics of History*. Columbia University Press.

Sen, A. (1990). Gender and Cooperative Conflict. In I. Tinker (Ed.), *Persistent Inequality: Women and World Development* (pp. 123–149). University Press Oxford.

Squires, J. (2005). Is Mainstreaming Transformative? Theorising Mainstreaming in the Context of Diversity and Deliberation. *Social Politics, 12*(3), 366–388.

Stratigaki, M. (2004). The Cooptation of Gender Concepts in EU Policies: The Case of 'Reconciliation of Work and Family.' *Social Politics, 11*(1), 30–56.

Strassmann, D. (1995). Creating a Forum for Feminist Economic Inquiry. *Feminist Economics, 1*(1), 1–5.

Strober, M. (1987). The Scope of Microeconomics: Implications for Economic Education. *The Journal of Economic Education, 18*(2), 135–149.

Strober, M. (1995). Do Young Women Trade Jobs for Marriage? A Skeptical View. *Feminist Economics, 1*(1), 197–205.

Strober, M. (2016). *Sharing the Work: What My Family and Career Taught Me about Breaking Through (and Holding the Door Open for Others)*. MIT Press.

Tronto, J. (1993). *Moral Boundaries: The Political Argument for an Ethic of Care*. Routledge.

Verloo, M., & Lombardo, E. (2007). Contested Gender Equality and Policy Variety in Europe: Introducing a Critical Frame Analysis Approach'. In M. Verloo (Ed.), *Multiple Meanings of Gender Equality: A Critical Frame Analysis of Gender Politics in Europe* (pp. 21–49). Central European University Press.

Walby, S. (2005). Gender Mainstreaming: Productive Tensions in Theory and Practice. *Social Politics, 12*(3), 321–343.
Welter, F. (2010). Contextualizing Entrepreneurship—Conceptual Challenges and Ways Forward. *Entrepreneurship Theory and Practice, 35*(1), 165–184.
West, R. (1999). *Caring for Justice*. New York University Press.
Willis, R. J. (1973). A New Approach to the Economic Theory of Fertility Behavior. *Journal of Political Economy, 81*(Part II), S14–S64.
Woolley, F. (1993). The Feminist Challenge to Neoclassical Economics. *Cambridge Journal of Economics, 17*(4), 485–500.
Woolley, F. (1996). Getting the Better of Becker. *Feminist Economics, 2*(1), 114–120.
Woolley, F. (1999). Economics of the Family. In J. Peterson & M. Lewis (Eds.), *The Elgar Companion to Feminist Economics* (pp. 328–336). Edward Elgar.
Woolley, F. (2003). Control over Money in Marriage. In S. Grossbard-Shechtman (Ed.), *Marriage and the Economy: Theory and Evidence from Advanced Industrial Societies* (pp. 105–128). Cambridge University Press.
World Economic Forum. (2023). *Global Gender Report Gap*. https://www.weforum.org/reports/global-gender-gap-report-2023/

Index

A

Abbott, Edith 100, 101, 106, 145, 151–154, 174
Abbott, Grace 174, 175
Abolitionism 62, 139, 147
Abortion 17, 59, 124, 173, 261, 264, 265
Adams, Abigail 135
Addams, Jane 110, 111, 146, 149, 175, 176
Alcoholism 72, 169–171, 175
Americanization 14, 119, 120, 124, 126
Androcentrism 14, 109, 113, 115
Androgynous model (in Bergmann) 256
Anthony, Susan B. 89, 139
Antis 137, 141, 143, 148, 149
Aristotle 5, 44
Astell, Mary 40–42
Austen, Jane 167

B

Baillie, Joanna 167
Balch, Emily Green 125, 126, 145
Beard, Charles 143, 144
Beard, Mary R. 143
Beccaria, Cesare 59
Becker, Gary 18–20, 22, 25, 192–194, 202–204, 208–216, 218, 219, 221, 224, 226, 235, 236, 247–251, 256, 258, 260–262
Beecher, Catharine 45, 141, 110, 195
Beecher, Harriet 195
Beecher, Isabella 110

G. Becchio, *The Doctrine of the Separate Spheres in Political Economy and Economics*, Palgrave Studies in Classical Liberalism,
https://doi.org/10.1007/978-3-031-51262-9

Benevolent (breadwinner) 8, 20, 155, 180, 215, 224, 249, 255, 259, 261
Bergmann, Barbara 23, 233, 236, 249, 250, 254, 256–262, 264
Biological differences (between genders) 193, 214, 217, 245, 251
Birth control 109, 123, 124, 160, 173, 205
Black Americans (people of color) 25, 144, 145
Bodichon, Barbara 90
Bosanquet, Helen Dendy 91, 159, 160
Boserup, Ester 245, 246
Breadwinners versus care-providers 12, 16, 18, 255, 261
Breckinridge, Sophonisba 13, 99–101, 145, 151–154, 167, 174, 197
Bronson, Minnie 150–153
Brown Adams, Anne 157
Brown, John 157
Bullock, Charles J. 143
Burke, Edward 44, 50

C

Cabanis, Pierre-George 57, 59
Cady Stanton, Elizabeth 89, 139, 140
Cain, Glenn 207, 226
Capability approach 242, 252
Capitalism 8, 15, 16, 35, 55, 87, 158, 161
Care; care work 6, 21, 22, 24, 36, 83, 90, 92, 120, 123, 135, 159, 172, 192, 201, 210, 216, 234, 235, 239–244, 248, 253, 254, 265, 274
Carver, Thomas Nixon 13, 142, 144, 149, 154
Caste system 23, 259, 260
Catholic Church 33, 74
Ceteris paribus assumption 208
Charity 14, 91, 105, 118, 169, 172
Child-caring 23, 197, 206, 215, 222, 247, 258, 260, 264
Clark, John Bates 172, 176, 204
Class 4, 7, 24, 92, 97, 118, 121, 161, 170, 227, 239, 250, 264
Classical liberal feminism 52
Classical liberalism 24, 35, 59, 70, 97, 236, 237, 263
Cleyre, Voltairine de 15, 161
Clubbing 136, 182
Coase theorem 211
Collet, Clara 13, 101, 106–108, 167, 168
Coman, Katherine 125, 145
Commons, John R. 91, 122, 176
Competitive advantage, theory of 19, 96, 148, 194, 210, 212–214, 222, 249, 250, 260
Condorcet, Nicolas 56
Cooperative games 221–223, 225, 248, 251, 252
COVID-19 pandemic 236, 273
Cult of domesticity 9, 14, 18, 23, 34, 88, 113, 136, 141, 162, 165, 180, 194, 196, 265
Culture 10, 15, 113, 117–120, 124, 180, 198, 201, 234, 245, 252, 263
Customs 40, 55, 62, 71, 76, 86, 105
Cycle of vulnerability 240

D

Davenport, Herbert J. 143, 144
De Beauvoir, Simone 9
Decision-making process 202, 268
Defoe, Daniel 42
De Grouchy, Sophie 12, 55–60
De Stael Necker, Anne-Louise Germaine 44, 57
Dewey, John 199
Dickinson, Clara 199
Discrimination 2, 20, 22, 53, 87, 90, 100, 104, 123, 146, 152, 177, 178, 194, 196, 204, 208, 210, 217, 218, 227, 235, 237, 245, 250, 252, 254, 256, 259, 260, 263, 266, 269, 270
Displacement principle 237, 238
Division of labor 2, 3, 9, 17, 19, 21, 34, 45, 70, 87, 92, 105, 143, 165, 193, 194, 200, 201, 211, 214, 215, 217, 223, 225–227, 234, 236, 239, 240, 245, 249–252, 254, 255, 257–260, 262, 272–274
Divorce 12, 17, 33, 39, 47, 48, 59, 65–67, 155, 156, 161, 163, 180, 194, 211, 212, 214, 216, 222, 223, 235, 239, 240, 244, 245, 248, 251, 252, 257, 258, 265, 273
Divorce legislation 156
Doctrine of the separate spheres 1–4, 6–11, 13, 14, 16, 17, 19, 20, 23–25, 33–36, 42, 44, 45, 63, 64, 67, 71, 83–85, 88, 91, 101, 104, 106, 110, 116, 126, 136–138, 143, 192, 195, 202, 210, 212, 213, 216, 223, 224, 226, 227, 234–236, 238–241, 249, 251, 256, 257, 260, 263, 272, 273, 275
Double burden (vocational divide) 24, 239, 240, 243, 255, 264, 268, 273
Douglass, Frederick 140
Du Bois, W.E.B. 108, 143–145, 177

E

Economics of gender 19, 25, 253, 254
Edgeworth, Francis Ysidro 12, 91, 93, 100
Edgeworth, Maria 167
Ely, Richard T. 91, 103, 142, 149
Empathy 248
Engels, Friedrich 15, 158
Enlightenment 44, 45, 49, 52, 56, 70
Ethnicity 4, 16, 35, 73, 122, 136, 170, 222, 225, 254, 264
Entrepreneurship (female) 84, 210, 268, 271, 272
Eugenics 14, 16, 108–110, 117, 121–123, 125, 176
Evans, Charles 146

F

Factory legislation 13, 90, 93
Family (economics of) 17, 18, 21–23, 192, 194, 203, 205, 226, 234, 244, 245, 256
Family (Victorian model) 3, 92
Family wage 13, 14, 88, 92, 98, 100, 102, 103, 127, 144, 159, 164, 210
Farnam, Henry W. 121, 122, 143

Fawcett, Millicent 13, 91, 96, 97, 100
Female entrepreneurship (businesswomen) 84
Femininity 35, 109, 167, 168
Feminism 9, 17, 34, 73, 108–110, 160, 180, 234, 237, 238, 256, 262
Feminist economics 21, 22, 25, 194, 200, 203, 233, 238, 244, 245, 250, 253–256, 266
Feminist philosophy 234, 244
Feminist policy 23
Fénelon, François 42, 43
Fertility 19, 121, 173, 205–207, 211, 215, 216, 220, 260, 261
Fetter, Frank 121, 122
Filmer, Robert 38, 39, 44
Fisher, Irving 121, 143, 145, 204
Fourier, Charles 15
Free-riding 21
French Revolution 45, 49, 56, 58, 59
Friedan, Betty 3, 257, 264
Friedman, Milton 18, 202, 218, 219, 226
Friendship 71
Fundraising 13

G

Gender inequality
  in education 265
  in labor market 252, 264, 265, 267
  in political realms 4
Gender pay gap 2, 13, 20, 85, 95, 101, 143, 252, 254, 267, 270
Gender-specialized education 235
Gender stereotypes 5, 17, 21, 22, 52, 91, 113, 116, 212, 224, 234, 251, 252, 256, 266, 271, 273
Gibson, Mary 119
Glass ceiling 150, 153, 196, 267, 269
Global datasets 267, 268
Global society 24, 275
Goldin, Claudia 1, 2, 17, 88, 239, 270
Goldman, Emma 161
Gouges, Olympe de 11, 45–48
Gournay, Marie de 35, 37
Green, Hetty 84
Grimké, Angelina 178
Grimké, Sarah M. 17, 178–180
Guilds 85, 86

H

Hadley, Arthur T. 143
Hammond, Matthew B. 91, 95
Harman, Lillian 15
Harman, Moses 160
Harper, Frances 139, 180, 181
Hayek, Friedrich 263
Heather-Bigg, Ada 91, 93
Herschell, Caroline 167
Heywood, Angela 15, 160
Hobbes, Thomas 38
Hobson, John A. 95
Hoffman, Frederick 176
Home economics 18, 119, 141, 191, 194–199, 220
Household 2, 5–8, 18–21, 35, 43, 45, 71, 86, 91, 105, 150, 157, 158, 165, 167, 191–193, 197–199, 201–203, 205, 206,

212, 214, 215, 217, 219–223, 225, 227, 240, 246, 249, 250, 252, 253, 257, 262, 263, 273, 274
Household economics 18, 19, 191, 192, 197–199, 203, 206, 209, 220
Housewife 3, 85, 193, 194, 205, 258, 259
Howard, George Elliott 141
Hoyt, Elizabeth 18, 191, 197, 198, 201, 202
Hull House 110, 111, 119, 165, 174, 175
Human capabilities 21, 247
Human capital 18–20, 92, 93, 192, 203–211, 213–215, 217, 220, 226, 249, 250, 254, 260
Hutchinson, Emilie 146, 153, 154

I

Immigrants 14, 98, 117–120, 122–124, 126, 127, 136, 171, 173, 193, 204
Immigrant women 13, 118–120, 125, 126, 173
Immigration 13, 89, 98, 100, 110, 117, 118, 120–122, 125–127, 171
Inclusion principle 237, 238
Industrial Revolution 7, 8, 84, 87, 105, 117
International Association for Feminist Economics (IAFFE) 233
Intersectionality 7, 118, 239, 254
Investment (educational) 91, 92, 206, 213, 220, 244

J

Jevons, William 13, 91, 93
Job discrimination 2
Job segregation 85, 88, 96, 255, 257, 258, 264, 270

K

Kelley, Florence 13, 98
Kelly, Gertrude 169
Kingsley, Charles 89
Knox, John 38
Kollantai, Alexandra 158
Kyrk, Hazel 18, 191, 197–202

L

Labor economics 18, 19, 125, 196, 203, 254
Lambs, Charles 155
Leaky pipeline 269
Leibowitz, Arleen 206
Lerner, Gerda 33, 156, 180
Libertarianism 15, 16, 159–161, 169
Locke, John 11, 35, 36, 38, 39, 44, 49, 57
Love 5, 6, 33, 46, 50, 55, 169, 209–211, 219, 235, 241, 263

M

Mainstream economics 21, 26
Marcet, Jane 11, 60, 61
Marriage 136, 155
Marriage (abolition) 159
Marriage (institution) 8, 9, 11, 12, 14, 33, 39, 49, 155, 159, 194, 235, 261, 272
Marriage legislation 17

Marriage market 10, 21, 209, 210, 219, 222, 245, 251
Marriage (theory of) 194, 209, 221, 235, 256, 257, 261
Marshall, Alfred 12, 91–93, 218
Martineau, Harriet 12, 60–63, 167
Marxism 15, 16, 158, 250
Masculinity 22, 243
Maternalism 13, 126, 138, 175
Matheolus 36
McMahon, Theresa 98
Microcredit 254, 272
Mill, James 54, 61
Mill, John Stuart 12, 61, 65, 67, 70–75, 91, 93
Mincer, Jacob 18, 19, 203–209, 226, 249
Mises, Ludwig 263
Mitchell, Wesley Clair 101, 143, 144
Modigliani, Franco 202
Montagu, Mary Pierrepont 40
Montaigne, Michele de 35
More, Hannah 167
Motherhood 6, 13, 34, 54, 55, 83, 85, 92, 97, 98, 102, 103, 106, 124–127, 138, 139, 144, 156, 163, 164, 166, 168, 172, 180, 195, 212, 242, 243, 247, 259, 264
Mott, Lucretia 140

N

Nash bargaining models (of marriage) 221, 225
Native (American Indians) 108
Native (Anglo-Saxons) 108, 122
Natural rights 12, 35, 38, 45, 49, 52, 62, 68, 69
Nerlove, Marc 192, 219
New home economics 18–20, 22, 25, 192, 193, 196, 202, 206, 209, 213, 219, 224, 226, 227, 233, 246, 249, 256, 259, 263, 265
New Woman 14, 17, 108, 109, 113, 115, 116, 126, 136, 155, 167, 172, 181
Nobel Prize 19, 213, 260
Non-cooperative games (in marriage) 221
Norms, social and cultural 9, 15, 17, 21, 22, 58, 60, 73, 137, 157, 165, 171, 174, 219, 227, 234, 235, 237, 239, 241, 247, 249, 261, 267, 268
Nussbaum, Martha 242, 263

O

Occupational segregation 13, 19, 21, 85, 87, 96, 101, 110, 173, 197, 250, 251, 256–258, 266, 267, 270, 271
Optimal sorting 210–212, 219
Optimization 193, 224, 226
Overcrowding theory 117, 120, 208, 257

P

Paine, Thomas 56
Pater familias 6, 8, 20, 247
Paternalism 13, 98, 102, 138, 244
Patriarchy (patriarchal system) 5, 6, 8, 15, 16, 22, 35, 38, 43–45,

70, 73, 111, 137, 138, 161, 204, 219, 227, 235, 241, 243, 255
Patten, Simon 121, 122, 143, 144, 199
Paul, Alice 104
People of color 13, 16, 173, 176, 177, 181, 204, 208
Perkins Gilman, Charlotte 14, 103, 109–116, 123, 161–168
Pearson, Karl 91
Persons, Charles 91, 120
Phelps, Charlotte 219
Pigou, Arthur 91
Pink collar sectors. *See* Discrimination
Pizan, Christine de 36, 37
Plato 5
Polygamy 33, 211, 239, 245, 260, 261
Post-modern feminism 238
Poullain de la Barre, François 35, 39
Power 5, 22, 36, 38, 45, 46, 49, 72, 161, 204, 235, 249, 250, 263
Preferences
  endogenous 22, 200, 245, 247, 252, 253
  exogenous 247, 254
  individual 21, 254, 255
Prenuptial agreements 161, 273
Prescott Hall 117
Progressive Era 13–15, 17, 85, 88, 97, 98, 108, 117, 126, 139, 146, 154, 169, 173, 176, 181, 193, 194
Prohibition 103, 139, 152, 170
Prostitution 12, 16, 26, 34, 53, 72, 97, 103, 111, 136, 138, 164, 168–175
Protestant Reformation 40
Push and pull effect 207, 208

Q
Quiet revolution 1, 2, 17

R
Race 7, 16, 24, 92, 102, 108, 109, 120–122, 124, 125, 139, 140, 147, 170, 177, 181, 204, 212, 225, 227, 244, 250, 254
Radcliff, Mary Ann 168
Rathbone, Eleanor 91, 97
Rational choice 22, 218, 219, 246, 250, 259, 263
Reid, Margaret 18, 191, 192, 197, 198, 202, 220, 221, 224, 226
Religion 3, 55, 212, 244, 267
Reversal principle 237
Ricardo, David 60
Richards, Ellen Swallow 195–198
Richardson, Samuel 42
Robinson, James Harvey 155, 246
Robinson, Mary aka Anne Frances Randall 55
Roland, Madame 57
Ross, Edward 122
Rousseau, Jean-Jacques 3, 43, 44, 51, 54, 56

S
Sabin, Pauline 170
Salons 10
Same-sex partnership 25
Samuelson, Paul 218, 220, 221
Sanger, Margaret 123, 173

Schmoller, Gustav 125
Schultz, Theodore 18, 202–206, 226
Seager, Henry R. 91, 98
Sen, Amartya 242, 252, 263
Sexual liberation 15
Sisterhood 9, 47
Slavery 12, 54, 71, 73, 110, 147, 160, 176, 178, 204
Smart, William 91, 95, 96
Smith, Adam 56–58, 60
Social capital 275
Social evil 164, 169, 170, 172
Socialism 125, 237
Social pressure 17, 21, 71, 110, 156, 162, 212, 234, 244, 246, 259, 268
Social reforms 97, 146, 147, 153, 154
Social settlements 110
Social well-being (welfare) 1, 36, 69, 76, 90, 91, 112, 114, 125, 145, 148, 149, 153, 166
Spooner, Lysander 161
Standard economics 18, 19, 22, 25, 203, 204, 218, 226, 227, 233, 234, 241, 244, 247, 252–254, 256, 266
Starr, Ellen Gates 110
State 16, 35, 44, 72, 91, 92, 161, 263
Steuart, James 60
Stewart, Maria W. 178
Stone, Lucy 15, 139
Suffrage (women's) 16, 49, 137, 139–148, 150, 153, 154, 265
Sumner, Helen 104, 105, 145, 150, 154
Sweating system 88, 89, 97
Sympathy 56–58

T

Talbot, Marion 18, 145, 149, 154, 166, 167, 191, 196–198
Talleyrand, Charles Maurice 50
Taussig, Frank 13
Taylor Mill, Harriet 65–70, 75
Tennessee Claflin 84
Thompson, William 54, 55
Threat point 222, 223, 225
Tocqueville, Alexis de 3, 45
True womanhood 14, 17, 23, 136, 155, 156, 172, 181, 192, 195
Truth, Sojourner 178
Tucker, Benjamin 161
Turgot, Anne-Robert Jacques 56, 59

U

Unpaid work 8, 21, 22, 240, 270, 273, 274
Urbanization 13, 110, 117, 118, 121, 127
Utility function (of a family/household) 20, 209, 210, 214–216, 218–220, 225, 247, 255
Utopian (novels, thinkers) 36, 111, 115, 155, 161

V

Van Etten, Ida 89, 125
Van Kleeck, Mary 91
Veblen, Thorsten 114, 143, 199
Voltaire (François-Marie Arouet) 56, 58

W

Wagner, Adolph 125

Walker, Edwin Cox 160
Walker, Francis Amasa 121
Webb, Beatrice 91, 94, 97, 99
Webb, Sidney 13, 91, 94, 95
Western society 17, 24, 33, 201, 227, 272
Wheeler, Anna Doyle 54, 55
Wicksteed, Philip 204
WiHo model 224
Willcox, Walter 176, 177
Wolfe, Albert B. 143, 145
Wollstonecraft, Mary 11, 49–55, 57, 60, 63, 162
Woodhull, Victoria Claflin 84
Women's economic independence 11, 33, 56, 60, 106, 109, 111, 113, 144
Women's education 11, 33, 34, 36, 42, 56, 60, 64, 91, 110, 141
Women's suffrage 15, 16, 39, 49, 67, 72, 103, 126, 127, 136, 139–155, 158, 161, 175, 181, 265
Wright, Carrol D. 89, 95

X

Xenophon 5

Y

Younger, Maud 104

Z

Zetkin, Clara 158

SPRINGER NATURE

GPSR Compliance

The European Union's (EU) General Product Safety Regulation (GPSR) is a set of rules that requires consumer products to be safe and our obligations to ensure this.

If you have any concerns about our products, you can contact us on ProductSafety@springernature.com

In case Publisher is established outside the EU, the EU authorized representative is:

Springer Nature Customer Service Center GmbH
Europaplatz 3
69115 Heidelberg, Germany

Kolibri 360 GmbH
Ferdinand-Jühlke-Straße 7
99095 Erfurt, Deutschland
produktsicherheit@kolibri360.de